LEGISLATED
LEARNING

THE BUREAUCRATIZATION
OF THE AMERICAN
CLASSROOM

ARTHUR E. WISE

University of California Press
Berkeley · Los Angeles · London

University of California Press
Berkeley and Los Angeles, California
University of California Press, Ltd.
London, England
© 1979 by the Regents of the University of California
First Paperback Printing 1982
ISBN 0-520-04792-3
Printed in the United States of America
1 2 3 4 5 6 7 8 9

Library of Congress Cataloging in Publication Data

Wise, Arthur E.
    Legislated learning.

    Includes index.
    1. Educational equalization—United States.
    2. Educational accountability—United States.
    3. Educational law and legislation—United States.
        I. Title.   LA210.W56   379'.151'0973   78-62844

To Sylvia and Marion

CONTENTS

PREFACE
TO PAPERBACK EDITION OF
LEGISLATED LEARNING

The major message of *Legislated Learning* and *Rich Schools, Poor Schools* is that promoting equal educational opportunity generally requires regulation by central government whereas improving the quality of education does not. Indeed, efforts to regulate the quality of education often have the effect of lowering its quality. Of course, central government may seek to improve education indirectly through research, development, and dissemination and through the encouragement of innovation. The distinction between how government should treat equal educational opportunity and educational quality is found in the legislation creating the U.S. Department of Education. The first two purposes of the legislation are:

(1) To *strengthen* the *Federal commitment* to *ensuring* access to equal educational opportunity for every individual;

(2) To supplement and complement the efforts of States, the local school systems and other instrumentalities of the States, the private sector, public and private educational institutions, public and private nonprofit educational research institutions, community-based organizations, parents, and students to improve the quality of education.[1]

The language of the first statement is quite strong. The statute speaks of a *federal commitment* in this area; it speaks of *strengthening* that commitment. And it speaks of *ensuring* access. In contrast, the language of the second statement is less strong. It calls upon the Education Department "to sup-

[1]P.L. 96–88 (emphasis added).

plement and complement" the efforts of those responsible for operating schools. In improving the quality of education, the Education Department is to have a subordinate and indirect role. These statements of purpose postulate a division of labor between the federal government and those who have the responsibility for operating schools.

Statements of principle cannot by themselves reorient the federal role. To bring about this reorientation, the legislation created a Presidentially-appointed Intergovernmental Advisory Council on Education. The Council is to provide a forum for representatives of government and education to discuss educational issues. It is to assess both the extent to which federal objectives are achieved and the adverse consequences of federal actions. Finally, it is to make recommendations for improvement to the Secretary of Education, the President, and the Congress. The Council, in short, is to be a focal point for sorting out the federal role in education.[2]

At this writing, the Council has been slow to commence action. Its operation has been overshadowed by the education policies of the Reagan Administration which, at their most extreme, call for the virtual elimination of the federal role in education. That is the certain result of combining budget reductions and unprincipled deregulation which will reduce access to educational opportunity; consolidations which limit the federal role in helping to improve education; dismantling the Education Department to further weaken the federal role; and the "new federalism" to eliminate the federal role in education. However, the Reagan Administration favors tax credits which perversely would both strengthen the federal role and promote unequal educational opportunity. While the Reagan Administration policies are superficially consistent with the concerns expressed in *Legislated Learning* about excessive rationalization and overcentralization, they clearly ignore some problems of unequal opportunity which only the federal government can solve. And they deemphasize the supplementary federal role in improving the quality of education. The education policies of the Reagan Administration have already generated a serious defense of previous federal policy.

[2]The author served as a consultant to President Carter's Reorganization Project to create the U.S. Department of Education.

In the end, I predict that the two central purposes of the federal role in education will remain.

In the space available, it is difficult to appraise developments in the courts and at state and local levels of school governance. While school finance reform litigation continues, it seems to be focusing on equal educational opportunity, as I argue it should. (See especially, *Somerset* v. *Hornbeck*, in Maryland.)[3] Unfortunately, statewide minimal competency testing continues, although its place as the central educational focus of state legislatures is being taken by competency testing for teachers. Rigid management systems based upon testing seem to be a central preoccupation of many local boards of education. Fortunately, educational malpractice lawsuits seem not to be making much headway.

While policy currents ebb and flow, the central message of *Legislated Learning* remains: economic, scientific, legal and bureaucratic rationality have their limits when applied to the operation of educational institutions. Economic efficiency models may not always apply; practices based upon scientific findings may be pseudo-scientific; quasi-legal procedures may not always be appropriate; and bureaucratic routines may not result in better education. Technocratic practices mandated by legislation too often have perverse effects. It is time to revive the ideas of responsible lay and competent professional leadership in education.

A. E. W.
March 1982

[3]Circuit Court of Baltimore City. Slip Opinion. Docket 119A; Folio 159; File No.: A-58438 (1981). The author served as an expert witness for the plaintiffs.

PREFACE

Most educational policies are based upon seemingly unassailable common sense. Most of us would agree that: to have clear objectives is a good thing; to plan is sensible; to coordinate is reasonable; to regulate ensures equal treatment; to follow procedures is to ensure fairness. Yet, not only do educational policies based upon these verities often fail to achieve their intended results, but they increasingly are becoming the cause of profound, unanticipated, and unexamined changes in the conception and operation of education in the United States today.

Why should this be so? The reason is that educational policy is more and more being determined by the states, by the federal government, and by the courts, rather than by the schools and colleges themselves. State legislatures, demanding accountability, impose upon the schools managerial accounting schemes adopted from industry. State boards of education, concerned about diffuse educational goals, endeavor to reduce these goals to the basic skills alone. State courts require that schools become "thorough and efficient" as mandated by their state constitutions.

At the federal level, Congress, concerned about unemployment figures, calls for career education. The executive branch, responding to concerns for equality, promulgates affirmative action procedures and goals. The federal courts demand that schools observe due process with regard to individuals. Unions, dissatisfied with the protections afforded by civil service and tenure provisions, seek additional procedural safeguards through collective bargaining. Educational researchers, unable to discover what effects the schools are actually having, create models of efficient and effective schooling.

All these influences are designed to rationalize—to tighten or standardize—the operation of educational institutions.

We are witnessing at least three changes in the structure for governing education: (1) federal and state governments are making policy in areas formerly reserved to local school boards and college boards of trustees; (2) general government is making policy in areas formerly reserved to educational government; and (3) as other levels of government make educational policy, schools are becoming more bureaucratic. Policy interventions strengthen hierarchical control where it exists, or require it to be created where it does not already exist. Despite the traditions of local control and institutional autonomy and the fact that the Tenth Amendment to the Constitution reserves education to the states, a hierarchy of control is emerging in the governance of education with the federal government at the top and state governments in the middle, leaving the local schools and colleges at the bottom.

The means by which higher levels of government come to control schools and colleges is by insisting that they rationalize their operations—that is, by requiring compliance with a growing number of regulations and procedures. Schools and colleges are already bureaucratically organized, of course, and their procedures, to some extent, have already been rationalized. As these procedures are multiplied and as more attention is given to them, schools are becoming more and more rationalized, sometimes leading to the phenomenon which I will call the hyperrationalization of the schools.

In my earlier book, *Rich Schools, Poor Schools: The Promise of Equal Educational Opportunity*, I suggested that the problem of intrastate inequalities in educational expenditures might be susceptible to constitutional attack. The problem of low school expenditures could not be solved locally, since it was caused by differences in the capacity of local school districts to raise funds. The solution—technically easy, if politically difficult—was the manipulation of state school finance formulas to equalize educational spending. Judicial intervention would, by requiring new school finance plans, force state legislatures to solve the problem.

Generally, problems associated with equality in education—with the distribution of opportunities or resources—are more political than technical. When schools or colleges discriminate on the basis of race, economic status, handicap, or sex, those who suffer discrimination will wish to invoke higher authorities to redress the imbalance. The goal of equality has been and is being promoted by court decisions, federal legislation, and state legislation. While the cost of equality is some centralization of educational decision-making, it is a cost which is justified by its benefits.

Now a new goal has begun to capture the attention of those who make policy for education—to make educational institutions more efficient and more effective. Sometimes this goal is invoked as a reaction to efforts to equalize the distribution of opportunities or resources, or to conjure images of waste and duplication. At other times, it is invoked to promote genuine educational achievement, and legislation or a court order is sought to solve the problem of low academic achievement.

Policy designed to solve the problem of low academic achievement is quite different from policy designed to solve the problem of unequal educational opportunity. The solution to the problem of low achievement is more technical than political. While it is true that some teachers do not teach and some students do not learn, the causes of low achievement may not respond to the kinds of policy interventions permitted by the current state of knowledge about teaching and learning. And each policy intervention contributes to the further centralization and bureaucratization of education. These are costs which may have no benefits. Most teachers do teach, and most students do learn. Policy interventions are not neutral in their effects upon good teachers and good students.

Many of the new educational policies draw upon the tradition of scientific management. For some time I believed in the probable utility for education of such procedures as systems analysis, cost-benefit studies, and management-by-objectives. In fact, I once took leave from the study of education to learn these procedures. That was in 1965, and many people believed then that quantitative approaches to decision-making would make government more efficient and more effective. Despite the fact that this promise has failed to be fulfilled, new techniques periodically emerge—and are applied to education. While the scientific management approach to public administration may have some promise, it seems doomed by premature application. If a technique is put to full-scale use as soon as it is devised, the consequences are now predictable.

Many of the new policies draw upon educational research and social science research relevant to education. While I have believed and continue to believe that education can be improved by systematic study, here, too, research findings and new techniques seem doomed by premature application. On the one hand, some investigators promote their discoveries prematurely. On the other hand, the operating educational system and the educational policy system demand and consume discoveries at a rapid rate. The phenomenon is not new—John Dewey observed it—and it operates to the continuing detriment of the educational system and the social sciences.

When I was associated with the National Institute of Education, we struggled to envision how to bridge the gap between the genuine information needs of policymakers and the state-of-the-art of educational research and development. The demand for information to improve education far exceeds the supply of scientifically established wisdom. What to do until such knowledge can inform policy—if that day should arrive—remains a fundamental issue for those who would make policy for education.

Educational policies represent the efforts of policymakers to improve the educational system. Elected and appointed officials, external to local school systems or institutions of higher education, concerned with the operation of the educational system, create policy to correct perceived deficiencies. Every educational policy expresses a promise—if not for reform, at least for change. And every educational policy has two components—the reform or change desired, and a theory (stated or unstated) that provides the basis for believing that the reform or change will occur. My purpose here is to analyze the goals and the theories of certain educational policies and their consequences for the present and future of education.

Under our structure of government, policymakers at all levels have authority to make policy for education—to set goals, to specify the means to achieve them, and to require that schools conform to various laws. Policymakers are experiencing a growing sense of responsibility for education, whether because of rising costs, growing aspirations, or increasing dissatisfaction with education as it is. Their task is not easy, because the technology for accomplishing school improvement by policy interventions is inadequate. The motivations which inevitably govern policymakers, however, cause them to push that technology to its limit, frequently resulting in unanticipated effects. Policymakers will be portrayed as struggling to use an inadequate technology to correct real and perceived deficiencies in the educational system.

At times policymakers may be motivated by a desire for reelection. Hence, their actions may be explained by a need to *appear* to be coping with an important educational or social problem. Doubtless, a political model will explain much of the behavior we observe. My focus on the substance of educational policy is designed to analyze the long-term consequences of policy interventions based upon the prevailing rationalistic view of educational institutions.

This book, then, is about educational policy; it is not precisely about the politics of education nor about education and politics. While I do not assume that policymakers have set about to centralize control over education, I do conclude that the cumulative impact of these educational policies may be either a national system of education or fifty state systems of education which are all but indistinguishable.

To explain many of the legislatively and judicially induced educational reforms which occurred between the mid-1960s and the mid-1970s, it is necessary to understand the underlying ideas of the policies of this period. The courts have rendered decisions about racial desegregation, school finance equalization, educational malpractice, and due process. The federal government has enacted compensatory education, the National Assessment of Educational Progress, the Equal Educational Opportunity Survey, the National Institute of

Education, systematic educational evaluation, and education for the handicapped. The states have legislated accountability, planning-programming-budgeting, other scientific management systems, competency-based education, assessment, and other data-based educational management systems, including, especially, minimal competency testing. Higher education has been specifically affected by data-based decision-making systems, coordinating commissions, regulation, and proceduralization. By examining the educational policies of this period, it will be possible to extrapolate their consequences into the future.

We are dealing with *ideas* about how education *should* occur. To what extent do these ideas affect practice? Often a succession of policies is designed to implement one underlying idea. When one policy has not seemed to work, it has been replaced by another. The succeeding policies may appear to be different, but the goals remain the same. If the policy-making system persistently adheres to an idea, eventually the operating system will be forced to conform, and education will change.

We will develop and analyze the following propositions:

1. The more educational policies are promulgated by higher levels of government, the more bureaucratic will become the *conception* of the school. Education is seen as serving narrowly utilitarian ends employing rationalistic means.

2. To the extent that educators reject the bureaucratic conception of the school, educational policies will fail. The beliefs that education must be liberating and that schools cannot be standardized buttress this rejection.

3. To the extent that educators accept the bureaucratic conception of the school, the more bureaucratic will the schools become *in fact*. Quasi-judicial procedures, rigid rules, pseudoscientific processes, and measurable outcomes *can* be implemented.

4. Problems of inequity in the allocation of educational opportunities, resources, and programs can be solved by policy intervention. They may be otherwise insoluble.

5. Problems of low productivity in the educational system generally cannot be solved by policy intervention. It is, of course, possible to reduce costs—with an indeterminate ef-

fect upon quality. It is also possible for schools to adopt pseudoscientific processes and measurable outcomes. Given the state-of-the-art of educational science, it is doubtful, however, that productivity will increase.

6. While teachers as individuals resist the conception of their role implied by excessive rationalization, teachers' organizations may contribute to it.

7. To the extent that the public or interest groups address demands to policymakers rather than to the educational system, centralization and rationalization will increase.

8. To the extent that the public or its representatives insist upon *measuring* the effects of educational policies, the goals of education will be narrowed to that which can be measured.

These developments challenge a number of traditions and traditional conceptions of education: (1) they challenge the principle of individual freedom by characterizing individual (student) welfare as subordinate to the welfare of the state; (2) they challenge the traditions of local control of the public schools and institutional autonomy in postsecondary and private education; (3) they challenge the traditional "separation of education from politics" as institutionalized in the existence of school boards; (4) they challenge teacher autonomy and professionalism in schools and academic freedom and collegial governance in colleges. In place of these traditions, they offer legislated learning—and its counterpart, judicially mandated learning. Whether legislation and court decrees can improve learning is questionable. But there is little question that *legislated learning* will increase *the bureaucratization of the American classroom.*

The traditional authority of local school boards, non-public school boards, and boards of trustees of postsecondary institutions is being increasingly challenged by state and federal authorities. There is an apparent growing belief by these central authorities that rules and regulations can make schools and colleges not only more equitable but also more efficient and effective. These central authorities require the measurement of learning, apparently believing that measurement will improve learning. Incidentally, of course, the application of yardsticks provides information to central authorities which increases their capacity to rule the schools. The imagery suggested by "ruling" is strong—stronger than its synonyms "administering," "managing," or even "leading." While the question of governance is obviously at stake, so are the more important questions of the proper relationships among the individual, the school, and the society.

ACKNOWLEDGMENTS

A number of people helped to make this book possible. Joel S. Berke, then director of the Education Policy Research Institute, invited me to be a "visiting scholar." James A. Kelly of the Ford Foundation thought that I might have something to say again. Happily for me, Harold Howe II and the Ford Foundation agreed. Educational Testing Service, the parent organization of EPRI, provided academic freedom. I owe a significant debt to my colleagues at EPRI—especially Joan C. Baratz, Terry W. Hartle, and Peter N. Skerry. J. W. Getzels, Samuel Halperin, and Howard Wainer will each find his specific suggestion here. Other intellectual debts are many: most are acknowledged in the pages to follow. June Cheit helped to make the manuscript more coherent. The number of typists who cheerfully contributed to the venture is too large to acknowledge individually, but I am grateful to them all. Fortunately for both of us, Susan did not have to help this time but her emotional support was unfailing. Jeffrey and Jodi were constant reminders of our need for an educational system that liberates rather than restricts. I alone am responsible for this interpretation of American educational policy.

CHAPTER 1
EDUCATIONAL POLICIES: FROM OPPORTUNITY TO ACHIEVEMENT; FROM EQUALITY TO ADEQUACY

*Americans are accustomed to inscribe their ideals in laws,
ranging from their national Constitution to their local traffic
rules. American laws thus often contain, in addition to the
actually enforced rules (that is, "laws" in the ordinary technical
meaning of the term), other rules which are not valid or
operative but merely express the legislator's hopes, desires,
advice or dreams. There is nothing in the legal form to distinguish the latter rules from the former ones. Much of the
political discussion has to do with the question of strengthening
the administration of laws or taking other measures so as to
enforce them. Between the completely enforced rules and the
unenforceable ones there are many intermediary types which are
sometimes, under some conditions, or in some part, only
conditionally and incompletely enforced.*

GUNNAR MYRDAL
An American Dilemma

In recent years the legislative, executive, and judicial branches of government have imposed a myriad of new policies upon
schools and colleges in order to improve their performance.
These policies are designed, on the one hand, to eliminate
inequities arising from discrimination on the basis of race,
sex, poverty, or other factors, and, on the other, to make the
schools perform more productively.

1

Minimum competency testing for advancement in or graduation from the public schools had been mandated by 33 states by mid-1978.[1]

Accountability laws calling for planning-programming-budgeting systems, management-by-objectives, and other "scientific management" systems had been enacted by at least 73 state laws by 1974.[2]

School finance reform and in certain instances the establishment of statewide educational standards had been ordered by a number of state courts by 1978.[3]

The number of pages of *federal legislation* concerning education increased from 80 to 360 from 1964 to 1976; and the number of pages of federal regulations increased from 92 in 1965 to nearly 1,000 in 1977.[4]

Federal court decisions affecting education proliferated from 112 between 1946 and 1956, to 729 between 1956 and 1966, to in excess of 1,200 in the next four years.[5]

Many of the policies to be examined in this chapter are efforts to define and mandate *equality* in the provision of educational services. Since equality of educational opportunity is related to the constitutional idea of equal protection of the laws, whenever government chooses to make education available it may be obliged to provide equal educational opportunity. Some of the policies interpret the meaning of equal protection of the laws and related legal concepts in the context of education.

We shall also examine policies which attempt to mandate fairness about who shall be *denied* access to certain educational services. Increasingly, schools must hold hearings affording due process to those who are to be excluded from educational programs.

Policymakers focus on two concerns with regard to the

1. Chris Pipho, "Minimum Competency Testing in 1978: A Look at State Standards," *Kappan* 59:9 (May 1978), 585–87.

2. See note 44 below.

3. Allan Odden, *School Finance Reform in the States: 1978.* Denver: Education Commission of the States, 1978.

4. Joseph A. Califano, Secretary of Health, Education, and Welfare, as quoted in *Higher Education and National Affairs*, August 25, 1978, p. 1.

5. John C. Hogan, *The Schools, the Courts, and the Public Interest.* Lexington, Mass.: Lexington Books, 1974, pp. 6–7.

productivity of schools in delivering educational services. The first concern is that the schools are inefficient—that they simply are not achieving as much as they should for the amount of money being spent on them. Efficiency is defined as "maximizing output for a given level of input" or "achieving a given level of output at least cost." Many policies are efforts to improve efficiency in the operation of schools.

The second concern is that schools are not performing as effectively as they might—that they are not attaining the goals or objectives that they should. Many policies attempt to establish the goals of education more precisely in the belief that more precise goals are more likely to be attained.

We shall first see how the U.S. Supreme Court has tended to shift concern from equality of educational opportunity to adequacy of educational achievement. We shall then see how the federal government has pursued equal educational opportunity by searching for means to improve the educational achievement of poor students and how state legislatures have tried to promote educational achievement through accountability legislation. Finally, we shall explore legislation and litigation intended to *mandate* learning.

Our examination will reveal the interplay among government, school reality, and the ideas connected with bureaucracy, economics, science, and law. We shall see how, through the proliferation and overlay of educational policymaking, the ideal of equality of opportunity has tended to be replaced by the concept of an adequate level of achievement.

THE U.S. SUPREME COURT: FROM EQUALITY OF EDUCATIONAL OPPORTUNITY TO MINIMAL EDUCATIONAL ADEQUACY

RACIAL DESEGREGATION

In *Brown* v. *Board of Education* in 1954,[6] the U.S. Supreme Court advanced four bases for the conclusion that blacks were being denied equal educational opportunity. The first

6. 347 U.S. 483, 1954.

involved a comparison of tangible resources.[7] This is a relatively easy comparison to make, since to ascertain compliance requires only that the resources available to two groups be tallied and compared.

The second basis was that the state, having created an "opportunity," was obliged to make it equally available to all.[8] This basis is problematical, since it requires an agreed-upon definition of an "opportunity" and a comparison of its availability.

The third basis was that the separation of the races was "inherently unequal."[9] This basis requires the compilation of statistics, although statistical comparisons do not distinguish between mere separation and segregation by intent.

The fourth basis was that segregation had a harmful effect upon black children.[10] The showing of harmful effects is the most problematical of all, for it leads to the expectation that desegregation will have beneficial effects. In turn, further efforts at integration must suffer the burden of proof that desegregation has beneficial effects. What ought properly to be dealt with as a moral issue becomes, instead, a pragmatic one. Thus, the groundwork is laid for the belief that efforts to improve the educational environment of black children should be reflected in *measures* of self-concept and academic achievement, and for the belief that changes in educational practices—whatever the motivation for them—should be reflected in measures of educational outcomes.

The original objective of *Brown* had been to remove barriers to equal educational opportunity. The Supreme Court could have found segregation on the basis of race unconstitutional simply because it involved a classification on the basis of race. In fact, with this precise reasoning, the Court struck down segregation in the District of Columbia on the same day as it ruled in *Brown*.[11] In *Brown*, however, the Court based its decision, in part, upon psychologically determined findings of harmful effects of segregation upon black children.

[*7]. Ibid., p. 492. Supplementary quotations from sources cited in this and other notes appear in the Appendix at the end of this chapter. The numerals for such notes are marked with an asterisk.

[*8]. Ibid., pp. 492–93. [*9]. Ibid., p. 495. [*10]. Ibid., p. 494.

11. *Bolling* v. *Sharpe*, 347 U.S. 497 (1954).

Whether the evidence of harm and the psychological testimony supporting it were necessary has been the subject of dispute.[12] This evidence raised the inevitable question: If segregation causes harm, does desegregation cure it?[13] Successful desegregation came to be measured by scores on tests of academic achievement rather than merely by the percentages of blacks and whites in schools. To the extent that this criterion is used to measure success, the consequence is less a concern for providing equality of educational opportunity than it is for the outcomes of the educational process.

SCHOOL FINANCE EQUALIZATION

The transition from a concern for equal educational opportunity to a concern for the outcomes of the educational process can also be seen in *San Antonio* v. *Rodriguez*.[14] This case, also concerned with equal educational opportunity, was brought to challenge unequal expenditures among the school districts of Texas. *San Antonio* remains the major Supreme Court decision regarding school finance reform.

The objective of the "school finance reform" movement is to equalize educational expenditures within a state. Before 1965, changes in school finance practices were debated politically in nearly every state legislature. Equalization was argued on the basis of fairness where the objective was to narrow the range of expenditures between high and low wealth districts. Beginning in the late sixties, however, reform of school finance practices was being argued on constitutional grounds. Equalization was called for by the equal protection clause where the objective was the elimination of expenditure differences which arose on the basis of wealth or geography.[15] An alternative objective was to eliminate expenditure

12. Edmond Cahn, "Jurisprudence," *New York University Law Review* (January 1955), pp. 150–69.
13. Audrey James Schwartz, "Social Science Evidence and the Objectives of School Desegregation," in John E. McDermott (ed.), *Indeterminacy in Education* (Berkeley: McCutchan, 1976), pp. 73–113.
14. 411 U.S. 1 (1973).
15. Arthur E. Wise, *Rich Schools, Poor Schools: The Promise of Equal Educational Opportunity* (Chicago: University of Chicago Press, 1968).

differences which arose on the basis of wealth differences alone, with the major goal being tax reform rather than school finance reform.[16]

But in *San Antonio*, which upheld the Texas school finance system, school finance reform was implicitly given a new objective. The decision turned, in part, on whether Texas provided an adequate education when judged by the future demands of citizenship.[17] According to the Court's reasoning, the imputed objective of state school finance plans is to provide an "adequate minimum [sic] educational offering,"[18] thus "assuring a basic education"[19] for every child in the state. The test of this objective would be that each child have "an opportunity to acquire the basic minimal [sic] skills"[20] necessary to exercise the fundamental rights of citizenship. The objective of state school finance plans as conceived by the Court in *San Antonio* is neither equal educational opportunity nor equalization of educational expenditures; nor, indeed, equalization of educational tax rates. It is, instead, the provision of a minimally adequate education as judged by an outcome standard.

Mr. Justice Marshall, in his dissent, criticized the Court's "retreat from [its] historic commitment to equality of educational opportunity."[21] He questioned the majority's acceptance of the argument that the state's minimum foundation program of state aid to local school districts guaranteed an adequate education to every child.[22] Finally, he wondered how the Court could know that the state aid program provided "enough" education when the Court elsewhere accepted the "expert opinion" that cost and quality are not related in education.[23] Marshall's dissent drew attention to the problem of defining an adequate level of educational achievement.

16. John E. Coons et al., *Private Wealth and Public Education* (Cambridge, Mass.: Belknap Press, 1970).
  *17. 411 U.S. 1, 35–37.
  18. Ibid., p. 45.
  19. Ibid., p. 49.
  20. Ibid., p. 37.
  *21. Ibid., pp. 70–71.
  *22. Ibid., pp. 86–87.
  *23. Ibid., pp. 89–90.

THE FEDERAL GOVERNMENT: SEARCHING FOR EDUCATIONAL ACHIEVEMENT

IMPROVING EDUCATIONAL ACHIEVEMENT

In 1965 the federal government began to launch a series of initiatives designed to improve educational achievement among poor students. That year the Congress enacted the landmark Elementary and Secondary Education Act, intended to "strengthen and improve educational quality and educational opportunities in the Nation's elementary and secondary schools."[24] Title I of that act called for financial assistance to school districts with "concentrations of children from low-income families" to meet "the special educational needs of educationally deprived children."[25]

Title I appeared to have three interrelated but distinct purposes:

1. To provide financial assistance to school districts in relation to their numbers of low-income children and within those districts to the schools with the greatest numbers of low-income students.

2. To fund special services for low-achieving children in the poorest schools.

3. To contribute to the cognitive, emotional, social, or physical development of participating students.[26]

Although Title I was concerned with the provision of educational opportunity, the expectation that it would lead to increased educational achievement was implicit.[27]

From the start, school districts which received Title I funds were required to engage in systematic evaluation of the effects of Title I funded projects. Each school district was to report specific student performance data to the state department of education so that the state could "perform its duties under this title."[28] This requirement for systematic evalua-

---

24. Public Law 89–10.
*25. Ibid., Title I, Sec. 101.
26. National Institute of Education, *Evaluating Compensatory Education: An Interim Report on the NIE Compensatory Education Study* (Washington, D.C.: HEW/NIE, 1976) pp. 1/8–1/10.
27. Ibid., p. 1/10.
*28. Public Law 89–10, Title I, Sec. 141.

tion of educational achievement is evidence that Title I was intended to do more than merely provide financial aid to school districts. It was also intended to improve the effectiveness of the educational system, that is, to increase the level of measured achievement among children from poor families.

SEARCHING FOR THE CAUSES OF
EDUCATIONAL ACHIEVEMENT: EFFORT 1

The enactment of the Elementary and Secondary Education Act was followed shortly by the *Equality of Educational Opportunity Report*—popularly known as the Coleman Report—which presented the results of a survey mandated by the Civil Rights Act of 1964.[29] The Commissioner of Education was to "... conduct a survey ... concerning the lack of availability of equal educational opportunities for individuals by reason of race, color, religion, or national origin in public educational institutions at all levels in the United States."[30] Since the mandate called for a survey of the "availability of equal educational opportunities," we can assume that the framers of the Act intended a survey of the availability of educational resources by race and the other designated characteristics.[31] But Mr. Coleman and the other researchers charged with carrying out the survey chose not to limit their investigation to a survey of the availability of school inputs. They decided instead to extend the inquiry to look at the determinants of variations in school outcomes as well. For their analysis, they chose as the measure of school outcomes a test of verbal ability (in reality, a test of verbal achievement).[32] The most surprising and most widely cited conclusion of the study was:

> that schools bring little influence to bear on a child's achievement that is independent of his background and general social

29. James S. Coleman et al., *Equality of Educational Opportunity* (Washington, D.C.: U.S. Government Printing Office, 1966).

30. Civil Rights Act of 1964, Sec. 402.

31. James S. Coleman, "The Evaluation of *Equality of Educational Opportunity*," in Frederick Mosteller and Daniel P. Moynihan (eds.), *On Equality of Educational Opportunity* (New York: Random House, 1972), pp. 146–67, especially p. 150.

32. Coleman et al., *Equality of Educational Opportunity*, p. 295.

context; and that this very lack of an independent effect means that the inequalities imposed on children by their home, neighborhood, and peer environment are carried along to become the inequalities with which they confront adult life at the end of school. For equality of educational opportunity through the schools must imply a strong effect of schools that is independent of the child's immediate social environment, and that strong independent effect is not present in American schools.[33]

Although widely differing judgments are held about the correctness of Coleman's conclusions, his report has, for many practical purposes, defined the policy debate in education.[34] Coleman himself has said that the study ". . . has had its major impact in *shifting* policy attention from its traditional focus on comparison of inputs . . . to a focus on output, and the effectiveness of inputs for bringing about changes in output."[35] Indeed, public policy attention has become virtually riveted upon outcomes rather than upon inputs or processes. Somewhat less obvious has been the shift to changes in scores on achievement tests, particularly tests of the basic skills, as the "legitimate" measure of school effectiveness.

MEASURING EDUCATIONAL ACHIEVEMENT

In 1969 the federal government entered into a contractual relationship with the Education Commission of the States to create the National Assessment of Educational Progress.[36] The clearly ambitious overall objective of NAEP is to ". . . examine achievement in 10 learning areas, to spot changes in level of achievement over the years and to apply the implications of those changes to national educational policy."[37] NAEP assumes that changes in achievement levels can be traced to specific policies.

33. Ibid., p. 325.

34. Mosteller and Moynihan, *On Equality of Educational Opportunity*; James W. Guthrie et al., *Schools and Inequality* (Cambridge, Mass.: M.I.T. Press, 1971). McDermott, *Indeterminacy in Education.*

35. Coleman, "The Evaluation of *Equality of Educational Opportunity*," pp. 149–50.

*36. National Center for Education Statistics, *The Condition of Education, 1976* (Washington, D.C.: U.S. Government Printing Office, 1976), p. 296.

37. Ralph Tyler, Foreword to *Update on Education* (Denver: Education Commission of the States, 1975), p. xi.

While the long-term benefits of NAEP are yet to be assessed, it has had some consequences:

> Its data are integral to the yearly reports on the condition of education mandated by federal law; 36 states have drawn upon the assessment materials or methodology for the establishment of their own assessment programs; assessment data have been used to document educational inequities and secure money for their remediation; professional educators have interpreted the results and discussed their implications for curriculum, textbook and classroom; and countless districts, schools and individuals have used National Assessment objectives as starting points for the creation of personal or local teaching objectives.[38]

In short, the most noticeable consequence of NAEP appears to be in giving legitimacy to the idea of assessment and helping to proliferate its application in thirty-six states.[39]

SEARCHING FOR THE CAUSES OF EDUCATIONAL ACHIEVEMENT: EFFORT 2

In 1972 the federal government officially concluded that none of its previous efforts nor those of local and state educational authorities had yet had the desired effects:

> The Congress hereby declares it to be the policy of the United States to provide to every person an equal opportunity to receive an education of high quality regardless of his race, color, religion, sex, national origin, or social class. Although the American educational system has pursued this objective, it has not yet attained that objective. Inequalities of opportunity to receive high quality education remain pronounced. To achieve quality will require far more dependable knowledge about the processes of learning and education than now exists or can be expected from present research and experimentation in this field. While the direction of the education system remains primarily the responsibility of State and local governments, the Federal Government has a clear responsibility to provide leadership in the conduct and support of scientific inquiry into the educational process.[40]

38. Ibid., pp. xi–xii.   39. Ibid., pp. 143–47.
40. Public Law 92–318, Sec. 405.

While Congress observed that there were "inequalities of opportunity," it declared the policy of the United States to be (only) "to provide to every person an equal opportunity to receive an education of high quality."

With this declaration, Congress brought into being the National Institute of Education (NIE), which was

> ... to improve education, including career education, in the United States through:
>
> (a) helping to solve or to alleviate the problems of, and achieve the objectives of American Education;
>
> (b) advancing the practice of education, as an art, science, and profession;
>
> (c) the strengthening of the scientific and technological foundations of education; and
>
> (d) building an effective educational research and development system.[41]

NIE was to search systematically and scientifically for the means to achieve the objectives of American education, which included an education of high quality for all regardless of race, social class, and other specified characteristics.

SEARCHING FOR THE CAUSES OF EDUCATIONAL ACHIEVEMENT: EFFORT 3

NIE had barely commenced operation when a bill was introduced in Congress which would have required a change in the method of allocating Title I funds.[42] These funds were being allocated on the basis of the number of poor families, on the assumption of a correlation between poverty and "educational disadvantagement." It was pointed out that some poor are not educationally disadvantaged and that many non-poor are educationally disadvantaged. The bill would have required that funds be allocated on the basis of the number of students performing poorly on tests in reading and arithmetic. While the bill did not pass, the Education Amendments of 1974 did call upon NIE to conduct a three-year study of the effectiveness of compensatory education programs.[43] NIE was to discover in three years how to allocate funds to improve

41. Ibid.   42. H.R. 5163.
*43. Public Law 93–380, Sec. 821.

reading and mathematics achievement—an objective not different from the major long-term objective of the Institute itself. The federal search for the causes of educational achievement was insistent.

THE STATE LEGISLATURES: ACCOUNTABILITY FOR EDUCATIONAL ACHIEVEMENT

At the state level, the striving for educational achievement resulted in the enactment of at least seventy-three laws in the years between 1963 and 1974.[44] These laws clearly revealed a concern for ensuring educational achievement rather than for providing educational opportunities, and a concern with adequacy rather than equality. To satisfy this mandate for accountability, the schools have turned to the techniques of management science.

SCIENTIFIC MANAGEMENT

The lexicon of the accountability movement includes at least the following terms:

accountability
planning, programming, budgeting systems (PPBS)
management-by-objectives (MBO)
operations analysis
systems analysis
program evaluation and review technique (PERT)
management information systems (MIS)
management science
planning models
cost-benefit analysis
cost effectiveness analysis
economic analysis
systems engineering
zero-based budgeting

44. Cooperative Accountability Project, *Legislation by the States: Accountability and Assessment in Education*, Report No. 2 (Colorado: CAP, 1974), p. 7. The Cooperative Accountability Project was a seven-state, 39-month project initiated in April 1972 and financed by funds provided under E.S.E.A. of 1965 (Public Law 89–10). Most of the legislation cited in this section is taken from the above-referenced publication.

These purely management techniques are perceived in some cases to be directly applicable to education, and the ideology which has given rise to their use has also given rise to derivative approaches adapting management science to education.

Perhaps more important, however, is the fact that management ideology has focussed concern upon the output of the educational system in two ways. First, numerous systems for focusing attention upon outputs have been devised. These include:

> competency-based education (CBE)
> performance-based education (PBE)
> competency-based teacher education (CBTE)
> assessment systems (federal, state, and local)
> program evaluation
> learner verification
> behavioral objectives
> mastery learning
> criterion-referenced testing
> educational indicators
> performance contracting

Second, rubrics for minimum expectations for school outcomes have been devised to describe the nature of that education which is designed to transform the "output" of the school system to the "input" of society. The term "functional literacy" best captures this transformation, but other dimensions of education are captured by: basic education, basic skills, career education, and moral education.

Let us look at how some of the lexicon of the accountability movement is used in legislation affecting the schools.

Accountability / The term "accountability" in short order became the generic term for the forms of legislation listed above. A good illustration of the specific use of the term is Colorado's Educational Accountability Act of 1971:

> (1) The general assembly hereby declares that the purpose of this article is to institute an accountability program to define and measure quality in education, and thus to help the public schools of Colorado to achieve such quality and to expand the life opportunities and options of the students of this state; further, to provide to local school boards assistance in helping

their school patrons to determine the relative value of their school program as compared to its cost.

(2) (a) The general assembly further declares that the educational accountability program developed under this article should be designed to measure objectively the adequacy and efficiency of the educational programs offered by the public schools. The program should begin by developing broad goals and specific performance objectives for the educational process and by identifying the activities of schools which can advance students toward these goals and objectives. The program should then develop a means for evaluating the achievements and performance of students. It is the belief of the general assembly that in developing the evaluation mechanism, the following approaches, as a minimum, should be explored:

(b) Means for determining whether decisions affecting the educational process are advancing or impeding student achievement;

(c) Appropriate testing procedures to provide relevant comparative data at least in the fields of reading, language skills and mathematical skills;

(d) The role of the department of education in assisting school districts to strengthen their educational programs;

(e) Reporting to students, parents, boards of education, educators, and the general public on the educational performance of the public schools and providing data for the appraisal of such performance; and

(f) Provision of information which could help school districts to increase their efficiency in using available financial resources.[45]

In addition, this act includes terms and references highlighted in other types of accountability legislation. The act seeks not only to promote accountability for results, but it also endorses "adequacy," "efficiency," " performance objectives," "evaluation," and "basic skills." It appears to strengthen the hand of the state in educational policymaking and implies that the accountability program will reveal how to make students learn.

The Florida Legislature has enacted an accountability law in every year between 1969 and 1976. The Educational Ac-

45. Chapter 123, S. 41, 1971.

countability Act of 1971 directed the Commissioner of Education and the State Board of Education to establish grade-by-grade standards in the basic skills and to use tests based on specific theories of testing.[46] Maryland enacted an accountability law in 1972 which contained a number of the familiar elements; it also underscored the idea that local objectives must conform to state objectives.[47] In 1975, Mississippi adopted "an act to establish a system of educational accountability and assessment of educational performance to assist in the measurement of educational quality and to provide information to school officials and citizens."[48] It directed that the State Department of Education establish the goals and that the schools attain the goals. In none of these mandates for accountability is a penalty associated with failure on the part of the student, the teacher, or the school.

Planning, Programming, Budgeting Systems (PPBS) / Because the accountability movement was not restricted to education, often government-wide accountability legislation included education within its scope. In 1973 the Texas Legislature enacted a bill directing the Legislative Budget Board to establish a planning, programming, budgeting system:

> The performance report shall analyze the operational efficiency of state agency operations and program performance in terms of explicitly stating the statutory functions each agency, department, commission and institution are to perform and how these statutory functions are being accomplished, in terms of unit-cost measurement, workload efficiency data, and program output standards as the Legislative Budget Board shall establish.[49]

The emphasis was on performance, and the clear intent was to develop measurable output standards. Subsequent resolutions of the Texas Legislature directed *program budgeting* and a study of *zero base budgeting* including *cost-benefit analysis*.[50]

˚46. House Bill No. 894, 1971.
˚47. Article 77, Section 28A, Senate Bill No. 166, 1972.
˚48. House Bill No. 35, 1975.
 49. House Bill No. 169, 1973.
 50. Cooperative Accountability Project, *Legislation by the States*, p. 89.

Management-by-Objectives (MBO) / Sometimes it is not clear under which accountability rubric a particular piece of legislation should be classified. In 1971, Virginia enacted a law "to revise certain standards of quality for the several school divisions determined and prescribed by the board of education and to specify certain objectives for the board of education and local school boards." The law appeared to be a basis for management-by-objectives. It prescribed, *inter alia*, performance objectives for the state and for school districts. One of the more ambitious, if enigmatic, of these was:

> The percentage of the student population achieving at or above grade level norms or the equivalent as measured by approved standardized achievement tests should equal or exceed the mean ability level of the student population as measured by appropriate scholastic aptitude tests.[51]

The language of the objectives appeared to be a mixture of exhortation and data-based management; the penalty for failure to attain the objectives is not specified. The presumption is that schools have not been trying hard enough or at least have not succeeded—and that the existence of the law will bring about the objectives. Presumably, barriers to the attainment of these objectives are removed by the legislation.

Systems Analysis / Some legislation directly orders the implementation of a specific management tool. In 1973, Oklahoma, for example, imposed systems analysis upon the school districts of the state, in a law which provided, *inter alia*:

> That each school district that wishes state accreditation shall initiate a systemwide needs assessment involving all grades under its jurisdiction.
> That the needs assessment shall be undertaken by the local staff in compliance with general direction and guidelines developed by the State Department of Education.
> That a systems analysis process including goals and objectives shall be utilized to plan the instructional program to fit the needs of the students of said district.[52]

---

*51. House Bill No. 845, 1972.
*52. House Concurrent Resolution No. 1027, 1973.

Here systems analysis, originally developed to manage defense expenditures, is linked to an education-specific term, "needs assessment."[53]

Management Information Systems (MIS) / While Oklahoma favored systems analysis, Ohio favored a management information system:

> The state department of education shall develop a comprehensive system for providing educational management information and accountability capabilities. The system shall be designed for eventual implementation on a state-wide basis and shall utilize the technology of the computer and related systems concepts. Developmental work by the department shall utilize pilot school districts and shall strive, with regard to all public and nonpublic elementary and secondary schools in the state, to (1) define those measurable objectives for which each facet and level of public education is to be held accountable; (2) identify pertinent data elements and devise methods and systems for fairly, accurately and uniformly measuring and reporting the extent to which the defined objectives are met; (3) develop uniform files, methods and systems for collecting, processing, sorting and analyzing data which will permit identification of those factors in the teaching-learning process which have the greatest relevance to student performance; (4) develop uniform accounting methods and systems which will relate the cost and the efficiency of those factors to the learning outcome; and (5) develop uniform systems of reporting the findings of the program to all interested persons.[54]

Lest the apparent intent of the act be misconstrued, the framers found it necessary to specify utilization of the computer and to garb an accountability law with the rhetoric of computer technology. Ohio schools were to be improved by a computer-based MIS.

53. "Needs Assessment" is a concept or technique which follows a sequence of dubious reasoning. Children or schools have different needs. Those differences can be precisely assessed. Instructional programs can be constructed to remedy those needs. However, needs are not absolute; they must be imputed by reference to a desired state. "Needs" are thus difficult both to conceptualize and to assess. Finally, it may not always be possible to construct instructional programs to meet these needs.
54. House Bill No. 475, 1972.

Management Science / California vies with Florida for the distinction of being the state with the greatest volume of accountability legislation. In an interesting variation, California, in 1971, created an Educational Management and Evaluation Commission. The State Board of Education was to appoint nine public members of this commission—three to "represent the field of economics," three to "represent the learning sciences," and three to "represent the managerial sciences":

> The commission shall assist and advise the State Board of Education in the evaluation of the program achievement of educational programs, in the determination of the relative cost effectiveness of educational programs, and shall make recommendations concerning the expanded use, modification, or replacement of educational programs so as to produce a higher degree of program achievement and cost effectiveness. The commission shall also serve as an advisory body to the State Board of Education on program budgeting and accounting systems for school districts.[55]

The composition of this commission and its mandate made clear that its purpose was the introduction of management science to education.

Planning Models / In 1971, Colorado adopted not only an Educational Accountability Act but a Comprehensive Educational Planning Act as well:

> (a) Comprehensive educational planning includes, but is not limited to, the following steps:
> (b) Evaluation of the present educational program and identification of the strengths and weaknesses of the district;
> (c) Delineation of the knowledge, skills, and attitudes which are the goals of the district's educational program;
> (d) Development of a plan for the district's educational program which will enable pupils in the district to meet the delineated goals.[56]

Colorado's accountability law called for "determining whether decisions affecting the educational process are advancing

55. Assembly Bill No. 2800, 1971.
56. Chapter 123, S. 43, 1971.

or impeding student achievement"; its planning act required "evaluation of the strengths and weaknesses of the district."

Rhode Island in 1973 adopted a law calling upon the Board of Regents to approve a master plan to encompass not only elementary and secondary schools but also colleges and universities; not only public education but also non-public education.[57] Presumably the Regents were also to define "what men should know and be able to do" with sufficient precision to be able to evaluate whether schools and colleges produce such men.

EDUCATION-SPECIFIC SCIENTIFIC MANAGEMENT

The legislation reviewed thus far embodies the application of scientific management developed in other sectors and applied without much modification to education. At the same time, the ideology of management science has spawned the development of techniques specifically directed to education. In turn, these techniques have frequently been imposed by legislation—often before they have been developed.

Performance-Based Education / In 1974, Georgia passed the Adequate Program for Education in Georgia Act, which called for performance-based criteria for operating the instructional program of each public school.[58] While the Act was designed to encourage performance-based education, a definition of PBE was not included in the law. Although the Act was titled "an adequate program," it called for both "equal" and "adequate" programs. The law apparently did not contemplate any inconsistency between these objectives; "economy" and "efficiency" were also featured objectives of the law.

Competency-Based Teacher Evaluation / A number of state laws were designed to require *competency-based or performance-based teacher education, certification, or evaluation.* The first of these was California's Stull Act, which mandated that the evaluation of teachers be based upon their competence. Each school district was "to develop and adopt

*57. Chapter 249, 1973.
*58. Senate Bill No. 672, 1974.

specific evaluation and assessment guidelines" which were to include:

> The establishment of standards of expected student progress in each area of study and of techniques for the assessment of that progress.
>
> Assessment of certificated personnel competence as it relates to the established standards.
>
> Assessment of other duties normally required to be performed by certificated employees as an adjunct to their regular assignments.
>
> The establishment of procedures and techniques for ascertaining that the employee is maintaining proper control and is preserving a suitable learning environment.[59]

The most interesting feature of this law was its requirement that the evaluation of teachers be based upon their contribution to their students' performance. That school districts have had difficulty in meeting this demanding standard is suggested by the fact that a less restrictive new law replaced the Stull Act in 1975.[60]

Assessment Systems / A major variation of accountability legislation has been programs of assessment. The state to attract the most attention in this regard is Michigan, which adopted its comprehensive assessment program in 1970. The law provided for:

> A statewide program of assessment of educational progress and remedial assistance in the basic skills of students in reading,

---

59. Chapter 361, 1971.

60. Chapter 1216, 1975. In "Research Basis for Performance-Based Teacher Education," Robert W. Heath and Mark A. Nielson conclude:

"First, the research literature on the relation between teacher behavior and student achievement does not offer an empirical basis for the prescription of teacher-training objectives.

"Second, this literature fails to provide such a basis, not because of minor flaws in the statistical analyses, but because of sterile operational definitions of both teaching and achievement, and because of fundamentally weak research designs.

"Last, given the well-documented, strong association between student achievement and variables such as socioeconomic status and ethnic status, the effects of techniques of teaching on achievement (as these variables are defined in the PBTE research) are likely to be inherently trivial." *Review of Educational Research* 44:4 (Fall 1974), 463–81.

mathematics, language arts and/or other general subject areas is established in the department of education, which program shall:

(a) Establish meaningful achievement goals in the basic skills for students, and identify those students with the greatest educational need in these skills.

(b) Provide the state with the information needed to allocate state funds and professional services in a manner best calculated to equalize educational opportunities for students to achieve competence in such basic skills.

(c) Provide school systems with strong incentives to introduce educational programs to improve the education of students in such basic skills and model programs to raise the level of achievement of students.

(d) Develop a system for educational self-renewal that would continuously evaluate the programs and by this means help each school to discover and introduce program changes that are most likely to improve the quality of education.

(e) Provide the public periodically with information concerning the progress of the state system of education. Such programs shall extend current department of education efforts to conduct periodic and comprehensive assessment of educational progress.[61]

The law directed attention to the basic skills and provided extra funds for students with the "greatest educational need." Michigan's assessment law differs from other laws in specifying a course of action upon the identification of need. The law did assume, as did others, however, that the state could induce educational improvement where local school districts could not.[62]

Program Evaluation / In 1969, California passed the Educational Improvement Act, which was designed to specify

61. Public Act No. 38, 1970.

62. The Michigan assessment law has been analyzed more than most. A few studies are: Ernest House, Wendell Rivers, and Daniel Stufflebeam, "An Assessment of the Michigan Accountability System," A Report to the Michigan Education Association and the National Education Association, March 1974. "A Staff Response to the Report 'An Assessment of the Michigan Accountability System,'" Michigan Department of Education, May 1974. Jerome T. Murphy and David K. Cohen, "Accountability in Education—The Michigan Experience," *Public Interest* 36 (Summer 1974), 53–81.

criteria and techniques for the evaluation of state and federal project grants:

> It is the intent of the Legislature that the funds provided by this chapter and the funds provided through Title I and Title III of the Elementary and Secondary Education Act of 1965 [and] the Miller-Unruh Basic Reading Act of 1965 be expended in the most effective way possible, and that cost effectiveness measures be employed in the approval and evaluation of all projects. It is the further intent of the Legislature that all projects be evaluated annually as to the degree of program achievement and cost effectiveness produced; that highly effective projects shall be expanded to further use in the district where operated and in other districts; and that less effective projects be replaced with ones of proven effectiveness, or by new projects which hold promise of high effectiveness.
>
> It is the intent of the Legislature that the effectiveness of a project be measured in terms of the objectives of the project, and that each district should be primarily concerned with the pupils' improvement in ability to read, to use and understand the English language and to use and understand the concepts of mathematics.[63]

This law, in effect, mandated that project grants were to focus upon basic skills, that they were to be evaluated, and that evaluation was to assess student improvement and cost effectiveness.

Learner Verification / Florida has adopted a law which seeks to guarantee in advance that textbooks and other instructional materials will work. The law, known as learner verification, requires, *inter alia*:

> Written proof of the use of the learner-verification and revision process during prepublication development and postpublication revision of the materials in question. For purposes of this section "learner verification" is defined as the empirical process of data gathering and analysis by which a publisher of curriculum material has improved the instructional effectiveness of that product before it reaches the market and then continues to gather data from learners in order to improve the quality and reliability of that material during its full market life. Failing

63. Assembly Bill No. 606 Chapter 784, 1969.

such proof, if the publisher wishes to submit material for adoption, he must satisfy the State instructional materials selection council that he will systematically gather and utilize learner-verification data to revise the materials in question to better meet the needs of learners throughout the state. Such text revision should be interpreted as including specific revision of the materials themselves, revision of the teachers' materials, and revision of the teachers' skill through retraining, it being the intent of the legislature that learner-verification and revision data shall include data gathered directly from learners; may include the results of criterion-referenced and group-normed tests, direct learner comments, or information gathered from written questionnaires from individual or small group interviews; and not preclude the use of secondary data gathered from teachers, supervisors, parents, and all appropriate participants and observers of the teaching-learning process.[64]

With the concept of learner verification, accountability seems to have touched nearly every aspect of education.[65]

The interest of all of these laws is to make schools accountable for results. The techniques they recommend are directed to the outcomes of the educational process. These education-specific techniques, together with the techniques of "pure" scientific management, are designed to promote educational achievement.

MANDATING EDUCATIONAL ACHIEVEMENT

As we have seen, the U.S. Supreme Court, as it has grappled with the issue of equal educational opportunity, has begun to evolve a standard of adequacy of educational achievement. It is a standard preferred by those who espouse it because it appears to be practical, specifiable, and attainable. The federal government, by supporting both the education of poor students and research on the determinants of educational achievement, has contributed to this standard. State legislatures, in their efforts to make schools accountable for results,

64. Chapter 233.25 (1974).

65. For a critical analysis of learner verification, see "Quality Control for Instructional Materials: Legislative Mandates of Learner Verification and Implications for Public Education," *Harvard Journal on Legislation* 12 (1975), 511–562.

have also made their contributions. Policymakers have not, however, been content merely to specify what learning they hope will occur. They have begun to mandate *that* learning occur.

Legislating Minimal Competency

California came close to mandating learning when it enacted the Guaranteed Learning Achievement Act of 1971. This act provided for "performance contracting" between private contractors and public school districts for the teaching of reading and mathematics,[66] and made payment to the private contractor contingent upon the acquisition by students of the basic skills.[67]

The idea of mandating learning actually began in 1976. In that year the *National Assessment of Educational Progress Newsletter* wrote that "one of the hottest issues in education today is minimal competency":

> Packed into those two words are images ranging from the simple implication that students need master only basic readin', writin' and rithmetic to a miscellany of complex, emotional and sometimes intertwined controversies.[68]

The reader will by now anticipate the connotations of minimal competency:

> The latter cover teacher accountability, costs and logistics of extensive remedial classes, potential loss of school revenue, increased parental demand for schools to prepare their children to manage—at least with some minimum success—their lives after formal education ceases and the specter of a country-wide testing program that is defined and controlled by the federal government.[69]

---

*66. Chapter 1600, Assembly Bill No. 1483, 1971.

67. For the generally negative evaluation of performance contracting, see Edward M. Gramlich and Patricia P. Koshel, *Educational Performance Contracting: An Evaluation of an Experiment* (Washington, D.C.: Brookings, 1975).

68. *NAEP Newsletter* 9:3 (June 1976), 1. Chris Pipho, associate director of Research and Information Services of the Education Commission of the States, operates a clearinghouse on minimal competency.

69. Ibid.

"Minimal competency," sometimes expanded to "minimal-competency-testing," joins together basic (minimum) skills, competency-based education, and assessment.

Perhaps the most comprehensive minimal competency testing legislation enacted in 1976 was Florida's Educational Accountability Act of 1976. The law mandated learning while preserving many other elements of accountability. Its intent was to:

(a) Provide a system of accountability for education in Florida which guarantees that each student is afforded similar opportunities for educational advancement without regard to geographic differences and varying local economic factors.

(b) Provide information for education decision-makers at the state, district, and school levels so that resources may be appropriately allocated and the needs of the system of public education met in a timely manner.

(c) Provide information about costs of educational programs and the differential effectiveness of differing instructional programs so that the educational process may be improved continually.

(d) Guarantee to each student in the Florida system of public education that the system provides instructional programs which meet minimum performance standards compatible with the state's plan for education.

(e) Provide a more thorough analysis of program costs and the degree to which the various districts are meeting the minimum performance standards established by the State Board of Education.

(f) Provide information to the public about the performance of the Florida system of public education in meeting established goals and providing effective, meaningful, and relevant educational experiences designed to give students at least the minimum skills necessary to function and survive in today's society.[70]

While the minimum performance standards may appear to be characteristics of programs, it soon becomes clear that they are standards for students to attain; in short, the system is to guarantee that each student attain a specified standard.

70. Chapter 76–223, Sec. 1 (1976).

The basic skills portion of the act specified what every student is to learn.[71] The law also specified the contingencies should a student fail to attain minimum performance standards.[72] In addition, it required educational planning (including the creation of a management information system);[73] research and development "to assess the effects of alternative educational practices";[74] educational evaluation;[75] procedures for diagnosis and placement of students in special programs for exceptional students to determine that the district is following the criteria for placement established by rules of the state board;[76] statewide assessment testing programs [sic];[77] school, district, and state reports;[78] and school advisory committees (but these shall not have "any of the powers and duties now reserved by law to the district school board").[79]

In 1976, Virginia enacted a law requiring "uniform statewide testing" of the "basic learning skills."[80] This law also called for career preparation.[81] Although both the acquisition of basic learning skills and career preparation were objectives of the law, testing was required only in the basic skills.

Minimal competency testing in the basic skills evolved out of the accountability movement. Earlier versions of accountability held out the promise of accommodating virtually any goal for education so long as that goal was, in principle, measurable. It was assumed that in time the appropriate measures would be developed. Measures were most readily available, however, only in reading and arithmetic. The collapse of the accountability movement into the minimal competency testing movement occurred because of the decline in certain test scores between the mid-60s and mid-70s.[82] A call arose

*71. Ibid., Sec. 13.   *72. Ibid., Sec. 15.   73. Ibid., Sec. 3.
  74. Ibid., Sec. 4.   75. Ibid., Sec. 5.   76. Ibid., Sec. 5.
  77. Ibid., Sec. 5.   78. Ibid., Sec. 6.   79. Ibid., Sec. 7,8.
*80. House Bill No. 256 (1976).   *81. Ibid.

  82. The National Institute of Education reported declines in the American College Test (Composite), Composite Test of Basic Skills, Iowa Tests of Basic Skills (later grades), Iowa Tests of Educational Development, Minnesota Scholastic Aptitude Test, National Assessment of Educational Progress (Science and Functional Literacy), and the Scholastic Aptitude Test, but *increases or no changes* in the Air Force Qualifications Test, American College Test (Science), Iowa Test of Basic Skills (early grades), National Assessment of Educational Progress (Reading Achievement), Pre-

for "back-to-the-basics" and was immediately translated into minimal competency testing legislation. The schools, of which so much had been asked, were now being directed to concentrate on instructing students in the basic skills.[83]

ASSURING THE EFFECTIVENESS OF EDUCATION

In 1975 the Education for All Handicapped Children Act was passed. Its stated purpose is:

> . . . to assure that all handicapped children have available to them . . . a free appropriate public education which emphasizes special education and related services designed to meet their unique needs, to assure that the rights of handicapped children and their parents or guardians are protected, to assist States and localities to provide for the education of all handicapped children, and to assess and assure the effectiveness of efforts to educate handicapped children.[84]

By this act the federal government is not merely making education available, it is *assuring* that the education provided will be effective. The law also requires certain educational practices, procedures, and regulations to achieve this goal.

Among the educational practices required is an "individualized education program" for every handicapped child. The program is defined as:

> . . . a written statement for each handicapped child developed in any meeting by a representative of the local educational agency or an intermediate educational unit who shall be qualified to provide, or supervise the provision of, specially designed instruction to meet the unique needs of handicapped children, the teacher, the parents or guardian of such child, and, whenever appropriate, such child, which statement shall include (A) a statement of the present levels of educational performance of each child, (B) a statement of annual goals, including short-term instructional objectives, (C) a statement of the specific

liminary Scholastic Aptitude Test, and Project Talent. *Declining Test Scores* (Washington, D.C.: DHEW/NIE, 1976), p. 28.

83. In 1977, Congressman Mottl introduced a bill which would have required states to establish basic standards of educational proficiency as a condition of receiving *any* aid under the Elementary and Secondary Education Act of 1965. The bill did not pass.

84. Public Law 94–142, Sec. 3. Emphasis added.

educational services to be provided to such child, and the extent to which such child will be able to participate in regular educational programs, (D) the projected date for initiation and anticipated duration of such services, and (E) appropriate objective criteria and evaluation procedures and schedules for determining, on at least an annual basis, whether instructional objectives are being achieved.[85]

The school district must "provide assurances" that it will establish an individualized education program for each handicapped child.[86] The State must "provide for procedures" for evaluating the effectiveness of these programs.[87] And the federal government must assess the effectiveness of individualized education programs.[88] In addition, the law requires that handicapped children be educated in the "least restrictive environment."[89]

The law also creates an elaborate system of procedural safeguards designed to assure that the child's parents are satisfied with his placement in school.[90] When a complaint arises under the procedure, the parents are entitled to a "due process hearing." If the parents are not satisfied with the outcome of the hearings, they can appeal to the State agency. At both hearings, they have the right to counsel and expert advice, the right to present evidence, the right to confront and cross-examine witnesses, and the right to hearing records.[91] If the parents remain unsatisfied by the outcome of the state-level hearing, they may bring action in State or federal court.

In sum, this law assures an effective education to all handicapped children and postulates that the result will be achieved—by the use of individualized education programs and in the least restrictive environment—when due process is followed.

DUTY TO TEACH: RIGHT TO LEARN

What happens if a student fails to attain the adequate level of achievement that the schools have been mandated to provide? In the early phases of the accountability movement,

85. Ibid., Sec. 4.   86. Ibid., Sec. 614.   87. Ibid., Sec. 613.
88. Ibid., Sec. 618.   *89. Ibid., Sec. 612.   *90. Ibid., Sec. 615.
91. Ibid.

it was implied that the school or the teacher was responsible if the child failed to learn, since they were being held accountable to the public or its representatives. In later phases of the accountability movement, it was implied that the student was at fault if he failed to learn. If the student does not become competent or attain the basic skills, he will not progress to the next grade or be graduated with a diploma.

Yet if a state mandates that students learn, does the student thereby gain a right to learn? In general, the rights of citizens and the duties of states are associated. By mandating that students acquire the basic skills, states may be assuming a legal obligation to teach. Indeed, this logical conclusion has been tested in litigation. In *Peter Doe* v. *San Francisco*, a youth sued the San Francisco Unified School District for educational malpractice.[92] His complaint alleged that the school district:

1. Negligently and carelessly failed to take notice of plaintiff's reading disabilities, despite evidence found in plaintiff's reading test scores, class performance, and parental inquiries from which defendants with exercise of reasonable care knew or should have known the existence of plaintiff's severe reading disabilities, disabilities from which serious injury to plaintiff would follow with near certainty unless adequate and competent reading instruction was promptly provided to him;

2. Negligently and carelessly assigned plaintiff to classes where the books and other materials were too difficult for a student of plaintiff's reading ability to read, when defendants knew, or with the exercise of reasonable care should have known, that said books and other materials were too difficult for a student of plaintiff's reading ability to read, comprehend, or benefit from;

3. Negligently and carelessly allowed plaintiff to pass and advance from a course or grade level although the defendants knew, or with the exercise of reasonable care and skill should have known, that plaintiff had not achieved the knowledge, understanding or skills required for completion of said course or grade level and necessary for him to succeed or benefit from subsequent course;

4. Negligently and carelessly assigned plaintiff to classes

92. First Amended Complaint, filed October 31, 1973, California Superior Court, Docket No. 653–312.

with instructors not qualified or unable to teach the particular subject, and to classes not geared toward students with his reading abilities and disabilities; and

5. Negligently and carelessly permitted plaintiff to graduate from high school although he was unable to read above the eighth grade level, as required by Education Code Section 8573, effective on the date of plaintiff's graduation from high school, thereby depriving him of additional instruction in reading and other academic skills.[93]

The case, which Doe lost on appeal, failed, in part because the duty of the school district had not been specified in as precise a manner as it would be under a minimal competency testing law.[94] Other educational malpractice suits have been and no doubt will be conceived and brought.[95] If a State promises an adequate education, it had better be prepared to deliver it.

THOROUGH AND EFFICIENT EDUCATION

The policies illustrated in this chapter have unfolded in rapid and dramatic form in New Jersey since 1972. There *Robinson* v. *Cahill*, and the legislative response to it, have provided the setting for several policy shifts.[96] *Robinson* v. *Cahill* began as a challenge to the State's pattern of inequality of educational opportunity—of unequal school expenditures. The Superior Court of New Jersey asserted that:

Providing free education for all is a State function. It must be accorded to all on equal terms. . . . Public education cannot be financed by a method that makes a pupil's education depend upon the wealth of his family and neighbors as distinguished from the wealth of all taxpayers of the same class throughout the State. . . .

Arthur Wise . . . first advanced this thesis in "Is Denial of Equal Educational Opportunity Constitutional?" . . . He elaborated upon it in *Rich Schools, Poor Schools.* . . . It was his contention

93. Ibid., pp. 7–8.   94. 131 Cal. Reporter 854, 1976.

95. See, for example, "A Graduate Who Says He Can't Read," *New York Times*, February 20, 1977. The article concerns a suit being brought against the Copiague Union Free Schools in New York. See also Joan C. Baratz and Terry W. Hartle, " 'Malpractice' in the Schools," *The Progressive* (June 1977), pp. 33–34.

96. 118 N.J. Supp. 223, 287 A. 2d 187, 1972.

that the present system of funding education of all states except Hawaii (which is funded entirely out of general state revnues) denies the equal protection of the laws. A similar thesis has been advanced by Coons, Clune and Sugarman, in "Educational Opportunity: A Workable Constitutional Test for State Financial Structures," . . . and in *Private Wealth and Public Education.* . . . It is this thesis that has been adopted by the Supreme Court of California in *Serrano.* . . .

The New Jersey system of financing public education denies equal protection rights guaranteed by the New Jersey and Federal Constitutions. In support of this conclusion I adopt the thesis of the foregoing authorities.[97]

The decision was affirmed by the New Jersey Supreme Court, not on the basis of equal protection, but on the article in the State constitution which mandates that "the legislature shall provide for the maintenance and support of a thorough and efficient system of free public schools." By the time the decision was implemented by state legislation, the result was comprehensive educational planning, emphasis upon the basic skills, statewide standards, and assessment. It remains to be shown how a suit concerned with equalizing educational expenditures could result in a demand for adequacy of educational achievement—known popularly in New Jersey as "thorough and efficient education." We shall look at *Robinson* v. *Cahill* in detail in Chapter 5.

Let us now turn to an analysis of some of the assumptions, ideas, and implications of educational policies imposed upon the schools from external sources.

97. 287 A. 2d 187, 214.

APPENDIX: SUPPLEMENTARY QUOTATIONS

NOTE 7.

Here, unlike *Sweatt* v. *Painter*, there are findings below that the Negro and white schools involved have been equalized, or are being equalized, with respect to buildings, curricula, qualifications and salaries of teachers, and other "tangible" factors. Our decision, therefore, cannot turn on merely a comparison of these tangible factors in the Negro and white schools involved in each of the cases. (347 U.S. 483, 492.)

NOTE 8.

Today, education is perhaps the most important function of state and local government. Compulsory school attendance laws and the great expenditures for education both demonstrate our recognition of the importance of education to our democratic society. It is required in the performance of our most basic public responsibilities, even service in the armed forces. It is the very foundation of good citizenship. Today it is a principal instrument in awakening the child to cultural values, in preparing him for later professional training, and in helping him to adjust normally to his environment. In these days, it is doubtful that any child may reasonably be expected to succeed in life if he is denied the opportunity of an education. Such an opportunity, where the state has undertaken to provide it, is a right which must be made available to all on equal terms. (Ibid., 492–493.)

NOTE 9.

We conclude that in the field of public education the doctrine of "separate but equal" has no place. Separate educational facilities are inherently unequal. Therefore, we hold that the plaintiffs and others similarly situated for whom the actions have been brought are, by reason of the segregation complained of, deprived of the equal protection of the laws guaranteed by the Fourteenth Amendment. (Ibid., p. 495.)

NOTE 10.

To separate [blacks] from others of similar age and qualifications solely because of their race generates a feeling of inferiority as to their status in the community that may affect their hearts and minds in a way unlikely ever to be undone. The effect of this separation on their educational opportunities was well stated by a finding in the Kansas case by a court which nevertheless felt compelled to rule against the Negro plaintiffs:

Segregation of white and colored children in public schools has a detrimental effect upon the colored children. The impact is greater when it has the sanction of the law; for the policy of separating the races is usually interpreted as denoting the inferiority of the negro group. A sense of inferiority affects the motivation of a child to learn. Segregation with the sanction of law, therefore, has a tendency to [retard] the educational and mental development of negro children and to deprive them of some of the benefits they would receive in a racial[ly] integrated school system. (Ibid., p. 494.)

NOTE 17.

Education, of course, is not among the rights afforded explicit protection under our Federal Constitution. Nor do we find any basis for saying it is implicitly so protected. As we have said, the undisputed importance of education will not alone cause this Court to depart from the usual standard for reviewing a State's social and economic legislation. It is appellees' contention, however, that education is distinguishable from other services and benefits provided by the State because it bears a peculiarly close relationship to other rights and liberties accorded protection under the Constitution. Specifically, they insist that education is itself a fundamental personal right because it is essential to the effective exercise of First Amendment freedoms and to intelligent utilization of the right to vote. In asserting a nexus between speech and education, appellees urge that the right to speak is meaningless unless the speaker is capable of articulating his thoughts intelligently and persuasively. The "marketplace of ideas" is an empty forum for those lacking basic communicative tools. Likewise, they argue that the corollary right to receive information becomes little more than a hollow privilege when the recipient has not been taught to read, assimilate, and utilize available knowledge.

A similar line of reasoning is pursued with respect to the right to vote. Exercise of the franchise, it is contended, cannot be divorced from the educational foundation of the voter. The electoral process, if reality is to conform to the democratic ideal, depends on an informed electorate: a voter cannot cast his ballot intelligently unless his reading skills and thought processes have been adequately developed.

We need not dispute any of these propositions. The Court has long afforded zealous protection against unjustifiable governmental interference with the individual's rights to speak and to vote. Yet we have never presumed to possess either the ability or the authority to guarantee to the citizenry the most *effective* speech or the most *informed* electoral choice. That these may be desirable goals of a system of freedom of expression and of a representative form of government is not to be doubted. These are indeed goals to be pursued by a people whose thoughts and beliefs are freed from governmental interference. But they are not values to be implemented by judicial intrusion into otherwise legitimate state activities.

Even if it were conceded that some identifiable quantum of education is a constitutionally protected prerequisite to the meaningful exercise of either right, we have no indication that the present levels of educational expenditure in Texas provide an education that falls short. Whatever merit appellees' argument might have if a State's financing system occasioned an absolute denial of educational opportunities to any of its children, that argument provides no basis for finding an interference with fundamental rights where only relative differences in spending levels are involved and where—as is true in the present case—no charge fairly could be made that the system fails to provide each child with an opportunity to acquire the basic minimal skills necessary for the enjoyment of the rights of speech and of full participation in the political process. (411 U.S. 1, 35–37.)

NOTE 21.

The Court today decides, in effect, that a State may constitutionally vary the quality of education which it offers its children in accordance with the amount of taxable wealth located in the school districts within which they reside. The majority's decision represents an abrupt departure from the mainstream of recent state and federal court decisions concerning the unconstitutionality of state educational financing schemes dependent upon taxable local wealth. More unfortunately, though, the majority's holding can only be seen as a retreat from our historic commitment to equality of educational opportunity and as unsupportable acquiescence in a system which deprives children in their earliest years of the chance to reach their full potential as citizens. The Court does this despite the absence of any substantial justification for a scheme which arbitrarily channels educational resources in accordance with the fortuity of the amount of taxable wealth within each district. (Ibid., pp. 70–71.)

NOTE 22.

Nor can I accept the appellants' apparent suggestion that the Texas Minimum Foundation School Program effectively eradicates any discriminatory effects otherwise resulting from the local property tax element of the Texas financing scheme. Appellants assert that, despite its imperfections, the Program "does guarantee an adequate education to every child." The majority, in considering the constitutionality of the Texas financing scheme, seems to find substantial merit in this contention, for it tells us that the Foundation Program "was designed to provide an adequate minimum educational offering in every school in the State," and that the Program "assur[es] a basic education for every child." But I fail to understand how the constitutional problems inherent in the financing scheme are eased by the Foundation Program. Indeed, the precise thrust of the appellants' and the Court's remarks are not altogether clear to me. (Ibid., pp. 86–87.)

NOTE 23.

Even if the Equal Protection Clause encompassed some theory of constitutional adequacy, discrimination in the provision of educational opportunity would certainly seem to be a poor candidate for its application. Neither the majority nor appellants informs us how judicially manageable standards are to be derived for determining how much education is "enough" to excuse constitutional discrimination. One would think that the majority would heed its own fervent affirmation of judicial self-restraint before undertaking the complex task of determining at large what level of education is constitutionally sufficient. Indeed, the majority's apparent reliance upon the adequacy of the educational opportunity assured by the Texas Minimum Foundation School Program seems fundamentally inconsistent with its own recognition that educational authorities are unable to agree upon what makes for educational quality. If, as the majority stresses, such authorities are uncertain as to the impact of various levels of funding on educational quality, I fail to see where it finds the expertise to divine that the particular levels of funding provided by the Program assure an adequate educational opportunity—much less an education substantially equivalent in quality to that which a higher level of funding might provide. Certainly appellants' mere assertion before this Court of the adequacy of the education guaranteed by the Minimum Foundation School Program cannot obscure the constitutional implications of the discrimination in educational funding and objective educational inputs resulting from the local property tax—particularly since the appellees offered substantial uncontroverted evidence before the District Court impugning the now much touted "adequacy" of the education guaranteed by the Foundation Program. (Ibid., pp. 89–90.)

NOTE 25.

In recognition of the special educational needs of children of low-income families, and the impact that concentrations of low-income families have on the ability of local educational agencies to support adequate educational programs, the Congress hereby declares it to be the policy of the United States to provide financial assistance . . . to local educational agencies serving areas with concentrations of children from low-income families to expand and improve their educational programs by various means . . . which contribute particularly to meeting the special educational needs of educationally deprived children. (Public Law 89–10, Title I, Sec. 101.)

NOTE 28.

Effective procedures, including provisions for appropriate objective measurements of educational achievement, will be adopted for evaluating at least annually the effectiveness of the programs in meeting the special educational needs of educationally deprived children.

The local educational agency will make an annual report and such other reports to the State educational agency in such form and containing such information (which in the case of reports relating to performance is in accordance with specific performance criteria related to program objectives), as may be reasonably necessary to enable the State educational agency to perform its duties under this title, including information relating to the educational achievement of students. . . . (Ibid., Sec. 141.)

NOTE 36.

The National Assessment of Educational Progress (NAEP) is an annual survey of knowledge, skills, understandings, and attitudes of selected groups of young Americans. It is the only national data base that periodically provides a comprehensive and systematic accounting of what the Nation is achieving educationally and whether the schools are meeting the needs of a modern, technological society. The project focuses on two main questions: (1) What is the educational attainment of various population groups in major school-related subject areas? and (2) What are the changes in attainment over time, if any, in these areas? From its inception, the National Assessment has been construed as a means for locating areas of unequal achievement similar in concept to the "pockets of unemployment" and has been providing achievement data for various disadvantaged groups as well as for other groups. More recently, NAEP is being adapted to provide data on achievement in career and occupational preparation and on mastery of basic skills and knowledge. (National Center for Educational Statistics, *The Condition of Education, 1976* [Washington, D.C.: U.S. Government Printing Office, 1976], p. 296.)

NOTE 43.

The Institute shall undertake a thorough evaluation and study of compensatory education programs, including such programs conducted by States and such programs conducted under title I of the Elementary and Secondary Education Act of 1965. Such study shall include—

(1) an examination of the fundamental purposes of such programs, and the effectiveness of such programs in attaining such purposes;

(2) an analysis of means to identify accurately the children who have the greatest need for such programs, in keeping with the fundamental purposes thereof;

(3) an analysis of the effectiveness of methods and procedures for meeting the educational needs of children, including the use of individualized written educational plans for children, and programs for training the teachers of children;

(4) an exploration of alternative methods, including the use of procedures to assess educational disadvantage, for distributing funds under such programs to States, to State educational agencies, and to local educational agencies in an equitable and efficient manner, which will accurately reflect current conditions and insure that such funds reach the areas of greatest current need and are effectively used for such areas. (Public Law 93–380, Sec. 821.)

NOTE 46.

(a) . . . establish basic, specific, uniform statewide educational objectives for each grade level and subject area including, but not limited to, reading, writing, and mathematics, in the public schools.

(b) The Commissioner shall develop and administer a uniform, statewide system of assessment based in part on criterion-referenced tests and in part on norm-referenced tests to periodically determine pupil status, pupil progress and the degree of achievement of established educational objectives.

(c) The commissioner shall make an annual public report of the aforementioned assessment results. Such report shall include, but not be limited to, a report of the assessment results by grade and subject area for each school district, and the state, with an analysis and recommendation concerning the costs and differential effectiveness of instructional programs. (House Bill No. 894, 1971.)

NOTE 47.

The purposes of this Act are to provide for the establishment of educational accountability in the public education system of Maryland, to assure that educational programs operated in the public schools of Maryland lead to the attainment of established objectives for education, to provide information for accurate analysis of the costs associated with public education programs, and to provide information for an analysis of the differential effectiveness of instructional programs. . . .

Education accountability program. The State Board of Education and State Superintendent of Schools, each Board of Education and every school system, and every school, shall implement a program of education accountability for the operation and management of the public schools, which shall include the following:

(1) The State Board of Education and the State Superintendent of Schools shall assist each local school board and school system in developing and implementing educational goals and objectives for subject areas including, but not limited to, reading, writing and mathematics.

(2) Each school, with the assistance of its local board of education and school system, shall survey the current status of student achievement in reading, language, mathematics, and other areas in order to assess its needs.

(3) Each school shall establish as the basis of its assessment project goals and objectives which are in keeping with the goals and objectives established by its board of education and the State Board of Education.

(4) Each school, with the assistance of its local board of education, the State Board of Education and the State Superintendent of Schools, shall develop programs for meeting its needs on the basis of priorities which it shall set.

(5) Evaluation programs shall concurrently be developed to determine if the goals and objectives are being met.

(6) Re-evaluation of programs, goals and objectives shall be regularly undertaken. (Article 77, Section 28A, Senate Bill No. 166, 1972.)

NOTE 48.

(a) Establish a procedure for the continuing examination and updating of adopted state goals for elementary and secondary education.

(b) Identify goal-related performance objectives that will lead toward achieving stated goals.

(c) Establish procedures for evaluating the state's and school district's performance in relation to stated goals and objectives. Appropriate instruments to measure and evaluate progress shall be used to evaluate student performance.

(2) The state's program shall provide for an annual review which shall include assessing the performance of students in at least the public elementary and secondary schools in such areas of knowledge, skills, attitudes and understandings, and other characteristics or variables that will aid in identifying relationships and differentials in the level of educational performance that may exist between schools and school districts in the state. (House Bill No. 35, 1975.)

NOTE 51.

For the state these objectives include:

1. A number of pupils equal to at least seventy percent of the pupils who entered the first grade twelve years earlier should be graduated from high school.

2. The percentage of the school population overage in the elementary grades should not exceed twenty percent of the enrollment in grades K−7.

3. The percentage of the student population achieving at or above grade level norms or the equivalent as measured by approved standardized achievement tests should equal or exceed the mean ability level of the student population as measured by appropriate scholastic aptitude tests.

4. At least thirty-one thousand, seven hundred fifty five-year-old children in the State should be enrolled in kindergarten.

5. At least one hundred thirty thousand pupils should be enrolled in summer programs.

6. At least fifty thousand eligible children should be enrolled in special education programs.

7. At least one hundred thirty-five thousand adults should be enrolled in continuing education programs.

8. At least seventy percent of the high school graduates should continue their education in programs provided by colleges and by schools such as business, nursing, data processing, and trade and technical.

9. At least ninety percent of the teachers should be assigned to teach only those subjects for which they have certificate endorsements.

10. At least twenty-three percent of the teachers should hold advanced degrees.

For the school district these objectives include:

1. High school graduates expressed as a percent of the first grade enrollment twelve years earlier should increase by at least three percent each year or until a level of seventy percent is reached. Appropriate adjustments will be made for school divisions with significant increases or decreases in school population.

2. The percentage of the school population overage in grades K−7 should be reduced by at least two percent each year or until a level not exceeding twenty percent is reached.

3. The percentage of the student population achieving at or above grade level norms or the equivalent as measured by approved standardized achievement tests should equal or exceed the mean ability level of the student population as measured by appropriate scholastic aptitude tests.

4. The percentage of teachers holding advanced degrees should increase by at least two percent each year or until at least twenty-three percent of the teachers hold such degrees. Work toward advanced degrees should be in the subject area to which the teacher is assigned.

5. The percentage of attendance of pupils should not fall below the average of the last three years or ninety percent of school membership.

6. Teachers shall be assigned to teach only those subjects for which they have certificate endorsements unless exceptions are granted by the Board of Education. (House Bill 845, 1972.)

NOTE 52.

Section 1. That the Oklahoma Department of Education be hereby requested to provide regulations within its accreditation process for the implementation of an educational-accountability program.

Section 2. That each school district that wishes state accreditation shall initiate a systemwide needs assessment involving all grades under its jurisdiction.

Section 3. That the needs assessment shall be undertaken by the local school staff in compliance with general direction and guidelines developed by the State Department of Education.

Section 4. That a systems analysis process including goals and objectives shall be utilized to plan the instructional program to fit the needs of the students of said district.

Section 5. That the needs assessment shall involve local patrons as well as school staff members of said district and shall encompass all of the curriculum areas at each grade level.

Section 6. That an evaluation shall be designed and conducted annually to determine whether or not and to what extent the objectives are being met.

Section 7. That the State Department of Education shall hold inservice training sessions for administrators, local school staff, and others involved to effect changes in the accreditation process. Furthermore, that these meetings shall be held periodically in planning regions throughout the State of Oklahoma. (House Concurrent Resolution No. 1027, 1973.)

NOTE 57.

(1) To approve a systematic program of information gathering, processing, and analysis addressed to every level, aspect and form of education in this state especially as that information relates to current and future educational needs so that current needs may be met with reasonable promptness and plans formulated to meet future needs as they arise.

(2) To approve a master plan defining broad goals and objectives for all levels of education in the state; elementary, secondary and higher. These goals and objectives shall be expressed in terms of what men should know and be able to do as a result of their educational experience. The regents shall continuously evaluate the efforts and results of education in the light of these objectives.

(3) To formulate broad policy to implement the goals and objectives established and adopted by the regents from time to time; to adopt standards and require enforcement and to exercise general supervision over all public education in the state and over non-public education in the state. . . . (Chapter 249, 1973.)

NOTE 58.

Performance based Criteria for Operation of Instructional Programs. The State Board of Education shall establish performance-based criteria upon which the instructional program of each public school will be evaluated so as to assure, to the greatest extent possible, equal and adequate educational programs, curricula, course offerings, opportunities and facilities for all students of Georgia's public schools, and economy and efficiency in administration and operation of each local unit of administration and public schools therein.

Statewide Assessment Program, Local Assessment Program, Funds for the Local Program. The State Board of Education shall adopt such instruments, procedures and policies as deemed necessary to assess the effectiveness of the educational programs of the State. Such assessments will be made at least once annually, at a minimum of three grade levels, and on a Statewide basis. The State Board shall annually cause a readiness test to be administered early during a child's first year in school. (Senate Bill No. 672, 1974.)

NOTE 66.

1. To increase significantly the achievement levels in reading and mathematics of children attending California public schools in the primary and elementary grades, as defined, through the use of contracts between public school districts and private contractors;

2. To provide that such contracting shall be on the basis of a "performance guarantee," whereby each private contractor is reimbursed on the basis of the performance and achievement of each child involved in the special experimental program;

3. To make the fullest use of federal funds which are or may become available for aid to public education in this state, especially for innovative and original public school programs;

4. To reinforce in public education the private enterprise concept of accountability for results, as measured by specific pupil achievement and mastery of basic skills, by holding the contractor and the school district directly responsible for a student's achievement and mastery of basic skills, or the lack thereof;

5. To demonstrate the effectiveness of new and innovative approaches to learning, which may later be capable of being transferred operationally to the public school system;

6. To reduce, consistent with quality and improved student achievement, future projected public school costs in this state. (Chapter 1600, Assembly Bill No. 1483, 1971.)

NOTE 71.

(1) The Legislature recognizes that the early years of a pupil's education are crucial to his future and that mastery of the basic skills of communication and computation is essential to the future educational and personal success of an individual. The first priority of the public schools of Florida shall be to

assure that all Floridians, to the extent their individual physical, mental, and emotional capacities permit, shall achieve mastery of the basic skills.

The term "basic skills," for the purposes of this section, means reading, writing, and arithmetic. Early childhood and basic skills development programs shall be made available by the school districts to all school age children, especially those enrolled in kindergarten and grades one through three, and shall provide effective, meaningful, and relevant educational experiences designed to give students at least the minimum skills necessary to function and survive in today's society.

(2) In implementing the intent of this section, each school district shall develop a program for early childhood and basic skills development. The early childhood and basic skills program shall be developed cooperatively by school administrators, teachers, parents, and other community groups or individuals having an interest in the programs or having expertise in the field of early childhood education or basic skills development.

(3) Each district's early childhood and basic skills development program shall be based on guidelines prepared by the Department of Education. . . . The Program shall assure that each pupil is enrolled in a program designed to meet his individual needs and that he achieves that level of mastery of the basic skills which his capacities permit. (Chapter 76–223, Sec. 13 [1976].)

NOTE 72.

(1) By July 1, 1977, each district school board shall establish a comprehensive program for pupil progression which shall be based upon an evaluation of each pupil's performance, including how well he masters the minimum performance standards approved by the state board.

(2) The district program for pupil progression shall be based upon local goals and objectives which are compatible with the state's plan for education and which supplement the minimum performance standards approved by the state Board of Education. Particular emphasis, however, shall be placed upon the pupil's mastery of the basic skills, especially reading, before he is promoted from the third, fifth, eighth and eleventh grades. Other pertinent factors considered by the teacher before recommending that a pupil progress from one grade to another shall be prescribed by the district school board in its rules.

(3) Beginning with the 1978–79 school year, each district

school board shall establish standards for graduation from its secondary schools. Such standards shall include, but not be limited to, mastery of the basic skills and satisfactory performance in functional literacy as determined by the State Board of Education, and the completion of the minimum number of credits required by the district school board. Each district shall develop procedures for the remediation of those students who are unable to meet such standards. Based on these standards each district shall provide for the awarding of certificates of attendance and may provide for differentiated diplomas to correspond with the varying achievement levels or competencies of its secondary students. (Ibid., Sec. 15.)

NOTE 80.

A. The General Assembly concludes that one of the fundamental goals of public education must be to enable each student to achieve, to the best of his or her ability, certain basic skills. Each school division shall, therefore, give the highest priority in its instructional program to developing the reading, communications, and mathematics skills of all students, with concentrated effort in the primary (kindergarten through grade three) and intermediate (grades four through six) grades. Remedial work shall begin for low achieving students upon identification of their needs.

B. By September, nineteen hundred seventy-eight, the Board of Education, in cooperation with the local school divisions, shall establish specific minimum Statewide educational objectives in reading, communications and mathematics skills that should be achieved during the primary grades and during the intermediate grades. (House Bill No. 256 [1976].)

NOTE 81.

The General Assembly concludes that a goal of public education must be to continue successfully a program of advanced education or to enter the world of work. Each school division shall, therefore, by September, nineteen hundred seventy-eight, provide programs, approved by the Board of Education, that offer:

1. Career guidance to all secondary students;

2. Adequate preparation to secondary students planning to continue their education and

3. Vocational education providing marketable skills for students who are not planning to continue their education beyond high school. Those students not completing their public school education should possess the basic skills and attitudes, com-

mensurate with their capabilities to obtain employment upon leaving school. (Ibid.)

NOTE 89.

... that, to the maximum extent appropriate, handicapped children, including children in public or private institutions or other care facilities, are educated with children who are not handicapped, and that special classes, separate schooling, or other removal of handicapped children from the regular educational environment occurs only when the nature or severity of the handicap is such that education in regular classes with the use of supplementary aids and services cannot be achieved satisfactorily. . . . (Public Law 94–142, Sec. 612.)

NOTE 90.

(a) Any State educational agency, any local educational agency, and any intermediate educational unit which receives assistance under this part shall establish and maintain procedures to assure that handicapped children and their parents or guardians are guaranteed procedural safeguards with respect to the provision of free appropriate public education by such agencies and units.

(b) (1) The procedures required by this section shall include, but shall not be limited to—

(A) an opportunity for the parents or guardian of a handicapped child to examine all relevant records with respect to the identification, evaluation, and educational placement of the child, and the provision of a free appropriate public education to such child, and to obtain an independent educational evaluation of the child;

(B) procedures to protect the rights of the child whenever the parents or guardian of the child are not known, unavailable, or the child is a ward of the State, including the assignment of an individual (who shall not be an employee of the State educational agency, local educational agency, or intermediate educational unit involved in the education or care of the child) to act as a surrogate for the parents or guardian;

(C) written prior notice to the parents or guardian of the child whenever such agency or unit—

(i) proposes to initiate or change, or

(ii) refuses to initiate or change, the identification, evaluation, or educational placement of the child or the provision of a free appropriate public education to the child;

(D) procedures designed to assure that the notice required by clause (C) fully inform the parents or guardian, in the parents' or guardian's native language, unless it clearly is not feasible to do so, of all procedures available pursuant to this section; and

(E) an opportunity to present complaints with respect to any matter relating to the identification, evaluation, or educational placement of the child, or the provision of a free appropriate public education to such child. (Ibid., Sec. 615.)

CHAPTER 2
HYPERRATIONALIZING THE SCHOOLS

"hyper" an element appearing in loan words from Greek, where it meant "over," usually implying excess or exaggeration.

"rationalize" 1. to ascribe (one's acts, opinions, etc.) to causes that superficially seem reasonable and valid but that actually are unrelated to the true, possibly unconscious causes. 2. to remove unreasonable elements from. 3. to make rational or conformable to reason. 4. to treat or explain in a rational or rationalistic manner. . . . 6. to reorganize and integrate (an industry). 7. to employ reason; think in a rational or rationalistic manner. 8. to invent plausible explanations for acts, opinions, etc., that are actually based on other causes.

"hyperrational" [listed but not defined]

*The Random House Dictionary
of the English Language*

As other and higher levels of government seek to promote equity and increase productivity in our educational institutions, important educational decisions are increasingly being determined centrally. The discretion of local officials is limited by their need to conform to policy decisions. The bureaucratic characteristics of the schools are strengthened as decision-making about people and resources is based on established rules and procedures; scientific management techniques are adopted to increase efficiency; and goals are specified in measurable outcomes. To the extent that this process causes more bureaucratic overlay without attaining the intended policy objectives, it results in what I shall call the *hyperrationalization of the schools.*

Whether rational systems of thought applied to educational planning lead to rationalization or hyperrationalization depends upon the adequacy of these systems. It is possible, certainly, for common sense, economic analysis, science, and legal reasoning, for example, to lead to sound educational policy. We shall see in this chapter, however, that such rational systems of thought contribute to strengthening the bureaucratic characteristics of educational institutions and often work to the detriment of the process they are intended to improve.

In the past, the local board of education was the final arbiter of institutional policies and practices. To be sure, some policies for local institutions were set elsewhere, but for all practical purposes most decisions were made at the local level. If a student, parent, or teacher had a problem with institutional policies or practices, it was everyone's expectation that that problem would be resolved locally or *not at all.*

Today that expectation has changed dramatically. A person with a grievance about the way in which he is being affected by his institution's policies or practices *may* try first to resolve it locally. However, should such efforts fail, he will often turn to authorities external to the institution. As the phenomenon of appealing to external authorities for the resolution of institutional problems has grown, our educational institutions have drifted toward centralization—when a state authority attempts to solve an educational problem, its solution is imposed on all schools in the state; and when the federal government attempts a solution, it imposes that solution on all schools in the nation.

The perceived failure of school officials to solve important educational and social problems, together with the realization that higher authorities are increasingly willing to intervene, is resulting in a growing diminution of local discretionary authority:

> In the past, if a parent were dissatisfied with the quality of the education his child was receiving, he either accepted it or tried to exert influence locally.
>
> In the past, if a child were not learning to read, his parents would appeal to local officials. If they were un-

willing or unable to deal with the problem, the search for a solution probably ended. Now, parents with such problems support state-level minimal competency testing in the belief that such testing may help their children learn to read.

In the past, if a female professor believed that she was being discriminated against in promotion decisions, she could only complain to the officials of the college. Now, because women resorted to the courts and to Congress, federally created protection exists.

In the past, if a parent were denied access to school records, he had little recourse. Now, federally created procedures regulate his access to his child's records.

In the past, a handicapped child might receive less than adequate treatment at the hands of the school. Recourse by the parents of handicapped children to the states, the courts, and the federal government now guarantees adequate treatment.

Students about to be suspended and teachers about to be dismissed no longer have to suffer the discretionary decisions of school officials. The courts have guaranteed that a hearing be held.

Schools no longer can segregate children by race.

Increasingly, states are losing the discretion to spend more money in rich school districts and less money in poor school districts.

While the objectives of the new educational policies are salutary, the tendency toward centralization is not only increasing but accelerating as recourse to higher authority is becoming habitual. Carried to its logical extreme, this tendency could result in a national system of education or fifty systems of education which are all but indistinguishable.

CENTRALIZATION AND EDUCATIONAL POLICYMAKING

The process of centralization is not new. Michael B. Katz has chronicled how, in 1876, the Boston schools were transformed from a sprawling collection of 160 primary schools, 50 grammar schools, and two high schools, led by a single superintendent and a school committee of 76 part-time lay members, into a large, coordinated, bureaucratic urban school system.[1] Control was centralized, a hierarchy was established, coordination was increased, and rules and procedures were established.[2] The administration assumed control over the many schools which formerly had operated rather autonomously. The forces that favored control, coordination, and consistency worked their will to create the Boston Public Schools.

Similar forces during this century have led to the reduction of the numbers of school systems in the United States from about 95,000 in 1947 to 16,730 in 1973–74.[3] Today these forces are operating to aggregate control at an even higher level. While the mechanism of centralization is no longer the consolidation of control within a school district or the consolidation of separate school districts, the growing influence of state and federal government may have similar effects. In a study published in 1976, Tyll van Geel presents a comprehensive report on who now has the authority to control the school program.[4] He analyzes the distribution and redistribution of authority over the school program, and details the growing influence of state and federal government, state and federal courts, and teachers' unions.

Whether the state or federal government will emerge with the greater amount of authority over education remains to be seen. However, the struggle appears to be between the federal and state governments, with local control receding. Joseph M. Cronin, State Superintendent of Education in Illinois, has written:

> The pleas for "local control" or the slogan, "education belongs to the states," may be uttered, even shouted, back home. But slowly, inexorably, and incrementally, the federal government is taking over education. Especially since 1965, the country has moved—almost every year—toward a national system

1. Michael B. Katz, *Class, Bureaucracy and Schools* (New York: Praeger, 1975), p. 66.

2. Ibid., pp. 59–73.

3. National Center for Education Statistics, *The Condition of Education 1976* (Washington: U.S. Government Printing Office, 1976), p. 186.

4. Tyll van Geel, *Authority to Control the School Program* (Lexington, Mass.: Heath, 1976).

of education. Furthermore, the potential opposition has almost conceded the inevitability of the trend. . . .[5]

And while the federal and state governments vie for control, the "imperial judiciary" also contributes to the trend toward centralization.[6]

CENTRALIZED POLICYMAKING

In the colonies the schools began as local institutions. When the U.S. Constitution was adopted, education was a matter reserved to the states; and when the state constitutions were adopted, *formal* responsibility over schools was vested in the state. Over the years educational government was separated from general government to "protect" schools from political decisions. Currently, *operational* control over schools is assumed to be at the local level, with the board of education creating policy and the professional staff operating the schools in conformity with that policy. Theoretically that is how American schools are organized and controlled.[7]

In practice, as we have seen, formal educational policy is developed at local, state, and national levels by all three branches of government. Indeed, no less than nine or ten official bodies—in addition to the board of education—can and do make educational policy. When those outside the traditional decision-making structure of the local school system are unable to secure a desired change from the traditional decision-making structure, they turn to these other bodies which, with increasing frequency, are willing to become educational policymakers.

Each of these bodies has a rationale or rationales which permit it to make educational policy: the federal courts are protecting constitutional rights; the Congress is acting pursuant to the general welfare clause; the executive branch is either proposing legislation to Congress or interpreting or

5. Joseph M. Cronin, "The Federal Takeover: Should the Junior Partner Run the Firm?" *Phi Delta Kappan* 57:8 (April 1976), 500.

6. Nathan Glazer, "Towards an Imperial Judiciary?" *The Public Interest*, No. 41 (Fall 1975).

7. For a complete description, see Roald F. Campbell et al., *The Organization and Control of American Schools* (Columbus, Ohio: Merrill, 1970).

implementing legislation or court decisions; the state legislature is exercising its formal authority; the state courts are
interpreting the state constitutions and statutory enact-
ments; the state board is exercising the formal authority delegated to it by the legislature; the state department is acting at
the behest of the legislature, the board, or the governor; and
local governments test the traditional separation of general
and educational government, typically over questions of
finance.[8]

The object of all of this attention is the local school
which, because of the arrangement of authority, organization,
and control, must formally accept policy generated by higher
authorities. What distinguishes legislative and judicial policy
from locally generated policy is that its principles are drawn
more from legal than educational imperative. The necessary
reliance upon law—as well as the dominance of those trained
in the law—tends to reinforce a legalistic conception of education and the school.

What accounts for the growing willingness of policymakers to engage education? In some measure, their success.
The policymaking system has overcome some problems
which the local schools were unwilling or unable to solve.
Other problems exist because power holders have no interest
in solving them. It required the intervention of the United
States Supreme Court to end segregation. It required an Act of
Congress to cause local school systems to pay special attention to the disadvantaged. It required federal action to draw
attention to the problem of sex discrimination. Court action
is necessary to redress inequalities in school expenditures.
The effect of the intervention of higher authority is to break a
political stalemate and to bring about a result which the normal decision-making process will not. Higher authorities in
the United States have been successful in solving some problems of equity and in calling attention to other situations in
which rights are being denied.

Success in solving problems of equity is encouraging
policymakers and those who appeal to them to try to solve
problems of productivity as well. The resolution of problems

---

8. See, for example, *Report of the Task Force on Budget Categories
to the Maryland State Board of Education*, December 22, 1976.

of equity requires only an alteration in the balance of power; it does not require arcane knowledge. Usually some statistical demonstrations are enough to reveal discrimination by race or by sex in the distribution of opportunities or resources. Statistical demonstrations are also sufficient to describe when discrimination has ended. To be sure, debates over parity and questions over intent sometimes remain, but scientific knowledge will not generally answer these.

With regard to productivity, however, the question becomes: With what degree of effectiveness or efficiency are opportunities and resources being employed? Perversely, the productivity question emerges from the concern for equity— often, but not always, at the instigation of those who would prefer the status quo. Will desegregation help minority children to improve their self-esteem and reading test scores? Will additional resources help poor children improve their reading scores?

The productivity concern extends beyond the socially disadvantaged to the general school population as well. If test scores are declining, and if children are not learning to read, the schools are not being productive. If schools can be directed to reassign children, reallocate resources, and hire certain classes of people, why can they not be required to improve themselves? Why can the schools not be made effective? The teachers accountable? The students prepared to perform well on tests? Why not sue if the school or the teacher fails to teach?

Productivity questions are intrinsically more difficult than equity questions because they arise not out of a political impasse but from a fundamental lack of knowledge about how to teach. Statistical demonstrations do not reveal how to increase productivity. Nonetheless, policymakers appear disposed to give it a try.

Once policymakers have intervened in educational policymaking, they are less inclined to defer to the local schools. Several rationales are offered to explain why this is true. For legislators, it is that overall responsibility for the public welfare and the public purse rests with them, but this has always been so. Another rationale is that, although it is seldom said in a loud voice, superior wisdom resides at the center. Whether or not one accepts this view is likely to depend upon one's location vis-à-vis the center. It is said that since schools have failed to reform themselves, reform must come from outside the schools. This is the most persuasive rationale—since it has already been noted that local institutions could not solve equity problems; that voluntary improvements to promote productivity have not been as effective as some would like; that emulation of lighthouse districts—typically wealthy districts—has not been possible or appropriate for poor school districts; and that the voluntary adoption of federally sponsored "improved curricula" has not solved the problem. If a voluntary system of school improvement has not worked, it would seem logical that improvement be required by law.

When the policymaking system perceives a lack of progress (or especially regress), it mobilizes to bring about change. It intervenes because it believes that the operating system is incapable of correcting itself. Once the policymaking system identifies a problem, it must act or at least give the appearance of action. Centralization, hyperrationalization, and goal reduction occur when the policymaking system believes that the alternatives have failed. Many of the serious problems in education exist because there is no highly developed science or technology of education to help confront a problem. The absence of such science or technology, however, does not prevent the policymaking system from acting. On the contrary, where no theory exists, the policymaking system constructs its own theory of education.

We are concerned here with the policymaking system as it is motivated to improve educational productivity and increase educational equity. It should be noted that other influences, which are not the focus of this discussion, also exert enormous influence on all policymaking, including educational policymaking. These, of course, are politics and the struggle to reallocate power, authority, and control.

AIMS AND THEORIES OF EDUCATION

No matter how educational policy is created, its purpose is to affect (presumably to improve) the practice of education. Inevitably, it must be based upon some theories or hypotheses about educational practice. If these assumptions are correct, the policy may have its intended consequence. If they are incorrect, it very probably will not.

An educational policy contains two elements—an aim to be achieved and a "theory of education" or set of hypotheses that explain how to achieve that aim.[9] Both must have some legitimacy in order for the policy to be successful. The aim may deal with the ends of education and be drawn from religion, ethics, tradition, the law, or other normative sources— i.e., the schools must prepare students to read, to face the world of work, to accept their place in society, or to question the current social order. The aim may deal with the means of education and be drawn from economic theory, the law, or other sources which prescribe how a society wishes to conduct its institutions—i.e., the schools must be efficient, treat all equally, provide due process, or maintain strict discipline. Whatever the aim, if it is not accepted as legitimate by the relevant parties, the policy probably will not work.

The theory of education may be drawn from "common sense," professional lore, or social science. Common sense tells us, for example, that a large organization cannot function effectively unless it has highly developed bureaucratic procedures.[10] From professional lore we know that a teacher cannot function as effectively in a large class as in a small one.[11] Social science shows us that integration works and that it does not.[12] Policies based upon incorrect assumptions probably will not work and may well have unintended (possibly undesirable) consequences.

Many educational policies of the 1960s and 1970s share a common rationalistic set of assumptions about schooling:

1. While numerous goals for education are imaginable, society must find a limited set upon which agreement is possible. The emerging consensus appears to be that the purpose

9. For a somewhat more elaborate definition, see Martin Rein, *Social Science and Public Policy* (Harmondsworth, England: Penguin, 1976), p. 103: "Policy paradigms are a curious admixture of psychological assumptions, scientific concepts, value commitments, social aspirations, personal beliefs and administrative constraint." Our definition is meant to subsume all of these elements.

10. Michael Crozier, *The Bureaucratic Phenomenon* (Chicago: University of Chicago Press, 1964), p. 1.

11. James S. Coleman, *Equality of Educational Opportunity* (Washington, D.C.: Government Printing Office, 1966).

12. Audrey James Schwartz, "Social Science Evidence and the Objectives of School Desegregation," in *Indeterminacy in Education*, ed. John E. McDermott (Berkeley, Calif.: McCutchan, 1976), pp. 73–113.

of schooling is to provide the student with basic and career skills. Establishing limited goals for schools is thought to facilitate goal attainment.

2. The goals must be put in a form which will permit assessment of the extent to which they are attained. Most effort has been given to defining the basic skills of reading and arithmetic. Such definition is thought to facilitate goal attainment.[13]

3. Tests are devised to assess performance. When the scores are available, they can be compared with other scores— districtwide, statewide, or nationwide. Such comparisons are thought to facilitate student, teacher, program, and school evaluation and improvement.

4. Some complexity is added by the realization that some children arrive at school less well-prepared than others. For such children, schools will either adjust expectations downward or provide supplementary educational services.

5. Education is to be conducted efficiently or in a cost-effective manner; the goals are to be attained at the lowest cost. Planning, resource allocation, and test results are to be tracked by ever more sophisticated evaluation and accounting systems.

6. Rules and procedures are superior to the exercise of judgment as means to promote equal and fair treatment in schools.

Regrettably, what is missing from this set of assumptions about education is any reference to the *process* of education—to how educational practice actually affects the child. The practice of education is thus to be altered without an understanding of how education occurs. How can such negligence be explained? Could it be that policymakers wish to leave the process of education to the professionals? This seems unlikely, since the policy they are making is designed to force change in professional practice. Could it be that policymakers do not yet possess the tools for legislating about the educational process? This seems plausible, since they do employ the tools that have already been furnished by educa-

---

13. John I. Goodlad, "A Perspective on Accountability," *Phi Delta Kappan* 57:2 (October 1975), 109.

tional research, as shown by the alacrity with which criterion-referenced testing has been adopted. A third explanation could be that policymakers think that legislating something to occur is sufficient to cause it to occur. At the very least, this explanation is not inconsistent with the behavior of some policymakers.

The theory of education which underlies much policy development includes at least the following additional rationalistic assumptions about human behavior and learning:

1. The child is pliable, at least within the range of normal aptitude and normal expectations. As noted, an ambivalent attitude is held toward children who arrive at school displaying less than normal aptitude.

2. The teacher is pliable and will modify his or her behavior to comply with legislation, court orders, regulations, or scientific knowledge about education.

3. A science of education exists which yields treatments that can be applied by teacher to student.

4. If shown the way, people will prefer cost-effective behavior over behavior which is not cost-effective. Since not all of these assumptions can be validated, one wonders whether a policy based on them could be expected to have its anticipated effects.

These kinds of assumptions were not needed in the past when most policymaking in education was restricted to prescribing inputs to education—to certification of teachers, school attendance, and dollars spent per child per year. As policymakers legislate about the process of education itself, however, more sophisticated assumptions are required. Recent federal legislation mandates that individualized education plans be prepared for every handicapped child.[14] Some state legislation effectively mandates the use of objectives-based education, requiring test-teach-test-reteach-test models of instruction as a matter of law. The belief that innovations such as these lead to improved goal attainment remains to be proved.[15] Since policymakers have begun to legislate actual

14. Public Law 94–142.
15. Phillippe C. Duchastel and Paul F. Merrill, "The Effects of Behavioral Objectives on Learning: Review of Empirical Studies," *Review of Educational Research* 43:1 (Winter 1973), 53–69.

output standards, an even more complex set of assumptions is needed. Courts are requiring "thorough and efficient" education, state school boards are requiring competency-based educational outcomes, and legislators are requiring minimum standards of attainment. Usually such policies do not encompass changes in financing practices. They apparently assume that there is enough slack in existing school budgets and an adequate (although unused) technology to achieve these ends.

Frequently the aim of a policy is only a dream of the policymaker—what he wishes will occur as a function of a legislative enactment, executive decree, or judicial pronouncement. If the policy is to be more than a dream, the policymaker must have some reasons or evidence for believing that it will have its intended effect.

But it is much more difficult to develop policy than it is, for example, to design new methods of instruction for classroom use. While a policy may involve or be dependent upon a new educational technology, whether the technology is effective is only the first question. Because the policymaker is far removed from the classroom, he is forced to make numerous assumptions about how a whole succession of organizations and sub-organizations will respond to the policy. At each level through which the policy must pass on its way to implementation, bureaucratic politics and incentives can and will affect how and if the policy will be implemented.

Goal Reduction

It is evident from the above that the broad purposes for which societies create formal educational institutions—to transmit and generate the cultural heritage, to educate their members for the betterment of society, and to have them become better producers and consumers of the culture—are not the subject of current educational policymaking. The imperatives of centralized educational policymaking lead to a substantially narrower view of the purposes of education. As policies are more and more centrally determined, abstract and salutary goals are reduced and trivialized, and only those goals which can be measured are implemented.

This phenomenon of goal reduction appears to be the result of three causes: First, it is believed that schools should accomplish at least the minimum expectations which society has for them. This belief leads to a focus upon the minimum agreed-upon objectives for schooling to the exclusion of other objectives. Second, it is believed that preeminence should be given to those educational objectives which appear, if attained, to help solve pressing social problems. Thus, if unemployment is high, emphasis is given to basic and career skills in the anticipation that the attainment by all students of these skills will resolve the social problem. Third, the tools for educational policy implementation are rudimentary.

In the past, policymakers were content to render goals for education abstractly, globally, and with the highest expectations that rhetoric could muster. Goals stated in such terms were not only difficult to put into operation—they were perhaps unattainable altogether. Policymakers now prefer goals which *appear* attainable and which are measurable. It may be that goals appear attainable because they are measurable, or it may be that they are chosen because they are measurable. At any rate, both the level of rhetoric and the expectations have been reduced.

In the drive to make educational institutions accountable, goals have become narrow, selective, and minimal. That which is measurable is preferred to that which is unmeasurable. Reductionism is also caused by efforts to give operational meaning to words which appear in legal documents. It is one thing for a state constitution to promise "thorough and efficient" schools; it is another to give that concept literal meaning.[16] It is one thing to assert that schools should provide "each child with an opportunity to acquire the basic skills necessary for the enjoyment of the rights of speech and full participation in the political process."[17] It is quite another to identify the necessary skills, to determine the capacity for enjoyment, and to assess full participation.

The goals which are receiving current attention view education instrumentally—not as an end in itself but as preparation for life, especially for the world of work. Elementary schools are to develop in students the basic skills—reading

16. *Robinson* v. *Cahill*. 62 N.J. 473, 303 A. 2d 273 (1973).
17. *San Antonio* v. *Rodriguez*. 411 U.S. 1 (1973).

and arithmetic—at the level minimally necessary to function effectively in society. Secondary schools are to continue instruction in the basic skills and provide vocational and career skills. Higher education continues vocational and career preparation. Neither colleges nor schools are viewed *by the policymaking process* as institutions for the generation or transmission of the cultural heritage, beyond that narrow sense encompassed by the basic skills and career education. Nor does the policymaking process view education as an end in itself—as the means to increase individual enlightenment and social welfare.

Consider how the available tools limit the goals of elementary schools. In education, there is no more highly developed technology than that of testing.[18] Consequently, tests have come to define the goals of education, and schooling has come to be evaluated by changes in test scores. The generalized goal that schools should teach children to read and do arithmetic is transformed into the objective that children should be able to prove their ability to read and to do arithmetic by taking an examination. The technology of testing forces the belief that there is a cutoff score which reveals a level of performance which is adequate.

Dissatisfaction with norm-referenced testing—which reveals only how a person performs in comparison to others—has led to criterion-referenced testing. This testing method is a technique for relating test items to absolute criteria, which, in turn, can be related to adult needs for reading and arithmetic skills. The technology of criterion-referenced testing, when combined with the ideology of basic skills, permits linking tests to the needs of adult life. The ideology of basic skills and the technology of criterion-referenced testing combine to allow the policy process to control the educational process. We need only determine the basic skills or minimum competencies in reading or arithmetic which are necessary for survival in adult life. In turn, these skills will be made operative by means of criterion-referenced tests. Through this process, the goal of schooling is reduced to the instrumental

18. Lee J. Cronbach and Patrick Suppes, eds., *Research for Tomorrow's Schools* (Toronto: Macmillan, 1969), p. 73.

value of providing just enough reading and arithmetic skill to get by as an adult. While the goal of schooling can be seen in instrumental terms without testing (it has always been so seen), policymakers would not then be able to control it. It is one thing to state abstractly that the goal of schooling is to prepare children to function in society, and quite another to state it in terms sufficiently precise for operational control.

The transformation of general goals for schooling into narrow instrumental objectives is most clearly seen in vocational and career education. One goal of education has always been to help prepare people for the world of work. However, as policymakers attempt to reach that goal through programs of career and vocational education, it becomes both narrower and minimal. The success of career education is measured by its results in entry-level job placements.

Similarly, in institutions of higher education one of the major goals has been to provide education to students. When this goal is made commensurate with the production of credit hours, the process of educational decision-making can be seriously affected. As policymakers allocate funds to institutions on the basis of credit-hour production, and as institutions allocate funds on a similar basis to colleges and departments, decisions begin to be made on a basis that assumes that the only goal of such institutions is the transmission of knowledge without regard to their broader purposes.

The narrow instrumental view of the goals of education which policymakers appear to hold as they make policy may stand in sharp contrast to their personal views of the purposes of education. The exigencies of the policymaking process, together with the limited technology for making policies, cause policymakers to adopt a narrow view. Their personal goals for the elementary schools may be not only to teach basic skills but to instill the desire to learn and to develop the potential of the child; for the secondary schools, not only to prepare students vocationally but also to develop their critical capacities and to cultivate various interests; for the colleges, not only to produce credit hours but also to preserve, create, and transmit our cultural and scientific heritage. In the real world of policymaking, however, these larger goals are not integral to the process.

EFFECTS OF BUREAUCRACY
ON EDUCATIONAL INSTITUTIONS

As we have seen, central authorities devise educational policy designed either to promote equity or to increase productivity in the schools. The concepts and tools upon which they rely to achieve these objectives are resulting in further and even excessive rationalization of the operation of our schools and colleges.

INFLUENCE OF BUREAUCRACIES

Michael Crozier has identified three meanings of the term "bureaucratic," each of which alerts us to developments in education:

> The first and the most traditional usage corresponds to a concept of political science: bureaucracy is government by bureaus. In other words, it is government by departments of the state staffed by appointed and not elected functionaries, organized hierarchically, and dependent on a sovereign authority. Bureaucratic power, in this sense, implies the reign of law and order, but, at the same time, government without the participation of the governed.[19]

At least two points should be made in connection with bureaucracy as government by bureaus. First, at all three levels of government, education competes for funds with other public functions. These other functions are organized into "bureaus." As the federal Office of Management and Budget and corresponding units in state government have increased in influence, the tendency has been for all *bureaus* to have to respond in similar ways to the pressures generated by these accounting-oriented agencies. The demand for performance-oriented data to accompany budget data—the manifestation of the scientific management which has accompanied the rise of budget agencies—has reinforced the bureaucratic elements of schools. Second, schools during this century have come to be governed by appointed professionals, organized hierarchically and reporting to school boards but insulated from the direct influence of those served. Crozier goes on:

19. Crozier, *The Bureaucratic Phenomenon*, p. 3.

The second usage originates with Max Weber and has been propagated especially by sociologists and historians: bureaucratization is the rationalization of collective activities. This bureaucratization is brought about by, among other means, the inordinate concentration of the units of production and in general of all organizations and the development within these of a system of impersonal rules, as much for the definition of functions and the repartition of responsibilities as for the ordering of careers.[20]

It is bureaucratization as rationalization which provides the basis for hyperrationalization. Crozier's third definition is also revealing:

The third usage corresponds to the vulgar and frequent sense of the word "bureaucracy." It evokes the slowness, the ponderousness, the routine, the complication of procedures, and the maladapted response of "bureaucratic" organizations to the needs which they should satisfy, and the frustrations which their members, clients, or subjects consequently endure.[21]

While schools display many of the negative characteristics associated with bureaucracy, their more interesting response to bureaucratization is to deny that education can be standardized and predicted:

In our modern world, the progress of standardization, of predictability, and of rationality in general paradoxically seems to be accompanied by an increasing dependence on the indispensable human means, who maintain their autonomy in regard to the goals of the organization much more easily than heretofore.[22]

(How teachers deal with bureaucratization is discussed in Chapter 3.) Crozier speaks also of the "pathology of organizations" which

develops from the relative incompatibility between their goals, which spring from a type of utilitarian rationality, and the means of social control, which are determined by the primary behavior and values characteristic of the cultural system of which the organizations are part.[23]

20. Ibid.
21. Ibid.
22. Ibid., p. 6.
23. Ibid., p. 8.

Chapter 3 also discusses the "utilitarian rationality" which generates the goals for education. The "means of social control," we shall suggest, may not only deny values characteristic of our culture but also may lie beyond the knowledge base.[24]

It has become fashionable to combine the word "bureaucracy" with the word "technology" to yield "technocracy." Theodore Roszak has dramatically defined the term:

> By the technocracy, I mean that social form in which an industrial society reaches the peak of its organizational integration. It is the ideal men usually have in mind when they speak of modernizing, up-dating, rationalizing, planning. Drawing upon such unquestionable imperatives as the demand for efficiency, for social security, for large-scale coordination of men and resources, for ever higher levels of affluence and ever more impressive manifestations of collective human power, the technocracy works to knit together the anachronistic gaps and fissures of the industrial society. The meticulous systemization Adam Smith once celebrated in his well-known pin factory now extends to all areas of life, giving us human organization that matches the precision of our mechanistic organization.[25]

A technocratic society strives to rationalize all social institutions, including education. Katz speaks of "incipient technocracy" in education as the point of view which stresses the importance to education of technological innovation, efficiency, and research.[26] What the technocracy literature reveals is the inexorable quality of technocracy. Once the process of technocratic rationalization begins, there appears to be no limiting it.

Francis E. Rourke has called attention to the fundamental paradox of bureaucracy:

> This is the fact that Weber and other early students of the subject saw bureaucracy as the ultimate triumph of rationality

24. Arthur E. Wise, "Teacher: Automaton or Craftsperson," in *Trends, Processes and Prescriptions in Inservice Education,* ed. Louis J. Rubin (Boston: Allyn-Bacon, 1978).

25. Theodore Roszak, *The Making of a Counter Culture* (Garden City, N.Y.: Anchor, 1969), pp. 5–6.

26. Katz, *Class, Bureaucracy and Schools,* p. 128.

while many critics see it as having characteristics that contribute instead to irrationality in decision.[27]

It is obvious that the irrationality which is associated with bureaucratization will increase as the bureaucratic characteristics of schools are strengthened.[28] We will not, however, be directly concerned with the irrationality in decision-making which is promoted by bureaucratization, except insofar as hyperrationalization itself is an irrational phenomenon. When rationalization becomes hyperrationalization, we may conclude that the policymaking system is engaged in irrational decision-making.

EFFECTS OF BUREAUCRATIC RATIONALIZATION

According to Max Weber, every act of bureaucratic rationalization involves either weighing the relationship between means and ends or ensuring that a practice conforms to norms.[29] Concerning the weighing of means and ends, we shall say that rationalization occurs when the relationship between means and ends is known, when the ends are attainable given the means, or when the means are reasonable given the ends. When the relationship between means and ends is not known and bureaucratic rationalization persists, we shall say that we are witnessing the phenomenon of hyperrationalization—that is, an effort to rationalize beyond the bounds of knowledge. This involves imposing means which do not result in the attainment of ends, or the setting of ends which cannot be attained, given the available means—imposing unproven techniques on the one hand, and setting unrealistic expectations on the other.

Ensuring that a practice conforms to norms requires replacing the exercise of administrative discretion either with procedures or rules. Rationalization occurs when procedures

27. Francis E. Rourke, *Bureaucracy, Politics, and Public Policy* (Boston: Little, Brown, 1969), p. 139.

28. See, for example, Willis D. Hawley, "Dealing with Organizational Rigidity in Public Schools: A Theoretical Perspective," in *The Polity of School*, ed. Frederick M. Wirt (Lexington, Mass.: Heath, 1975), pp. 187–210.

29. Max Weber, *From Max Weber: Essays in Sociology*, trans. and ed. H. H. Gerth and C. Wright Mills (New York: Oxford University Press, 1946), p. 220.

and regulations ensure conformity to norms and have the intended effects of fairness and equality. Hyperrationalization occurs when conformity to norms is not achieved by the procedures and rules imposed—when procedures are followed but the norm of fairness is not necessarily attained; when rules are obeyed but the norm of equality is not necessarily attained.

Having accepted Weber's distinction between rationalization as the weighing of means and ends and as conformity to norms, it must be noted that an act of bureaucratic rationalization is not always clearly either one or the other. Consequently, the characteristic that marks the transition from rationalization to hyperrationalization in the one case may also be associated with the other.

Many policies appear, on the surface, to be appropriately designed to change schools. But they are often inappropriate because they proceed from rationale to action without adequate reason or evidence. Apparent logic becomes the basis for action; what is not contradicted by evidence is assumed to be possible. Too often what appears logical may or may not have a connection to reality. Where the connection to reality is absent, a policy intervention will lead to hyperrationalization. Let us look at a few examples:

Excessive prescription / Policies may prescribe either (1) the inputs to the system; (2) the process the system is to employ; or (3) the outcomes the system is to achieve. As we noted earlier, state policymakers restricted themselves to prescribing inputs such as the minimum expenditure level, the required number of days of school, and the minimum qualifications of teachers. Recently, however, various policies have begun to prescribe the expected outcomes of schooling—basic and career skills, for example. Other policies—such as individualized instruction, objectives-based education, and class size—are intended to prescribe the process of education. Typically, these prescriptions are contained in separate pieces of legislation. Hyperrationalization occurs when, for example, an outcome prescription is made without considering whether it is attainable given resource constraints. Numerous logical and practical inconsistencies are the likely result of efforts to prescribe input, process, and outcome controls.

Procedural complexity / In the past decade, many efforts have been made to decentralize school systems, provide for community participation, and allow community control. But long before these reforms were called for, school systems had already developed procedures for arriving at decisions which did not share authority. If those in authority do not wish to surrender authority and simply add new concepts of sharing decision-making without removing the old procedures, the objective of sharing authority will not be achieved, and the decision-making procedure becomes hyperrationalized.

Inappropriate Solutions / A prevailing view holds that schools exist to prepare a child to enter society, and it is occasionally observed that schools are not doing this job adequately. This observation gives rise to the suggestion that schools should be better articulated with the needs of society, which leads to the creation of a program or a curriculum to further that articulation. If high school graduates cannot find jobs, a career education program is created. If crime is on the rise, a moral education program is created. Such programs may be inappropriate solutions to the problems they are designed to solve because they have their genesis in the social structure rather than in individual behavior. Or these programs may be inappropriate because the informal curriculum of the school or extra-school socialization is a more powerful influence than the school curriculum. The solution to the problem, in other words, may lie in reforming society or the school rather than in creating a specific program or curriculum. The logic that connects the problem to the program solution may be faulty—another form of hyperrationalization.

First-order solution / Sometimes a first-order analysis of a problem yields a solution; it may be hyperrational when the solution is but a restatement of the problem. If schools are not accountable, create an accountability program. If high school graduates are incompetent, create a competency-based high school graduation program. If teachers are incompetent, create a competency-based teacher education program. The creation of a program with the same name as the problem may give the appearance of coping with the problem.

In fact, if these kinds of problems have solutions at all, they lie at the very core of the educational enterprise. If schools, teachers, and students are not performing according to expectations, the reasons may lie in a lack of knowledge of how to teach, of how to learn, or of how to organize a school. Tinkering in superficial ways with the expected outcomes of schooling may lie very far from the real solution to the fundamental problem.

Wishful Thinking / When policymakers require by law that schools achieve a goal which in the past they have not achieved, they may be engaging in wishful thinking—another form of hyperrationalization. Here policymakers behave as though their desires will be accomplished simply by decree. The assumption appears to be that school officials are engaged in nonfeasance or malfeasance. For example, in 1965 the federal government enacted legislation designed to address the failure of schools to adequately serve the needs of some children, particularly poor children and children of certain racial minorities. School systems would receive federal funds to be spent on the education of poor children. The legislation required that school systems describe how those funds would be used to alter the education of poor children. The assumption was that change from preexisting educational practices would have beneficial educational consequences. School systems which presumably did not previously have the knowledge or will or wherewithal to teach such children would, with federal funds, discover the knowledge, gain the will, and acquire the wherewithal to solve the problem. Suffice it for now to say that these beneficial consequences have not quickly followed modest federal investment. One result, and a second example of wishful thinking, has been that state legislatures and state courts have been requiring by law specified levels of performance on the part of school-people and schoolchildren. Competency-based graduation requirements and rulings for "thorough and efficient education" demand that the schools produce outcomes which they may not be able to achieve.

Scientism / To buttress their interventions, policymakers often turn to educational and social science research.

Although research is seldom able to settle important policy issues, policies are often defended by reference to a body of research which has been selected as one selects a biblical text—to support one's position. Such inappropriate reliance on research may be going beyond science to scientism—yet another manifestation of hyperrationalization.

OTHER RATIONALITIES

In addition to bureaucratic rationality, policymakers bring other kinds and combinations of rationality to bear upon education as well:

Commonsense rationality / The close familiarity which most members of society have with education leads some of them to believe that they have sufficient knowledge to make educational decisions and policy. Often parents, particularly middle-class or educated parents, are quite prepared to criticize the schools and to suggest changes. Lay school board members frequently are not hesitant to intervene in operational decisions. Reformers have suggested that anyone can become a teacher or school administrator. Familiarity, coupled with the perceived lack of a need for special expertise, seduces many into believing that they can easily make educational policy. Policymakers, called upon to remedy an educational problem, do not prescind. Moreover, they often act without the deference to experts which they might display in other arenas.

Common experience with schools becomes the data base for educational policymaking; commonsense rationality provides the needed means for analyzing the data and making prescriptions. Educational policy is made by using the modes of thought of everyday life. Common sense can be highly rational. An educational policymaker

> may search a present situation for its points of comparability to situations that he knew in the past and may search his past experience for formulas that have yielded the practical effects he now seeks to bring about. In this task he may pay close attention to these points of comparability. He may anticipate the consequences of his acting according to the formulas that recommend themselves to him. He may "rehearse in imagination" various competing lines of action. He may assign to each

alternative, by a decision made prior to the actual occasion of choice, the conditions under which any one of the alternatives is to be followed. Along with such structurings of experience as these, the person may intend through his behaviors to realize a projected outcome. This may involve his paying specific attention to the predictable characteristics of the situation that he seeks to manipulate. His actions may involve the exercise of choice between two or more means for the same ends or of a choice between ends. He may decide the correctness of his choice by invoking empirical laws. And so on.[30]

The problem with common sense is that while it sometimes yields accurate predictions, it often does not.

Commonsense rationality often has added persuasiveness because its characteristics shade into the characteristics of scientific rationality. The sure solution to a problem or the sure accomplishment of a task requires that

... the "means-ends relationships," be constructed in such a way (1) that they remain in full compatibility with the rules that define scientifically correct decisions of grammar and procedure; (2) that all the elements be conceived in full clearness and distinctness; (3) that the clarification of both the body of knowledge as well as the rules of investigative and interpretive procedure be treated as a first priority project; and (4) that the projected steps contain only scientifically verifiable assumptions that have to be in full compatibility with the whole of scientific knowledge.[31]

The problem with scientific rationality is that its conditions can almost never be satisfied in everyday educational settings. The construction of means-ends relationships that are the core of an educational policy must usually rest on less than full scientific rationality.

Professional rationality / The rational processes which teachers bring to bear on education are also those of common sense, although since the data base of education for teachers is

30. Harold Garfinkel, "The Rational Properties of Scientific and Common Sense," *Behavioral Science* 5:1 (January 1960), 76. See also Dale Mann, *Policy Decision-Making in Education* (New York: Columbia University Teachers College, 1975), especially pp. 33–45.

31. Garfinkel, "Rational Properties," p. 76.

probably different from that of the general public, their roles as professionals cause them to view educational reality differently. Has the application of teachers' common sense to their classroom experience yielded a corpus of knowledge which can be called professional lore? The answer appears to be no.

There is no common technical vocabulary which would indicate that the profession has a lore,[32] leading to the conclusion that teachers do not have a body of practical knowledge upon which to draw.[33] It is also taken to mean that teachers have an uncomplicated view of causality and an intuitive and conceptually simple approach to classroom events.[34]

For the present analysis, it is not necessary to settle the question of whether there is professional rationality or professional lore. What is important is that the fruits of professional rationality do not appear to be guiding the construction of educational policy. Indeed, the application of other kinds of rationality may be the proof that professional lore does not exist.

Economic rationality / It is not surprising that economic thinking has been employed in educational policymaking. Education consumes resources; resources are scarce; decisions about the allocation of resources must be made. Businessmen have always served on the boards of schools and colleges and have insisted that these institutions function according to sound business principles. Increasingly, policymakers have recognized that they must decide how to allocate public funds. They have looked to economics as a source of concepts and tools for managing educational expenditures. It has been hoped that economic analysis would reveal means to control costs or at least to calculate cost-benefit ratios.

But the assumptions required for economic analysis are better satisfied in the commercial sector than in the public

32. Emil J. Haller, "Teacher Socialization: Pupil Influences on Teachers' Speech" (Unpublished Ph.D. Dissertation, University of Chicago, 1975), p. 73. Philip W. Jackson, *Life in Classrooms* (New York: Holt, Rinehart and Winston, 1968), p. 144.

33. Dan C. Lortie, *School Teacher: A Sociological Study* (Chicago: University of Chicago Press, 1975), p. 73.

34. Jackson, *Life in Classrooms*, pp. 144–47.

sector. Dale Mann has specified five conditions which economic rationality requires:

> (1) ends that, although different, are comparable; (2) resources freely assignable among competing ends; (3) fairly complete information about how the system works (production functions); (4) resource allocations governed by marginal utility; and (5) actors who can carry out allocations.[35]

To what degree does eduation match these conditions? None is fully satisfied in education; indeed, they are hardly satisfied at all. In a firm, the ends are comparable by the metric of dollars. In education they are uncommensurable, for we have yet to find a common metric for learning to read, self-development, and career preparation. In schools, resources are not freely assignable among competing ends. Seniority, union contracts, and specialization, for example, militate against the free transfer of teachers. In some industries, production functions are known, i.e., the mix of capital, labor, and raw materials required to produce a given product can be specified with precision. In education, even rudimentary production functions are unknown. If production functions are unknown, how can resource allocation be governed by marginal utility? Finally, if the proper allocation is not known, then the ability to carry it out is moot. In practice, economic analysis per se is seldom invoked in educational policymaking, but is implicit in the various techniques of scientific management which are applied to education.

Scientific rationality / In most facets of modern life, the belief is pervasive that scientific rationality should be brought to bear on decisions. Education is no exception; indeed, at least the appearance of scientific rationality has been part of educational decision-making for most of the twentieth century.[36] The mental testing movement, the most highly developed aspect of education treated scientifically, has profoundly affected American education:

35. Mann, *Policy Decision-Making in Education*, p. 23.
36. Lawrence A. Cremin, *The Transformation of the School* (New York: Vintage, 1961). Cronbach and Suppes, *Research for Tomorrow's Schools*.

The relationships between knowledge, conceptualization, and practice are well illustrated in the mental-testing movement, in which scientific work has moved steadily forward for a century. Because objective and reproducible techniques are the heart of the movement, an investigator is almost always able to confirm the findings of predecessors. Because investigators in this field have insistently criticized each other's work, the inquiry has been better disciplined and the findings better substantiated than most other research treating educational matters. But excesses of interpretation have been as common here as elsewhere; perhaps more common, because a certain scientism has flourished in the field.

The prevailing view of differences among men changes over and over. What a given finding signifies depends upon who is interpreting it and, to a large degree, on the climate of opinion of his decade. When the prevailing thought accepts a competitive model of society, the mental test is a sort of tipsheet that helps decision-makers get their bets down on the likely winners. When ultra-equalitarianism reigns, the mental test is condemned as being an instrument of favoritism and privilege. Mental tests and the findings based on them have influenced social thought, but equally the prevailing thought has influenced the tests—the choice of tests for development, the questions asked about them, and the uses to which they are put. Testing was the first full-fledged "educational technology," and its history suggests something of the likely successes and excesses of technologies now emerging.[37]

Empirical inquiry in education has a long and checkered history. From studies of learning transfer to HEW's planned variation experiments, education has been studied and restudied.[38] Estimates differ on the extent to which systematic inquiry has affected education.[39] Yet the scientific approach to education is active and pervasive. Hardly anyone will undertake an educational innovation without an "evaluation" of it. The federal government will implement no new educational program without "scientific" evaluation of the results. Courts

37. Cronbach and Suppes, eds., *Research for Tomorrow's Schools*, p. 73.

38. Ibid., pp. 96–110; Alice Rivlin and Michael Timpane, *Planned Variation in Education* (Washington, D.C.: Brookings, 1975).

39. J. W. Getzels, "Examples of Successful Research Related to Education," informal paper, 1970.

and legislative bodies demand scientific evidence before ruling on education.[40] Today, as years ago, scientific research in
education suffers from the persistent demand that findings be
implemented immediately.[41]

At least two ironies are apparent with regard to scientific
rationality and educational policymaking. First, at the very
moment when state legislators are enacting rationalistic models of education, national legislators are failing to provide
funds to support research needed for their implementation.[42]
Second, at the very moment when state and federal legislators
are demanding rationalistic models, many educational researchers are beginning to attack their feasibility. John Goodlad has said:

> There is not a science of education sufficient to give credence
> to the scientism necessarily indicated if any model of account-
> ability of the kind described here is to function effectively. It is
> an idea whose time has not yet come, whatever rhetorical and
> political support it is able to muster. But it will be back again,
> probably in new trappings.[43]

A collection of essays by a number of educational researchers,
entitled *Regaining Educational Leadership: Critical Essays
on PBTE/CBTE, Behavioral Objectives, and Accountability*,
attacks "the technical ideology that fails to do justice to the
complexity of educational enterprise."[44]

> If schooling goes the way of technique, then its technocratic
> leaders must answer for the adoption of a questionable model
> of educational planning and operation (the industrial model), a
> questionable behavioral theory (behaviorist), and a question-
> able evaluation system (objective tests and measurements).[45]

40. John E. McDermott, ed., *Indeterminacy in Education* (Berkeley,
Calif.: McCutchan, 1976).

41. John Dewey, *The Sources of a Science of Education* (New York:
Liveright, 1929), pp. 17–18.

42. Arthur E. Wise, "The Taming of the National Institute of Education," *Phi Delta Kappan* 58:1 (September 1976), 62–64.

43. Goodlad, "A Perspective on Accountability," p. 110.

44. Ralph A. Smith, *Regaining Educational Leadership: Critical Essays on PBTE/CBTE, Behavioral Objectives, and Accountability* (New
York: Wiley, 1975), p. 1.

45. Ibid., p. 13.

James W. Guthrie argues:

> The complexity of a human endeavor such as learning defies simple cost-effectiveness analysis. Questions regarding the measurement of pupil learning potential and effective teaching techniques are vastly complicated. For example, to inquire if schools are effective assumes that (1) we have agreement on what it is schools should do, (2) we concur on how to measure these outcomes, (3) there exist means for diagnosing particular students' abilities to accomplish school objectives, and (4) we have knowledge of the instructional settings and techniques capable of moving a student, or groups of students, from what he or she now knows to where he or she should be or wants to be on the knowledge spectrum.[46]

Scientific rationality has been applied to education for some time. In the past, the implicit focus of research was likely to be the individual, the classroom, or the school. In recent years, as higher levels of government have endeavored to solve educational problems, research has focussed rather upon school systems—local, state, and national. It would appear that education faces at least as great a challenge at the macroscopic level as it does at the microscopic level in meeting the conditions of scientific rationality.

Legal rationality / Education has not escaped the growing litigiousness of modern America. Indeed, litigiousness appears to be one of the prime causes of the hyperrationalization of education. Constitutional, statutory, and case law yield formal statements of educational purposes as well as the norms by which education should be conducted. Legal challenges are brought when an aggrieved party can claim that educational practice does not conform to legal prescription. Most education cases have questioned whether educational practices conform to legal norms. Did segregation violate the norm of equal protection? Do resource inequalities violate equal protection? Does dismissal of students or teachers without a hearing violate the norm of due process?

46. James W. Guthrie, "Social Science, Accountability, and the Political Economy of School Productivity," in *Indeterminacy in Education*, pp. 260–61.

Cases involving the norms by which education is conducted must sometimes inquire into educational purpose in order to ascertain whether equal protection or due process is being denied.[47] Does society establish schools for its own or the individual's good? Increasingly, legal challenges question whether the schools are achieving the educational purposes for which they were designed. Does the law require the school to cause a high school graduate to be functionally literate? What is a minimally adequate education?[48] What skills are the schools required to develop?

The legal process demands that authority be found for judicial decisions. The body of law contains promises and premises which either have some apparent meaning or can be interpreted to have some meaning. In this fashion, the legal process can divine educational purposes. The promises contained in judicially derived educational policies are logical deductions from the promises found to be contained within the law. The legal process also contains its own theories of human behavior and of organization. Ordering the school administrator or teacher to alter his behavior is deemed sufficient to induce behavioral change. When the order is to cease a behavior, it may work; when the order is to perform a behavior, it may not. Schools are assumed to be organized according to the Weberian ideal of hierarchical authority.

Legal rationality is important not only for the obvious effects which court decisions have upon schools and colleges, but because the principles which emerge from court decisions become important in the internal operation of these institutions. As the result of court decisions, and to avoid future court challenges, school and college administrators must function in a judicial manner. Important school decisions such as those regarding the suspension of students and the firing of teachers must be made in quasi-judicial proceedings. School decision-making comes to resemble judicial decision-making,

47. Arthur E. Wise, *Rich Schools, Poor Schools: The Promise of Equal Educational Opportunity* (Chicago: University of Chicago Press, 1968), pp. 112–18.

48. Arthur E. Wise, "Minimum Educational Adequacy: Beyond School Finance Reform," *Journal of Education Finance* 1:4 (Spring 1976), 468–83.

and the educational administrator begins more and more to look like a judge.

Combined rationalities / In practice, these various rationalities are not applied in pure form to education, and at times they are explicitly amalgamated. Thus, "scientific management" links economic, bureaucratic, and scientific rationality. Concepts such as "education production function" link economic rationality, scientific rationality, and education.[49] At other times, one kind of rationality blends into another—the assumptions of scientific rationality might be relaxed and give way to commonsense rationality, for example. It is difficult to characterize some concepts such as "circumscribed authority" or "delegation of authority" as either legal or bureaucratic rationality. Most interesting are those instances in which the use of one type of rationality leads to the use of other types—"accountability" schemes invoke bureaucratic, legal, and scientific rationality; "management-by-objectives" invokes bureaucratic and scientific rationality.

Legislatures and courts invoke scientific management when they wish to become very precise about educational objectives and their attainment by students in schools. Laws requiring minimal competency tests[50] or competency-based education or basic skills acquisition necessitate planning, management, and evaluation systems. Court decisions requiring "thorough and efficient" education, where this phrase is taken to have substantive meaning, likewise necessitate scientific management. A successful malpractice lawsuit which demanded that schools teach literacy skills would have the same effect.

What we are witnessing is a linkage between the "new cult of efficiency"[51] and the growing litigiousness of society. Where the old cult of efficiency[52] was implemented by vote of business-dominated local school boards, the new cult of

49. J. Alan Thomas, *The Productive School* (New York: Wiley, 1971).

50. "How Much Must a Student Master," *Time*, February 28, 1977.

51. H. Thomas James, *The New Cult of Efficiency and Education* (Pittsburgh: University of Pittsburgh Press, 1969).

52. Raymond E. Callahan, *Education and the Cult of Efficiency* (Chicago: University of Chicago Press, 1962).

efficiency is implemented by legislation and litigation. Indeed, hyperrationalization results from the conjunction of legal, economic, bureaucratic, and scientific rationalities.

In general, education has failed to yield tools and concepts which are both policy-relevant and responsive to the unique conditions of education. Educational policies to improve equity or increase productivity must rely on tools and concepts spawned in other arenas. These tools and concepts are based upon rational paradigms which are only partially relevant to education; yet each is pushed to its theoretical limit as the educational policymaking system tries to control the operating educational system. Experts who advise policymakers about education have struggled not only to adopt concepts and tools to education but also to create education-specific concepts and tools. These inventions—minimal competency testing, competency-based education, program evaluation, and learner verification—generally fail to have the effects which are predicted for them, for the reasons we have seen. Education has spawned testing which is perceived by many to be a policy-relevant tool. The major deficiency of testing for policy purposes, however, is that it deals with the *results* of education and not the *workings* of education.

Limits of the rationalistic model / Educational policymakers behave as though they believe that schools operate according to the rationalistic model. That model postulates that schools operate by setting goals, implementing programs to achieve these goals, and evaluating the extent to which the goals are attained. The goal-oriented process is assumed to be effectuated through a bureaucratic distribution of formal authority and work responsibility. It is further assumed that the attainment of goals provides sufficient incentives to drive the system. Policies emanating from a belief in this model are designed to improve the operation of the goal-oriented process. Policies which promise to increase productivity and equity are imposed on the existing structure of the school in the anticipation that they will improve education.

To those who believe that reform of procedures will lead to reform of education, the rationalistic model of schooling looks unquestionably correct. If only the schools are given clear objectives to achieve, the objectives certainly will be achieved. If only the schools will tighten up this or that procedure, good educational results will follow. Since, in practice, such changes do not inevitably lead to the predicted result, it is possible that something is wrong with the self-evident rationalistic model.

> The sociology of knowledge argues that scientific thought, and especially thought on social and political matters, does not proceed in a vacuum, but in a socially conditioned atmosphere. It is influenced largely by unconscious or subconscious elements. These elements remain hidden from the thinker's observing eye because they form, as it were, the very place which he inhabits, his *social habitat*. The social habitat of the thinker determines a whole system of opinions and theories which appear to him as unquestionably true or self-evident. They appear to him as if they were logically and trivially true, such as, for example, the sentence "all tables are tables." This is why he is not even aware of having made any assumptions at all. But that he has made assumptions can be seen if we compare him with a thinker who lives in a very different social habitat; for he too will proceed from a system of apparently unquestionable assumptions, but from a very different one; and it may be so different that no intellectual bridge may exist and no compromise be possible between these two systems. Each of these different socially determined systems of assumptions is called by the sociologists of knowledge a *total ideology*.[53]

What may be wrong with the rationalistic model is that those who are attempting to change or control schools by reference to it are implicitly basing their actions on a set of assumptions that may be different from the assumptions, opinions, and theories under which the schools actually operate.

The failure of schools to conform to the rationalistic model may be seen in the failure thus far to create models which help explain the process of schooling empirically. The history of disciplined inquiry in education is a search to describe, analyze, and predict the effects of the interactions of the many elements which comprise schooling. Research on

53. Karl Popper, "The Sociology of Knowledge," in *The Sociology of Knowledge: A Reader*, ed. James E. Curtis and John W. Petras (New York: Praeger, 1970), p. 650.

teaching has been a search for the effects which schooling has. Yet, as we know so well by now, research on teacher effects and school effects has failed to explain much of the reality of schooling.

The Coleman Report epitomizes the use of the rationalistic model in the search for school effects.[54] In abstracting reality, the study accepts the basic input-process-output paradigm that has become the basis for thinking about education. It assumes that aggregate achievement test score maximization is the goal of the schools; that resources are effectively deployed; that efficiency principles operate in schools. Yet all of these assumptions are most likely violated in the way schools operate. Given this disjuncture between the model and reality, improvements in measurement, methodology, and research design will not yield great increases in the explanation of schooling. Moreover, increased efforts to explain by means of experimental modifications of schooling would be beside the point; schooling as it now operates may defy the kind of logical assumptions which we are accustomed to make.

Further corroboration of the disjuncture between the rationalistic model and school reality is to be found in the continual failure of the various scientific management models. Accountability, PPBS, and other such models have not had much effect upon the schools. On the one hand, the scientific management models may have been poorly conceived and poorly executed, and better conceptions and better executions may work. On the other hand, the operation of schools may be inconsistent with the assumptions of the scientific management models. In this case, there is no reason to expect improved scientific management models to have the predicted effects upon schools.

We have seen how the failure of a policy may be due to its hyperrational conception of how schools operate. The disjuncture between some educational policies and school reality is explored further in Chapter 3.

54. Coleman, *Equality of Educational Opportunity.*

CHAPTER 3
COMPLETING THE BUREAUCRATIZATION OF THE SCHOOLS

While you and I have lips and voices which are for kissing and to sing with who cares if some one-eyed son of a bitch invents an instrument to measure Spring with?

e. e. cummings
1926

In the past two decades, as we have seen, court decisions and government regulations have exerted an enormous influence on the stated goals of education as well as on the schools and colleges themselves. We now turn to an examination of how mandated policies have affected the way in which schools are to be administered and teachers are to teach.

As the schools have gradually evolved from rudimentary to full-fledged bureaucracies, those who are responsible for goal attainment have been treated increasingly as bureaucrats. If schools are not performing well, they are instructed to tighten specific operations—a phenomenon we call "bureaucratic rationalization." If teachers are not performing well, they are to be precisely instructed on what to teach and how to teach—we call this view "rationalistic teaching." The bureaucratization of schooling, teaching, and learning will be referred to as the "rationalistic model" or "rationalistic paradigm" of the process of education.

In this chapter we shall discover some of the deficiencies of the rationalistic paradigm as seen in historical perspective and by describing some of the dimensions of reality that it omits. It is important to state at the outset that we are dealing here with ideology—with sets of ideas about how to manage schools. While it is not easy to determine the extent to which this ideology has affected the practice of education in different periods, we shall see that it has been around for some time and is growing more and more pervasive.

SOME HISTORICAL PERSPECTIVE

Few elements in the drift toward hyperrationalization do not have their historical antecedents in early twentieth-century history. In Raymond E. Callahan's detailed account of the infiltration into education of scientific management, one is continually struck by contemporary parallels.[1] Each "new" system—whether it is the planning-programming-budgeting systems of the 1960s or the competency-based education systems of the 1970s—is intended to bring order out of chaos, to bring rationality to education. The model of a successful factory is persistent although less explicit today. Callahan's account gives the reader a sense of how small a distance we have come in this century with regard both to the rationales invoked and the techniques employed. The most tragic aspect of the contemporary effort to rationalize education is the near total ignorance of history which each wave of reform displays. Only a few can be reviewed here.

Scientific management applied to the schools led to the use of the dollar as the criterion for educational decisions as early as 1913. Callahan reports on a superintendent of the Newton, Massachusetts, Public Schools who, by that year, had devised an elaborate system for making the schools more efficient, which permitted him to deal with a variety of school problems.[2] One was how to determine the relative value of various subjects. He did this by calculating the cost of a "pupil-recitation" in each subject. He found "that 5.9 pupil-recita-

1. Raymond E. Callahan, *Education and the Cult of Efficiency* (Chicago: University of Chicago Press, 1962).
2. Ibid., pp. 67–79.

tions in Greek are of the same value as 23.8 pupil-recitations in French; that 12.0 pupil-recitations in science are equivalent in value to 19.2 pupil-recitations in English; and that it takes 41.7 pupil-recitations in vocal music to equal the value of 13.9 pupil-recitations in art."[3] How was this information put to use?

> Thus confronted, do we feel like denying the equivalency of these values—we cannot deny our responsibility for fixing them as they are? This is a whole-some feeling, if it leads to a wiser assignment of values in future. Greater wisdom in these assignments will come, not by reference to any supposedly fixed and inherent values in these subjects themselves, but from a study of local conditions and needs. I know nothing about the absolute value of a recitation in Greek as compared with a recitation in French or in English. I am convinced, however, by very concrete and quite local considerations, that when the obligations of the present year expire, we ought to purchase no more Greek instruction at the rate of 5.9 pupil-recitations for a dollar. The price must go down, or we shall invest in something else.[4]

Note how, after implying that the actual values of subjects may vary, the superintendent uses cost alone as the basis for decision. The reader will be forgiven if he cannot distinguish between the old simplistic notion of cost per pupil-recitation and the new, sophisticated notion of cost per credit hour.

Again in 1913, Franklin Bobbitt applied scientific management to defining the roles of the administrator and the teacher in the publication of a set of principles for the operation of schools in which he described his expectations for the teacher (N.B.: "worker"):

> Principle I. — Definite qualitative and quantitative standards must be determined for the product.
>
> Principle II. — Where the material that is acted upon by the labor processes passes through a number of progressive stages on its way from the raw material to the ultimate product, definite qualitative and quantitative standards must be determined for the product at each of these stages.

3. *Proceedings of the National Education Association* (1913), quoted in ibid., p. 73.
4. Ibid.

Principle III. — Scientific Management finds the methods of procedure which are most efficient for actual service under actual conditions, and secures their use on the part of the workers.

Principle IV. — Standard qualifications must be determined for the workers.

Principle V. — The management must train its workers previous to service in the measure demanded by its standard qualifications, or it must set up entrance requirements of so specific and detailed a nature as to enforce upon training institutions the output of a supply of workers possessing the desirable qualifications in the degree necessary for entrance into service.

Principle VI. — The worker must be kept up to standard qualifications for his kind of work for his entire service.

Principle VII. — The worker must be kept supplied with detailed instructions as to the work to be done, the standards to be reached, the methods to be employed, and the appliances to be used.[5]

The process begins by developing standards; it is worth noting how the standards are to be developed:

A school system can no more find standards of performance within itself than a steel plant can find the proper height or weight per yard for steel rails from the activities within the plant. . . . In the case of the instructions of our general society to its agent, the school, specifications must be equally definite. . . . The commercial world can best say what it needs in the case of its stenographers and accountants. A machine shop can best say what is needed in the workers that come to it.[6]

We have here, in 1913, not a precursor but an exact statement of what will later be called accountability, functional literacy, career education, competency-based education, competency-based teacher education, and more. What are we to make of this? Is it that between the first quarter and the last quarter of the twentieth century, this logical-deductive model has never been implemented? Or is there some other explanation?

5. Franklin Bobbitt, "The Supervision of City Schools: Some General Principles of Management Applied to the Problems of City-School Systems," *Twelfth Yearbook of the National Society for the Study of Education, 1913*, Part I (Bloomington, Illinois), quoted in ibid., pp. 81–90.
6. Bobbit, "The Supervision of City Schools," quoted in ibid., p. 83.

The early efficiency movement was accompanied by an unadulterated orientation to a narrow utilitarian vocationalism. Callahan quotes an educator speaking in 1909:

> Ordinarily a love of learning is praiseworthy; but when this delight in the pleasures of learning becomes so intense and so absorbing that it diminishes the desire, and the power of earning, it is positively harmful. Education that does not promote the desire and power to do useful things—that's earning—is not worth the getting. Education that stimulates a love for useful activity is not simply desirable; it is in the highest degree ethical. . . . Personally I would rather send out pupils who are lop-sided and useful, than those who are seemingly symmetrical and useless. A man without a vocation is more to be pitied than "the man without a country." . . . And the country of which he is an inhabitant is to be commiserated, too.[7]

How far we have progressed from a narrow, utilitarian view of education can be seen by examining a statement made by the U.S. Commissioner of Education in 1975:

> The college that devotes itself totally and unequivocally to the liberal arts today is just kidding itself. Today we in education must recognize that it is also our duty to provide our students with salable skills. . . . To send young men and women into today's world armed only with Aristotle, Freud, and Hemingway is like sending a lamb into the lion's den. It is to delude them as well as ourselves. But if we give young men and women a useful skill, we give them not only the means to earn a good living but also the opportunity to do something constructive and useful for society. Moreover, these graduates will experience some of those valuable qualities that come with meaningful work—self-respect, self-confidence, independence.[8]

The attitudes, planning models, and concepts which are espoused as revolutionary today were with us at least by the first two decades of this century.

Callahan's *Education and the Cult of Efficiency* is a catalog of the steps which educators took to devise means for

---

7. *Proceedings of the National Education Association* (1913), quoted in ibid., p. 10.

8. Terrell H. Bell, "Should Colleges Teach Salable Skills?" *The Chronicle of Higher Education*, April 7, 1975, p. 32.

accounting for educational expenditures. These steps led to efforts to operate schools on a more businesslike basis, and to have them prepare students to take their place in the world of work. In the process, to use Callahan's terms, instruction followed accounting, efficiency was demonstrated through records and reports, and schools prepared educational cost accounts and balance sheets and bound themselves in red tape. What was missing then, as now, was the integration of sound concepts of education into these managerial schemes. Educational quality could not be measured; reducing costs could be—therefore efficiency became economy. Increasing class size then was said to be increasing efficiency; today it is called improving productivity. Preparing young people for the world of work was called vocationalism; today it is called career education.

BUREAUCRATIC SCHOOLS

Early Models

The relationship between society and the school was not always mediated by a bureaucratic structure. As Michael B. Katz has pointed out, during the nineteenth century four different models of education competed for attention.[9] By the end of the nineteenth century, however, "incipient bureaucracy" was well on its way to ascendency as the model by which education was to be organized in the United States.

Paternalistic voluntarism, as represented, for example, by the New York Public School Society, provided free school to the very poor. The Society was administered by an unpaid, self-perpetuating board of leading citizens. Voluntarism "rested on faith in the individual talented amateur and, at an overall administrative level, scorned the need for elaborate organization, state control, or professional staff."[10]

Democratic localism sought to bring to the cities the kind of intimacy represented by local school districts in rural

9. Michael B. Katz, *Class, Bureaucracy and Schools* (New York: Praeger, 1975).
10. Ibid., p. 9.

areas. Its proponents "subordinated both efficiency and organizational rationality to an emphasis on responsiveness, close public control, and local involvement."[11] They were hostile to the professionalization of education, opposed normal schools, and feared state intervention, centralization, and indoctrination.

Corporate voluntarism was "the conduct of *single* institutions as individual corporations operated by self-perpetuating boards of trustees and financed either wholly through endowment or through a combination of endowment and tuition."[12] Katz argues that "for a time it appeared as though corporate voluntarism in the shape of the academies would become the general pattern for secondary education."[13] Its virtues, according to Katz, were:

> Without the stigma of lower-class affiliation, it offered disinterested, enlightened, and continuous management that kept the operation of education out of the rough and unpredictable field of politics. At the same time, by placing each institution under a different administrative authority, it retained the limited scope essential to institutional variety, flexibility, and adaptation to local circumstance.[14]

THE BUREAUCRATIC MODEL

Corporate voluntarism, like the other models, gave way to *incipient bureaucracy*:

> Bureaucracy retained a legacy from the organizational models that it superseded. It bowed in the direction of the democrats by accepting their redefinition of voluntarism and consequently placing educational institutions under boards that were publicly elected rather than self-perpetuating. It innovated in its rejection of a loose, personalistic style of operation in favor of organizational rationality, impersonality, and professionalism. Nevertheless, in two respects the path from paternalistic voluntarism is direct. First, bureaucracy retained the notion of a central monopoly and systematized its operation through the creation of elaborately structured schools and school systems. Second, bureaucracy continued, and even strengthened, the notion that education was something the

11. Ibid., p. 17.   12. Ibid., p. 22.   13. Ibid.   14. Ibid.

better part of the community did to the others to make them orderly, moral, and tractable. Unfortunately, the embodiment of that idea in compulsory, bureaucratic monopolies has continued to characterize American education.[15]

Bureaucracy appears to permit those in power to control the school system. The elaborated bureaucracy of the present century appears to permit the state to achieve its ends in the schools. It emphasizes "professionalism" in operation and underscores this emphasis by separating the school from the direct influence of parents. Indeed, the elaborated bureaucracy is a testament to the belief by those in power that the individual parent cannot be trusted to provide or select the right kind of education for his child.

Katz argues that bureaucracy is inevitable only if social complexity is approached with certain values and priorities: "If order, efficiency, and uniformity are preferred to responsiveness, variety, and flexibility, then, indeed, bureaucracy is inevitable."[16] But today as in the past, order, efficiency, and uniformity are strongly valued, at the same time as added control over the means and ends of education from the center is less feared and more accepted.

Bureaucracy is itself a complex form of organizing activities. Over the years bureaucratization has become more complex as the activities which it organizes have become correspondingly more sophisticated. Although scientific understanding of the way in which bureaucracies operate has also increased, that understanding has not directly led to practical prescriptions. Moreover, since public understanding here, as elsewhere, lags significantly behind scientific understanding, one result is that policymakers are often forced to act only upon their private understanding of how bureaucracy operates. Undoubtedly, their private set of hypotheses about the operation of bureaucracy is close to the Weberian classical model of bureaucracy. At the same time and in important ways, that model has been found inadequate as a basis for describing and predicting life in a bureaucracy. When an inadequate model is used as a basis for constructing educational

15. Ibid., p. 48.
16. Ibid., p. 108.

policy, we should not be surprised when that policy does not have its intended consequences.

THE RATIONALISTIC MODEL

One way to gain perspective on the bureaucratic model is to look at models of organization which have been devised to study the schools. Two have dominated—the rationalistic model and the natural systems model.

Ronald G. Corwin, in a comprehensive review of theory and research on organization in education, notes the basic assumptions which underlie the rationalistic model:

> 1. Organizations have clear-cut goals that are understood and subscribed to by the members.
> 2. Activities are planned.
> 3. Activities are closely coordinated.
> 4. The necessary information is available for making the informed decisions necessary to achieve the goals.
> 5. Officials have sufficient control over the organization to ensure compliance with long-range plans.[17]

Even these most basic assumptions are contradicted by the normal operation of schools. Schools do not have clear-cut goals that are understood and subscribed to by all. Goals are multiple, vague, general, and contradictory, and are given different interpretations by different school personnel who inevitably choose the goals to which they subscribe. School activities may be planned or unplanned; coordinated or uncoordinated. Information (scientific or other) to make informed decisions may or may not exist. And, so far, mechanisms of control in schools have not ensured compliance with long-range plans.

Not only are schools taken to be rationalistic, they are taken to be bureaucratic as well. Corwin enumerates the assumptions of a bureaucratic model:

> Domination-subordination, the division of labor, clique structure, and group size are all concepts central to this model, although they are not unique to it. The bureaucratic ideal type presumes goal consensus. Power is centralized, authority is

17. Ronald G. Corwin, "Models of Educational Organizations," *Review of Research in Education* 2 (1975), 247–95.

based on expertise as well as incumbency of office, there is close-knit coordination and extensive planning, and the components of organization are highly interdependent. Bureaucracies can be relatively autonomous and impervious to outside attempts to influence them, although in a larger sense they are products of society.[18]

Just as schools fail to conform to the assumptions of the rationalistic model, so do they fail to conform to the more detailed bureaucratic model. Consensus on goals is lacking. Formal power may be centralized, but its influence at the classroom level is attenuated. Authority residing in the administration tends to be based upon position rather than special expertise; the scientific management movements have been a search for special expertise. Increasingly, analysts question whether schools are or can be closely coordinated, what the effects of planning are, and how interdependent the components of school organization are. Hyperrationalization, of course, is a movement to ensure that schools conform to the bureaucratic model.

The Natural Systems Model

Corwin goes on to observe that the bureaucratic model oversimplifies the complexities of schools. Noting "accumulating evidence that organizations frequently do not conform to the rational model,"[19] Corwin observes that social scientists have adopted the natural systems model:

1. Members in different parts of an organization (math teachers, coaches, or janitors) often place the interests and objectives of their own unit above those prescribed for the overall organization.

2. One's status and activity in an organization take on value as ends in themselves (indeed, salary schedules for teachers are based on their seniority, independent of demonstrated contributions to explicit goals).

3. The official goals tend to become distorted and neglected as the organization strains to survive or expand.

4. Decisions are the outcomes of bargaining and compromise among competing subgroups.

18. Ibid., p. 253.   19. Ibid., p. 255.

5. No one group has sufficient information or power to compel a high degree of coordination among the subgroups.[20]

The natural systems model begins to describe how schools actually operate. Schedules are arranged for janitorial convenience rather than educational convenience. Some teachers are hired for their coaching rather than for their scholastic skills. The salaries of competent and incompetent teachers rise at the same rate. Easily attainable goals displace goals which are difficult to attain. Decisions are intelligible as the result of compromise rather than principle. Subgroups withhold information to protect their autonomy. While the model more nearly approximates the reality of how schools operate, educational policies continue to assume that schools operate on the rational or bureaucratic model.

OTHER MODELS

As Corwin reviews additional models for studying educational organization, the inadequacy of the rational model is laid ever more bare. "Open" and "closed" models underscore the extent to which the school functions independently of the environment. Organic models assume that schools are organic wholes, "with each part dependent upon every other part; a change in one element of the system alters all of its elements."[21] Specific variations of the organic model include the social systems model, the functional model, the cybernetic model, and the exchange model, each of which takes a slightly different view of how the elements relate to one another. "Conflict" and "political" models deal with how the school copes with riots, unions, strikes, and other pressure tactics. Role performance models deal with how the different persons who occupy the same position play different roles. Whether teachers and administrators view themselves as professionals or bureaucrats can alter their behavior. As Corwin builds toward a synthesis of a complex organizational model for schools, he even distinguishes between "formal" and "complex" organizations. Other factors which affect the relationships within each of the models include the environ-

20. Ibid.   21. Ibid., p. 270.

ment, technology, and organizational size. The point of this excursion into the variety of theoretical approaches to the study of schools is to underscore how complex schools actually are. Educational policies must assume implicitly that schools operate according to one or more of these models; yet, too often, they assume the correctness of the bureaucratic model.

LOOSE COUPLING

An important new concept—the idea that schools are "loosely coupled systems"—has entered the literature of organizational theory. This concept is meant to imply that the elements of the school system are not necessarily rationally or tightly related. Karl E. Weick had described loose coupling as:

> the image that coupled events are responsive, but that each event also preserves its own identity and some evidence of its physical or logical separateness. Thus, in the case of an educational organization, it may be the case that the counselor's office is loosely coupled to the principal's office. The image is that the principal and the counselor are somehow attached, but each retains some identity and separateness and that their attachment may be circumscribed, infrequent, weak in its mutual affects, unimportant, and/or slow to respond. Each of those connotations would be conveyed if the qualifier loosely were attached to the word coupled. Loose coupling also carries connotations of impermanence, dissolvability, and tacitness, all of which are potentially crucial properties of the "glue" that holds organizations together.[22]

The idea of loose coupling provides another challenge to the rational model of the school. It also provides a way to describe the disjuncture between the rational model and school reality.

In fact, the concept of loosely coupled systems helps to make explicit at least four aspects of hyperrationalization: (1) It explains why manipulating some elements in the sys-

22. Karl E. Weick, "Educational Organizations as Loosely Coupled Systems," *Administrative Science Quarterly* 21 (March 1976), 3. See also Michael D. Cohen and James G. March, *Leadership and Ambiguity: The American College President* (New York: McGraw-Hill, 1974).

tem of the school may have no consequences for other elements. (2) It directs attention to the possibility that the educational policymaking system may be loosely coupled to the operating educational system. (3) It reveals that researchers have often incorrectly assumed that schools operate as rational organizations. (4) It suggests that hyperrationalization may be evidence that loose coupling exists.

Efforts to rationalize the processes or the goals of schools frequently do not have the anticipated effects because the schools lack mechanisms which will facilitate rationalization. Two mechanisms which couple some non-school organizations are "technical core"—an automobile factory is coupled by its technical core as embodied in its assembly line, for example—and "authority of office"—a military organization is coupled by its authority of office as embodied in the chain-of-command. The school may be coupled by neither of these mechanisms.

New policies which hold schools accountable for attaining specified goals may have no effect upon the *processes* of education if the elements of the school system are only loosely coupled. Without changes in the process of education, it is difficult to understand how the goals of education can better be attained. A requirement that an individualized education plan be developed for every handicapped child will, of course, have no effect upon the education of that child if it is not tied to budget and program decisions which affect that child. It is possible to change one element in a school and not achieve the predicted consequences for other elements (indeed, to achieve unpredicted consequences) when the elements are not tightly related.

If educational policymakers are inclined to embrace the rationalistic model of the school while teachers are inclined to embrace less rationalistic models of schooling, then the policymaking system may not be communicating with the operating system. The two systems, because they are based on different ideologies and theories of education, are only loosely coupled. Policymakers create policies which are consistent with the rationalistic model and which would work if the model were a good representation of school reality. Practicing educators do not believe in the rationalistic model and do not share its assumptions. The policies do not work as intended because educators are unwilling or unable to accommodate their behavior to the model.

The idea of loose coupling alerts us to the possibility that researchers may learn more about schools if they do not make the traditional assumption that schools are rationalistic. Ironically, the propensity of policymakers to view education rationally is reinforced whenever they turn to researchers for advice, since the researchers have constructed rational models of schools in order to study them. Policymakers, seeing that schools have been studied rationalistically, believe that they can be made to conform to the researchers' model. In this fashion, research models prematurely become the basis for accountability and assessment programs.

Weick has suggested that overrationalization (his term) may be evidence that loose coupling exists.[23] When the couplings between elements receive excessive attention, it may be because they are loose. In this light, we can understand the monumental efforts occasionally undertaken by state superintendents of education to identify the goals of education. Arguably, because state superintendents lack influence over schools, they undertake ritual efforts to develop such statements of goals. More recently, state legislatures, frustrated at the poor match between the competencies of high school graduates and the demands of society, have required the generation of lists of expected competencies for high school graduates. Efforts to rationalize in detail what the schools are to accomplish may reveal the loose coupling of the legislature and the school.

RATIONALISTIC TEACHING

As we have already suggested, the policymaking process has an affinity for a rationalistic conception of teaching and the teacher. The reasons are simple: the will of the policymakers must be implemented; the expectations for what schools are to accomplish must be translated into action; the workers (teachers) in the factory (school) must perform their assigned tasks; and the bureaucracy must be peopled

23. Weick, "Educational Organizations," p. 9.

by bureaucrats who will implement the official goals of the institution.

CBTE

It is easy to characterize and even easier to caricature the movement known as competency-based teacher education.[24] Its fundamental principles are simplistic deductions from the view that the schools are creatures of society established to execute the will of society. Competency-based teacher education may be viewed as the embodiment of the set of expectations which the policymaking process would like to have about potential teachers. While there is no definitive conception of CBTE, definitions commonly include the following elements:

> 1. "Competencies" mean knowledge, skills, and behaviors that the teacher (or would-be teacher) must have.
> 2. Competencies are based on what teachers actually do in the classroom.
> 3. Criteria for determining competence are explicit and public.
> 4. Performance is the major source of evidence of competence.
> 5. Rate or progress through the program is determined by demonstrated competency (not time, semester hours, or some other standard).[25]

If colleges of education could train people to behave in the manner implied by these principles, then educational policy objectives would be self-executing. It would remain only for substantive educational goals to be specified.

The compatibility of CBTE with the school conceived as a bureaucracy is evident. Charles Bidwell has sketched the bureaucratic characteristics of schools as follows:

> 1. a functional division of labor (e.g., the allocation of instructional and coordinative tasks to the school system roles of teacher and administrator);

24. Ralph A. Smith, *Regaining Educational Leadership: Critical Essays on PBTE/CBTE, Behavioral Objectives, and Accountability* (New York: Wiley, 1975).

25. John G. Merrow, II, *Politics of Competence: A Review of Competency-Based Teacher Education* (Washington, D.C.: National Institute of Education, 1975), p. 14.

2. the definition of staff roles as offices, that is, in terms of recruitment according to merit and competence, legally based tenure, functional specificity of performance, and universalistic, affectively neutral interaction with clients;

3. the hierarchic ordering of offices, providing an authority structure based on the legally defined and circumscribed power of officers, a system of adjudication of staff disputes by reference to superiors, and regularized lines of communication;

4. operation according to rules of procedure, which set limits to the discretionary performance of officers by specifying both the aims and modes of official action.[26]

CBTE promises to specify the tasks which a person must be able to perform in order to enter the role of teacher. It promises to provide an operational basis for assessing competence for entry, for defining functional specificity of performance, and for circumscribing authority. It can be used to set minimum and maximum limits to performance by specifying aims and means. In short, CBTE promises to make operational the role of teacher conceived as bureaucrat.

TEACHERS' VIEWS

Teachers, of course, do not, for various reasons, readily accept a rationalistic characterization of their roles. Teacher training programs in the past may have failed to inculcate an appreciation of rationalistic thinking. Current teacher training programs may not be long or intensive enough for potential teachers to integrate this mode of thinking. Teachers may simply be resistant to bureaucratic rationalization of their role. The rationalistic mode of thinking may be dissonant with the reality of teaching. Substantial evidence suggests that the primary reason is that the rationalistic conception of teaching is perceived by teachers as not salient, useful, or relevant to the demands of their work.

How teachers view teaching has been the subject of two important books—Philip W. Jackson's *Life in Classrooms*[27]

26. Charles E. Bidwell, "The School as a Formal Organization," in *Handbook of Organizations*, ed. James G. March (Chicago: Rand McNally, 1965), p. 974.

27. Philip W. Jackson, *Life in Classrooms* (New York: Holt, Rinehart and Winston, 1968).

and Dan C. Lortie's *Schoolteacher*.[28] From these works emerges a picture of teaching and teachers which stands in dramatic contrast to the concept of rationalistic teaching. Teachers are rational, but not in the ways implied by bureaucratic rationalization.

Those who believe in the rationalistic model assume that the process of education rests on an underlying order. Lortie found that teachers may not share this "scientific" assumption:

> A scientific approach, however, normally begins with the assumption that there is an underlying order in the phenomena under study. It is not clear that all or most teachers make that assumption about their world. Some see teaching outcomes as capricious and describe short-term results in almost mysterious terms. If that viewpoint is widespread, it is not surprising that teachers do not invest in searching for general principles to inform their work. If they suspect that classroom events are beyond comprehension, inquiry is futile.[29]

Not only does the rationalistic model assume predictability in behavior, but it also simplifies reality:

> Those trained in behavioral science are used to accepting short-run measurements as evidence of effectiveness; it would be easy to assume that these teachers do not want to confront the possibility of low impact on students. But one wonders: styles of thought which pervade science may not work for those who take personal responsibility for the development of children. Science moves ahead through deliberate and sophisticated simplifications of reality, but there is little to suggest that this is the approach of classroom teachers.[30]

While the rationalistic model abstracts and simplifies reality, a teacher will not, cannot; because a teacher is responsible for a whole, real child.

Conceptions of education are formed well before exposure to teacher training. Lortie argues that a powerful determinant of the orientation of teachers is what they observe

28. Dan C. Lortie, *Schoolteacher: A Sociological Study* (Chicago: University of Chicago Press, 1975).

29. Ibid., p. 212.

30. Ibid., pp. 146–47.

over the years about their own teachers. The rationalistic model implicitly adopts a view of education drawn from the behavioral sciences:

> Teacher training is increasingly influenced by ideas drawn from behavioral science. Those trained in behavioral disciplines are inclined to conceptualize teaching in instrumental terms—to talk of "treatments" and "options" and to assess outcomes in terms of measurable and discrete objectives. One wonders how effectively such professors communicate with the many students who, it appears, see teaching as the "living out" of prior conceptions of good teaching. Students who conceive of teaching (consciously or not) as expressing qualities associated with revered models will be less attuned to the pragmatic and rationalistic conceptions of teaching found in behavioral science. The two groups—students and professors— may talk past one another.[31]

Teacher training fails to alter teachers' prior conceptions of education.

TEACHERS AND GOALS

The rationalistic model makes important assumptions about how the school operates. For example, it assumes that the goals of education are set politically, transmitted through the school district and school hierarchies, and then come to rest with the teacher for implementation. To what degree does this assumption accord with reality? To what extent do the formal goals of the school system guide the actions of teachers? According to Lortie:

> If teacher pride were ordered in strict adherence to organizational, formal goals, we would expect to find heavy emphasis on results attained with entire classes; school systems present themselves as concerned with the learning of all students. It is provocative, therefore, that most of these did so in an offhand manner. Such responses seemed to occur with teachers working in particular subjects and grades—the more tangible and visible the learning they were seeking to promote, the likelier they were to emphasize general gains with students. Examples are initial reading, physical education skills, typing, and skill subjects in home economics. A few elementary teachers linked

31. Ibid., pp. 66–67.

pride to favorable outcomes on achievement tests, but they seemed hesitant to do so.[32]

Perhaps surprisingly, teachers do not naturally emphasize objective group results. Yet the rationalistic model assumes that the underlying objective of the teacher is to maximize aggregate achievement test scores. Advocates of the rationalistic model will argue that accountability schemes are designed to focus the teacher's attention on output measures. And indeed, teaching for the test has occurred. However, whether the teacher has altered his orientation fundamentally is quite another matter. Until we understand why teachers eschew tests as a gauge of successful teaching, policies which assume that teachers are trying to maximize test scores are not likely to improve education.

Formally stated goals will only affect students as they are mediated by teachers. Currently, teachers translate formal goals into personalized objectives:

> Educational goals are often stated in global, even utopian terms. . . . [W]e observed that teachers "reduce" such goals into specific objectives they use in their daily work. This reduction apparently involves two conservative tendencies: relying on personal convictions and obtaining high satisfaction from outcomes that are less than universalistic. When teachers cannot use stated goals to guide their actions, organizational objectives give way to personal values; the personal values of teachers, as we saw . . . are heavily influenced by past experience.[33]

Unless either teacher training or the underlying system is altered and the behavior of teachers modified, the process of goal redefinition will likely continue.

As we struggle to understand the disjuncture between the rationalistic model of education and the reality of life in the classroom, the work of Jackson is particularly instructive. Jackson's impressions are derived from interviews of fifty teachers identified as outstanding by their superiors. Like Lortie, he found that teachers do not gauge their success by means of either commercial or teacher-made tests:

> In the most global terms, the goal of the schools is to promote learning. Thus, ideally we might expect teachers to derive

32. Ibid., p. 127.
33. Ibid., p. 208.

a major source of their satisfactions from observing growth in achievement among their students. Further, the students' performance on tests of achievement (commercial or teacher-made) would seem to provide objective and readily obtainable evidence of this growth. Logically at least, the conscientious teacher ought to point with pride or disappointment to the gains or losses of students as measured by test performance. But, as is often true in human affairs, the logical did not occur. One of the most interesting features of the interview material was the absence of reference to objective evidence of school learning in contexts in which one might expect it to be discussed.

Testing, when it is mentioned at all, is given little emphasis. These teachers treat it as being of minor importance in helping them understand how well they have done.[34]

That teachers do not naturally use tests to gauge their effectiveness is crucial to an understanding of the limits of reform through policy changes, the effectiveness of which are to be judged by test score changes. Time and again we find that what we predict or expect on the basis of logic or on the basis of experience in other sectors fails to occur in education.

Generations of educational researchers have tried to devise rational models of the act of teaching; increasingly, educational policies are devised which presuppose the utility of these models. Yet a rationalistic description of the act of teaching fails to emerge from interviews with teachers.

Sometimes teaching is described as a highly rational affair. Such descriptions often emphasize the decision-making function of the teacher, or liken his task to that of a problem-solver or hypothesis-tester. Yet the interviews with elementary teachers raise serious doubts about these ways of looking at the teaching process. The immediacy of classroom life, the fleeting and sometimes cryptic signs on which the teacher relies for determining his pedagogical moves and for evaluating the effectiveness of his actions call into question the appropriateness of using conventional models of rationality to depict the teacher's classroom behavior.

This questioning of the usefulness of rational models is not intended to imply that teaching is totally irrational or that the

34. Jackson, *Life in Classrooms*, p. 123.

customary laws of cause and effect somehow fail to operate in the classroom. Obviously events are as lawful there as they are in any other sphere of human endeavor. But the activities assumed to accompany rational thought processes—activities such as the identification of alternative courses of action, the conscious deliberation over choice, the weighing of evidence, the evaluation of outcomes—these and other manifestations of orderly cognition are not very salient in the teacher's behavior as he flits back and forth from one student to another and from one activity to the next.[35]

THE LIMITS OF THE RATIONALISTIC MODEL

That the rationalistic model does not fit the reality of classroom life does not, of course, imply that the teaching act is irrational. What it suggests is that the rationalistic paradigm is too simple. To understand teaching is at least as difficult as understanding human behavior. Like any human being, a teacher's purposive behavior is governed not only by a simple planning model but also by individual disposition, social circumstances, and institutional factors. In the classroom the quantity of human behavior is large and social interactions numerous:

> Anyone who has ever taught knows that the classroom is a busy place, even though it may not always appear so to the casual visitor. Indeed, recent data have proved surprising even to experienced teachers. For example, we have found in one study of elementary classrooms that the teacher engages in as many as 1000 interpersonal interchanges each day. An attempt to catalogue the interchanges among students or the physical movement of class members would doubtlessly add to the general impression that most classrooms, though seemingly placid when glimpsed through the window in the hall door, are more like the proverbial beehive of activity. One way of understanding the meaning of this activity for those who experience it is by focusing on the teacher as he goes about channeling the social traffic of the classroom.[36]

Imagine the teacher rationally calculating each of those thousand interactions and mentally or mechanically recording the

35. Ibid., p. 151.   36. Ibid., p. 11.

result of each against a long list of behavioral objectives!

The limits of the rationalistic approach to teaching are well described by Jackson:

> The major weakness of the engineering point of view as a way of looking at the teaching process is that it begins with an oversimplified image of what goes on in elementary school classrooms. The business of teaching involves much more than defining curricular objectives and moving toward them with dispatch; and even that limited aspect of the teacher's work is far more complicated in reality than an abstract description of the process would have it seem. When it is remembered that the average teacher is in charge of the twenty-five or thirty students of varying abilities and backgrounds for 1000 hours a year and that his responsibilities extend over four or five major curricular areas, it is difficult to see how he could be very precise about where he is going and how to get there during each instructional moment. He may have a vague notion of what he hopes to achieve, but it is unreasonable to expect him to sustain an alert awareness of how each of his students is progressing toward each of a dozen or so curricular objectives.[37]

This picture of school reality stands in stark contrast to the school reality envisioned by the rationalistic model.

The point is not so much that teachers cannot be trained to think more rationalistically and to judge their effectiveness by objective group results, although research does not support the idea that CBTE will improve learning.[38] Rather, the point is that teachers do not now view the rationalistic approach as particularly efficacious. This is so despite a number of facts which would appear to support a rationalistic approach to teaching. The rationalistic model has been around for a long time and periodically receives renewed attention. Instruction in curriculum planning and test construction has been a part of teacher training programs. Most schools appear to require teachers to maintain planning books; most schools require standardized testing periodically. Most teachers do

37. Ibid., p. 165.
38. Robert W. Heath and Mark A. Nielson, "The Research Basis for Performance-Based Teacher Education," *Review of Educational Research* 44:4 (Fall 1974), 463–81.

give tests. Yet, although teachers observe the forms of rationalistic teaching, they do not appear to accept it as a guide to their teaching.

The Organization of Teachers

Teachers and professors *individually* resist the forces associated with hyperrationalization by invoking professionalism. On the one hand, they argue that only their professional expertise should guide their actions. Individualism and autonomy are the preferred professional norms. On the other hand, they argue that their work is too subtle and complex to be ordered, standardized, routinized, and easily evaluated. Thus, individual teachers resist central determination of educational ends and especially means, excessive rationalization of procedures, and goal reduction and reductionism, all of which limit their autonomy.

However, the sentiments of individual teachers are not necessarily reflected by teachers *collectively*. While teachers individually resist the forces associated with hyperrationalization, collectively they may well contribute to them. Teachers' organizations do not intend to contradict the sentiments of their members, but they, like governmental bodies, have only a limited set of techniques for achieving their ends.

The major strategy of organized teachers has been to constrain hierarchical authority.[39] Their principal technique has been to create rules limiting administrator discretion. Their collective bargaining agreements call for appointment, assignment, and resource allocation decisions to be made on the "objective" basis of seniority. Teachers seek to limit

> specific administrative behavior by writing proscriptions into the contract. Yet if such restrictions are made general rules they can have unintended consequences. A rule designed to prevent administrators from calling unnecessary meetings may turn into a maximal statement on teachers' readiness to participate in staff meetings. Some teachers, fearing collegial displeasure, may hold back from initiating activities which require joint planning.[40]

39. Dan C. Lortie, *Schoolteacher: A Sociological Study* (Chicago: University of Chicago Press, 1975), p. 206.
40. Ibid., p. 207.

Rules, even when the result of the collective bargaining process, can limit professional autonomy.

Teachers' organizations have not limited their collective bargaining goals merely to "wages, hours, and working conditions" as has traditionally been the case in the private sector.[41] Collective bargaining agreements now cover provisions relating to class size; teacher evaluation, promotion, assignment, and transfer procedures; utilization of paraprofessionals and student interns; and teacher participation in instructional policymaking and the design of in-service programs.[42] As collective bargaining agreements confront the substance of education, they must be reconciled with school district policy as well as with policies emanating from federal, state, and court sources. The prescriptions and proscriptions of collective bargaining agreements challenge and are challenged by rules and procedures devised elsewhere. The resolution of compatible and incompatible provisions will shape the nature of education. While the exact resolution is difficult to foresee, it seems likely that more rather than less rationalization will be the result.

As organized teachers come to rely upon legalistic procedures to limit administrator discretion, they may well be inviting legalistic retaliation:[43]

> It appears that teachers have received a degree of "ritual pity" in the past; it was conventional to lament their low pay and refer to them as "dedicated"—workers who gave more than they received. The moral position of teachers made it difficult for others to demand more of them; teachers subsequently were exempted from high performance expectations and rigorous public scrutiny. But such relationships undergo change when teachers assert their collective power and win significant gains. The use of calculative strategies invites the use of calculative counterstrategies.[44]

It is no accident that accountability legislation and programs have emerged as teachers' organizations have become more

41. Lorraine M. McDonnell, "NEA Priorities and Their Impact on Teacher Education," Washington, D.C.: American Association of Colleges for Teacher Education, 1977, p. 4.

42. Ibid.

43. Lortie, *Schoolteacher*, p. 206.

44. Ibid., p. 221.

active. Accountability is management's demand for increased productivity in the educational system. In the private sector, economic concessions are sometimes granted in exchange for increases in productivity.

In this fashion, teachers' organizations contribute to the further rationalization of education. Directly, they devise their preferred rules and procedures. Indirectly, they precipitate retaliatory policies. The potential contribution of teachers' organizations to the centralization of education is very great. Teachers' organizations have begun to turn their attention away from collective bargaining with the local school board:

> Both the NEA and the AFT turned to political action because they realized there are real limits on what can be gained through the collective bargaining process alone. Not only are more resources available at higher levels of government, but by going outside the traditional board of education/teacher organization relationship, organized teachers believe they have a better chance of accomplishing their aims.
>
> The first goal of political action by teachers is to insure that they achieve more of their demands vis-à-vis the collective bargaining process. At the same time, however, both the AFT and the NEA realize that in some instances it is more efficient to lobby the state and federal governments. For example, instead of fighting with each Local Education Agency (LEA) for the right to bargain collectively, the teacher organizations are working for the passage of state and federal laws mandating collective bargaining for teachers. This strategy is a much more effective use of their organizational resources. In addition, both groups realize that, given the present inability of local jurisdictions to provide for all of the costs of public education, demands must be made on the state and federal governments to assume a greater responsibility for financing public education. In a sense, the AFT and the NEA are attempting to "level-up" the locus of educational decision making to higher levels of government.[45]

As political action occurs outside the local school district, the position of policymakers vis-à-vis the schools will be strengthened. Moreover, since policymakers are already accustomed to dealing with other kinds of bureaucrats, the tendency will

45. McDonnell, "NEA Priorities," pp. 7–8.

be to treat teachers as bureaucrats and schools as bureaucracies. The movement for statewide accountability laws will be strengthened. While, on the surface, teachers' organizations may oppose accountability legislation, legislators will perceive themselves under pressure to protect the public interest through the demand for increased productivity.

Similar patterns are evident in higher education as the collegial system of governance is supplanted by the bureaucratic system. As institutions and state systems of higher education become increasingly bureaucratic, faculty unionization can be expected to increase.[46] In turn, faculty unionization will reinforce the bureaucratization of higher education. In some state institutions, faculty unions already negotiate directly with state officials.[47] Thus faculty unionization becomes not a force for professionalism, but a force for rationalization and centralization.

INSTRUMENTAL EDUCATION

The policymaking process views education as the means by which the child is prepared to take his place in society. The school and the teachers are the instruments which will transform the child into a productive, literate, law-abiding citizen. The notions that education is important in its own right, that education may lead a person to challenge rather than accept society, and that education is a gift which society bestows upon the individual are absent from the instrumental view of education. It is conceivable that policymakers believe that the schools must be made accountable for the instrumental goals of education and that other goals may be left to local option. However, as the influence of policymakers becomes more pervasive, the risk is that the instrumental goals will become the exclusive goals.

CBE

Just as CBTE encapsulates the view of the teacher that the policymaking process prefers, so does competency-based

46. Donald M. Stewart, "The Not-So-Steady State of Governance in Higher Education," An Occasional Paper of the Aspen Institute for Humanistic Studies, 1976, p. 5.
47. Ibid.

education encapsulate the view of the process of education that the policymaking process prefers. CBE promises that relevant elements of education will be delivered by the school conceived of as a bureaucracy. It appears to provide a means to allocate instructional tasks, to specify expectations for performance, to circumscribe authority and responsibility, and to specify the aims of official action.

William G. Spady has developed an ideal definition of CBE.[48] Let us examine this definition in the context of school as bureaucracy to see how CBE can link education, the school, and the teacher to the demands of policymakers and to utilitarian goals for education.

> CBE [is] a data-based, adaptive, performance-oriented set of integrated processes that facilitate, measure, record, and certify within the context of flexible time parameters the demonstration of known, explicitly stated, and agreed upon learning outcomes that reflect successful functioning in life role.[49]

The definition requires that:

> the outcome goals of a CBE process be stated in terms that are clear and explicit with regard to the criteria of performance that are expected and that they be known and agreed upon by *all those with a direct interest in the student's educational progress.*[50]

By stating goals in clear, explicit, and operational terms, CBE makes the expectations for students apparent and, by direct implication, also the expectations for teachers.

In short, CBE provides a technology for prescribing learning outcomes to anyone with an interest in the education of the child—including, of course, policymakers.

In logical terms, CBE is devoid of ideological bias; presumably it can accommodate any goals for education. Indeed, its acceptance in the first instance may result from this ideological neutrality. The adoption of CBE requires a commitment only to a process, although, as we shall see, that process shapes the goals of education. Having found a tool,

---

48. William G. Spady, "Competency-Based Education: A Bandwagon in Search of a Definition," *Researcher* 6:1 (January 1976), 9–14.
49. Ibid.
50. Ibid. (emphasis added).

policymakers and others must then decide how to define competency:

> This approach, therefore, defines *competencies* as indicators of successful performance in life-role activities (be they producer, consumer, political citizen, driver, family member, intimate friend, recreational participant, or life-long learner) and distinguishes them from the discrete cognitive, manual, and social *capacities* (such as reading and computational skills, speaking ability, and motivation) that, when integrated and adapted to particular social contexts, serve as the enablers of or building blocks on which competencies ultimately depend.[51]

The idea of "competencies" means that the policymaker need not rely on proximate capacities. But CBE requires that learning outcomes be performance-based, measurable, and hence certifiable. Presumably competencies would be preferred to capacities except when the former cannot be easily measured. Capacities, because they are more closely related to the conventional and traditional curriculum of the school, may be easier to measure. Indeed, conventional testing and even criterion-referenced testing have been developed largely to test conventional curriculum outcomes. Their availability and technical quality (reliability and validity) may even lead to the selection of what they measure as the goals for education.

CBE requires that there be a consensus about goals. In our democratic, pluralistic, secular society, the setting of goals for education is an inherently provocative activity. There are three ways to avoid controversy in goal-setting, all of which have been employed at different times in different places in American education. One strategy is to state goals at a high level of abstraction—the general goal of equal educational opportunity is a good example. Controversy concerning equal educational opportunity was avoided until school systems began to test its meaning operationally. A second strategy for avoiding controversy is to state goals exhaustively. State superintendents of education, as an example, occasionally devise long lists of goals for the schools. So long as goals perceived as important by any group are not omitted from the list, controversy is averted. The problem with this strategy is that an exhaustive list is no guide to policy. The

51. Spady, "Competency-Based Education," p. 10.

third strategy, and the one most vigorously being pursued currently, is to select goals upon which there is general agreement.

The CBE ideology has at least one further effect upon the selection of goals:

> The basic tension in a CBE certification structure between "required minimums" and "desirable maximums" is probably unavoidable. Inherent in any certification process is the establishment of a performance floor which students must meet in order to receive institutional endorsement. But where exit rules allow one to receive a diploma once those minimums are met, the minimums may also serve as the maximums, and many students may choose to leave as soon as possible.[52]

Built into the CBE concept is the tendency to state goals in terms of minima. This tendency is strongly reinforced by the idea that schools are to prepare students to enter society, for entry expectations or requirements are inevitably stated in terms of minima.

The preference is then for minimum, agreed-upon, measurable, instrumental goals. What is difficult to determine is the exact nature of the interaction between CBE and the policymaking process. Is CBE merely an operational statement of the preferences of the policymaking process? Or is it a technical invention which facilitates the policymaking process? To what extent do they simply mirror one another? To what extent do they shape one another? A precise answer to these questions is impossible for several reasons: (1) one cannot identify an intellectual genesis for CBE; (2) the policymaking process has been affected by CBE; and (3) the line between the artifact known as CBE and the logical constructs used "naturally" by policymakers is impossible to locate. The essential point here, however, is that policymakers now behave as though they have a tool for affecting education in local schools.

Basic Skills

The policymakers' preference for preparing students to function successfully in adult roles is the starting point for the substance of educational policy. The ability to read has

52. Ibid., p. 12.

always been seen as the cornerstone goal of education and of preparation for adult roles. It is the preeminent educational goal over which there has been the least dispute, beginning perhaps with the passage by Massachusetts of the Old Deluder Satan Act in 1647. In recent years, public concern for reading has been embodied in the terms "basic education," "functional literacy," and "basic skills." Of these three terms, only functional literacy is exclusively concerned with reading. Functional literacy nicely captures the idea that students are to acquire the *minimum* reading skills necessary to *function* in society. Dissatisfaction with a total preoccupation with literacy occasionally has led to the coining of such phrases as "functional numeracy." Functional literacy may have outlived its usefulness as an expression because it is too limited. In its place we have basic education and, more recently, basic skills. These expressions are somewhat broader, although discussions of them generally begin with reading and seldom progress beyond arithmetic.

Basic education and basic skills, as goals for education, embody the properties desired by the policymaking process. They refer to minima, they generate consensus, they are measurable, and they are instrumental. "Basic" can be construed as a synonym for minimum; basic is basic; basic is not advanced; basic is without frills, without extras. No one can be opposed to basic education; some may want more, but no one can object to providing at least the minimum. Basic does not generate dissent, at least not until the specification of its contents goes beyond the mere listing of literacy and computational skills. The outcomes of basic education or basic skills instruction, at least in reading and arithmetic, are readily measurable by conventional tests. They can even be measured by modern criterion-referenced tests. The latter compare a student's performance not to his peers, but to the performance of a criterion list of capacities, the building blocks of competencies which are the indicators of successful performance in life-role activities. Thus, basic education and basic skills are instrumental. Indeed, they are frequently defined, in circular fashion, as leading to that set of outcomes minimally necessary for effective functioning in society.

As we have already suggested, the rationalistic paradigm

reappears every few years under a new name. The account-ability movement reemerges as the competency-based education movement. Competency-based education reemerges as the basic skills movement. Basic skills has reemerged as "minimal competency":

> More and more states and school districts across the nation are requiring students to prove competence in the 3Rs before they can get high school diplomas. This trend toward minimum competence tests and legislation mandating such action is moving like a "grass fire" through state capitols catching many educators in a web of controversies.[53]

Basic skills and minimal competency testing are one substantive thrust which the rationalistic paradigm encompasses. A school's, a teacher's, or a student's success in the basic subjects is measured by scores on a test of capacities to read and do arithmetic. The policymaking process is satisfied by a proximate indicator of competence probably because tests are well developed in this area and because it is difficult to certify competence in the adult-role demands for reading and arithmetic.

VOCATIONAL AND CAREER EDUCATION

Reading and computational skills do not exhaust the policymakers' substantive concerns for education, however. Their second major concern has been for vocational or career education—terms which some have suggested are interchangeable.[54] There is a straightforward reductionism in the advocacy of career education. Career education is the quintessence of instrumental education, for through it the student is transformed into the productive worker, and thus one of the major goals of the schools—to prepare productive citizens—is reached. If students are graduated from schools and are unemployed, it is assumed that is because they lack vocational skills. Since the schools can teach vocational skills, the acquisition of which will ensure that graduates will be

53. *A Summary of the 10th Annual Meeting of the Education Commission of the States* (1976), p. 30.

54. W. Norton Grubb and Marvin Lazerson, " 'Rally 'Round the Workplace': Continuities and Fallacies in Career Education," *Harvard Educational Review* 45:4 (November 1975), 451–74.

employable, it remains then only to enumerate the skills and inculcate them.

The motivation for vocational or career education is most easily understood in historical context. As W. Norton Grubb and Marvin Lazerson have put it so well:

> Within this context, the vocational education movement gathered support from businessmen, educators, social reformers, and labor. Its advocates argued that vocational education would produce a skilled labor force, contribute to further economic development, elevate manual labor to a higher status, and restore relevance to the schools. By teaching industry, discipline, submission to authority, respect for property rights, and acceptance of one's place in the industrial order, vocational education would combat social decay, industrial unrest, and alienation from work. Pupils would cease to drop out of school because vocational training would give them the skills they would need as adults in the labor market.[55]

In present terms:

> [C]areer education calls for a dramatic reorientation of the entire educational system toward the world of work so that all phases of the curriculum would be job-oriented. It would require that students leaving the educational system at any level be knowledgeable about available jobs and the skills they demand and, more important, that students possess immediately marketable skills.[56]

Vocational and career education have received periodic attention from the Congress since 1917 and increasingly from state governments. In addition to their attraction as instrumental and apparently feasible solutions to the recurrent problem of unemployment, these programs also satisfy the other tests for substantive educational policy. In the first place, career education can be made as broad as necessary to generate a wide consensus. Indeed, one definition of career education is "preparation for all meaningful and productive activity, at work or at leisure, whether paid or volunteer, as employee or employer, in private business or in the public sector, or in the family."[57] But when career education is con-

55. Ibid., p. 457.   56. Ibid., p. 453.
57. Kenneth Hoyt et al., *Career Education and the Elementary School Teacher* (Salt Lake City: Olympus, 1973), p. 2.

strued as all education, it loses its meaning. More narrow conceptions must be employed in order to make the concept operative.

Second, career education generally refers to minima. The school is discharged of its responsibility when the student is certified as competent for entry-level jobs. Third, as just noted, the learning outcome, if not measurable, is at least certifiable. Because career education emphasizes on-job competence rather than certification by the school, successful functioning on the job is the measure of a career education program's success.

In the case of basic education, policymakers must mandate statewide testing or assessment programs in order to monitor the effects of mandated instruction in the basic skills. In the case of career education, the impact of legislation is measured by placement into entry-level jobs.

Despite the obvious appeal that career education holds for better articulating the worlds of education and work, it rests on two faulty assumptions. The first is that it is in fact possible to identify and inculcate skills which will serve a person well as he seeks to make a *career.* No skills have been so identified, unless one considers them to be those usually associated with liberal education. Second, career education is supported by policymakers because they believe that better-trained school graduates will lead to reduced unemployment. Generally, however, the causes of unemployment lie not in the deficiencies of individual workers but in the structure of the economy.[58]

MORAL EDUCATION

Schools are expected to prepare not only literate and productive adults but also law-abiding citizens—an expectation reinforced by the belief that deficiencies in society result from deficiencies in individual citizens.[59] If there is moral decay in society, so this reasoning goes, it can be repaired by ensuring that the next generation of citizens has the skills developed by appropriate curricula in the schools to overcome moral decay.

58. Grubb and Lazerson, " 'Rally 'Round the Workplace,' " p. 465.
59. Samuel Bowles and Herbert Gintis, *Schooling in Capitalist America* (New York: Basic Books, 1976), p. 115.

But moral education is a particularly troublesome issue—
where is the consensus on what values should be taught and
how? According to John E. Coons:

> [O]ur adult society is characterized by indeterminacy con-
> cerning both the objectives and means of child rearing; in-
> deed, even where there is agreement on goals . . . there is often
> disagreement respecting the means to achieve them. . . . On
> some issues adult society can be simply puzzled as to what
> should be hoped for or done to children; today, perhaps the
> principles of sexual morality are in this state of ambiguity. On
> other issues—abortion policy may be an example—most adults
> hold strong and clear opinions, but these individual opinions
> conflict, preventing the formation of a policy consensus. . . .
> One might with slight distortion describe these contrasting
> conditions as puzzlement and pluralism. . . .[60]

A note on "Schools should teach a course on _____" in
The Legislative Review of the Education Commission of the
States illustrates how much indeterminacy is involved in try-
ing to enact moral education legislation:

> Filling in this blank space is getting legislative attention in
> a number of states. In *Florida* HB 1026 would require high
> schools to teach a course in "American democracy" to all stu-
> dents. It would also make the current Americanism versus
> Communism course voluntary. HB 1683 would require a high
> school course of the American legal system, including rights
> and duties of the citizen under criminal law and the state and
> the United States Constitutions. The Sunshine State also
> has two joint resolutions, HCR 240 and SCR 138, encouraging
> schools to offer programs assisting students to better under-
> stand their legal obligations, rights and responsibilities.[61]

This note reveals but a few of the problems inherent in the
attempt to prepare law-abiding citizens by means of moral
education. How one construes the problem that moral education is supposed to solve will determine how the blank is
filled in and which curriculum will be prescribed. The problems to be addressed by moral education, citizenship educa-

60. John E. Coons, "Law and the Sovereigns of Childhood," *Kappan*
58:1 (September 1976), 20.
61. Education Commission of the States, *Legislative Review* 6:9
(April 12, 1976), 2.

tion, or legal education have always been with the schools. Shall we teach the theory of democracy or only the American version? Shall we teach the virtues of capitalism? With or without reference to the vices of communism? Shall we teach students that they have rights? If so, how much balance do we give to teaching about responsibilities?

PREDICTION FOR SUCCESS

There are several problems with the assumption of the rationalistic paradigm that basic skills instruction, career education, and moral education will prepare literate, productive, and law-abiding citizens. Its major problem is that it assumes that it is possible to arrive at a list of skills, capacities, or competencies which, when attained, will guarantee success in adult roles.

First of all, it is not easy to secure agreement about the adult roles with which the schools should be concerned—should we be preparing people for work or for further education? Second, it is not easy to agree upon what constitutes success in adult roles. For example, if functional literacy training should prepare people to complete federal income tax forms, which form should we use—the short one or the long one? Third, it is frequently difficult to draw a connection between school-trained capacities and life-role competencies. There is no evidence that introducing the rationalistic paradigm will help students whom the schools are now failing. The rationalistic paradigm in its various manifestations contains no new theory of education, nor is there much evidence to support the *assumption* that students will learn more or better under such a system of education.[62]

Despite the evidence of its limitations, the belief in instrumental education is so persistent that one is compelled to inquire further into its causes. We have seen how instrumental education and the rationalistic paradigm satisfy the technical demands of the policymaking process and yield a conception of the school as bureaucracy and the teacher as bureaucrat. Samuel Bowles and Herbert Gintis see a more

62. Phillippe C. Duchastel and Paul F. Merrill, "The Effects of Behavioral Objectives on Learning: Review of Empirical Studies," *Review of Educational Research* 43:1 (Winter 1973), 53–69.

fundamental force at work.[63] They note that liberal educational theory posits three functions for the educational system:

> First and foremost, schools must help integrate youth into the various occupational, political, familial, and other adult roles required by an expanding economy and a stable polity. . . . We refer to this process as the "integrative" function of education.
>
> Second, while substantial inequality in economic privilege and social status is believed by most liberals to be inevitable, giving each individual a chance to compete openly for these privileges is both efficient and desirable. . . . We shall refer to this role of schooling in the pursuit of equality of opportunity, or of equality itself, as the "egalitarian" function of education.
>
> Lastly, education is seen as a major instrument in promoting the psychic and moral development of the individual. Personal fulfillment depends, in large part, on the extent, direction, and vigor of development of our physical, cognitive, emotional, aesthetic, and other potentials. . . . We refer to this as the "developmental" function of education.[64]

Liberal educational reformers believe that the integrative, egalitarian, and developmental functions are, if not necessarily associated, at least compatible. Bowles and Gintis argue, on the contrary, that these functions are incompatible, given the values of corporate capitalism:

> The educational system serves—through the correspondence of its social relations with those of economic life—to reproduce economic inequality and to distort personal development. Thus under corporate capitalism the objectives of liberal educational reform are contradictory: It is precisely because of its role as producer of an alienated and stratified labor force that the educational system has developed its repressive and unequal structure. In the history of U.S. education, it is the integrative function which has dominated the purpose of schooling, to the detriment of the other liberal objectives.
>
> More fundamentally, the contradictory nature of liberal educational reform objectives may be directly traced to the dual role imposed on education in the interests of profitability

63. Bowles and Gintis, *Schooling in Capitalist America.*
64. Ibid., p. 21.

and stability; namely, workers' productive capacities and perpetuating the social, political, and economic conditions for the transformation of the fruits of labor into capitalist profits. It is these overriding objectives of the capitalist class—not the ideals of liberal reformers—which have shaped the actuality of U.S. education and left little room for the school to facilitate the pursuit of equality or full human development. When education is viewed as an aspect of the reproduction of the capitalist division of labor, the history of school reforms in the United States appears less as a story of an enlightened but sadly unsuccessful corrective and more as an integral part of the process of capitalist growth itself.[65]

Whether or not one wishes to accept the full implications of this critique of capitalism, the analysis does provide a persuasive explanation of the preference of the policymaking process for the instrumental function of education. The rationalistic paradigm fails to make a place for the school as an institution for learning; it fails to make a place for a humanistic teacher; and it fails to provide a place for education conceived as self-development.

Let us now look at yet another aspect of hyperrationalization of the schools—how legal reasoning creates and reinforces the trends we have already discussed.

65. Ibid., pp. 48–49.

CHAPTER 4
LEGALIZING THE SCHOOLS: THE IMPACT OF THE COURTS

A school is an academic institution, not a courtroom or administrative hearing room.

UNITED STATES SUPREME COURT
Missouri v. *Horowitz*

Court decisions about education, important in themselves, also have furnished a model for legal reasoning in educational matters. In fact, legal reasoning has become a major way of thinking about educational institutions. It characterizes not only litigation but legislation, collective bargaining, and regulations and procedures designed to influence the schools as well. Legal reasoning is seen as an important mode of thought not only for regulating the schools, but also for changing and improving them.

The legalization of education proceeds apace with the bureaucratization of education; indeed, the two processes seem inextricably connected. As Max Weber observed, the demands of the law become the procedures of the bureaucracy:

> "Equality before the law" and the demand for legal guarantees against arbitrariness demand a formal and rational "objectivity" of administration, as opposed to the personally free discretion following from the "grace" of the old patrimonial domination.[1]

1. Max Weber, *From Max Weber: Essays in Sociology*, trans. and ed. H. H. Gerth and C. Wright Mills (New York: Oxford University Press, 1946), p. 220.

As the legal process operates to ensure that society's institutions conform to the law, these institutions become more legalistic in their operations.

Nathan Glazer has argued in a provocative article, "Towards an Imperial Judiciary," the increasingly pervasive influence of the law.[2] Not only is the reach of the law being extended by court decisions, but by the response of the executive and legislative branches as well. In turn, the actions of courts, legislatures, and executives have a powerful effect upon social institutions like the schools. The process is reciprocal, mutually reinforcing, and in the end, circular.

Once courts insist that due process be granted, "the logic of that position must be worked out."[3] Legislatures begin to draft legislation; executives begin to draft guidelines. The schools begin to develop procedures to conform to the court ruling, to the legislation, and to the guidelines. The procedures, if they are to satisfy the legal concept of due process, must mimic the judicial process. If the procedures fail to guarantee due process, appeal is made again to the courts. Successive iterations of this process in situations involving decisions about students, teachers, administrators, and board members can only cause the schools to function according to the dictates of legal reasoning.

Litigation about schools has a strong potential for shifting the locus of control over local schools (and colleges) to the state. Under the federal constitution, education is a function reserved to the states. State constitutions, in turn, typically vest responsibility for education in the state legislature. In their turn, state legislatures typically delegate operational control to local agencies. However, delegation of operational control does not absolve the state of its obligation to conform to state and federal constitutions. In disputes concerning race and school finance, the state has been reminded of its obligation to conform to the federal constitution.[4] In other disputes, local agencies have been reminded that they are

2. Nathan Glazer, "Towards an Imperial Judiciary?" *The Public Interest*, No. 41 (Fall 1975), pp. 104–23.

3. Ibid., p. 113.

4. Arthur E. Wise, *Rich Schools, Poor Schools* (Chicago: University of Chicago Press, 1968), especially Chapter 2.

agencies of the state and subject to its control.[5] One important possible effect of the increasing volume of education litigation is the centralization of educational control at the state level.

ADJUDICATION AND HYPERRATIONALIZATION

How does a lawsuit begin in a bureaucratic setting? Most frequently, a person or a group wishing to solve a problem will draw it to the attention of those in authority. Although the majority of problems appear to be solved in this manner, there are, of course, exceptions. For example, the authorities may not recognize a problem; they may not acknowledge the legitimacy of the person or group that raises the issue. They may not consider a problem serious enough to warrant solution; or they may feel that it has low priority in relation to their other responsibilities. They may feel that the solution is too costly or that it will, in turn, raise other problems in the future. Or the authorities simply may not know how to produce an appropriate solution. Confronted with any of these conditions, the aggrieved party may turn to the courts.

Many of the attributes of adjudication which Donald L. Horowitz analyzes in *The Courts and Social Policy* may contribute to the hyperrationalization of education.[6]

Courts must dispose of cases / Once a litigant can successfully define his problem as a legal one, he is often assured of a "solution."

There is an undeniable attractiveness to the judicial method. In its pristine form, the adversary process puts all the arguments before the decision maker in a setting in which he must act. The judge must decide the case and justify his decision by reference to evidence and reasoning. In the other branches, it is relatively easy to stop a decision from being made—they often effectively say no by saying nothing. In the judicial process, questions get answers. It is difficult to prevent a judicial

5. Ibid., especially Chapter 3.
6. Donald L. Horowitz, *The Courts and Social Policy* (Washington, D.C.: The Brookings Institution, 1977).

decision. No other public or private institution is bound to be so responsive.[7]

Executives and legislatures have numerous means to avoid making difficult decisions. When the reason for not acting is a lack of knowledge of the consequences attendant to a policy initiative, a study can be initiated. When ideas about policy objectives are in conflict or knowledge of policy consequences is uncertain, a commission can be appointed. Courts frequently make decisions and create policy in the absence of knowledge.

The court must rationalize its decision in accordance with constitutional, statutory, or case law / A court must have a principled basis for its decision. Moreover, the decision must be rationalized not against any possible legal principle, but only against those which precedent permits.

> The requirement that judges justify their decisions by reference to reason may mean that adjudication is not appropriate for those problems best resolved by a process of negotiation. Compromise outcomes are often not defensible by resort to reason.[8]

Yet, in education, most issues are problematic. They involve conflict, for example, between liberty and equality, individual and group interests, or professional and lay judgments. While court decisions frequently defer to only one side of the conflict, schools generally must compromise.

The judicial process is more rational than the legislative process / Political considerations less often are determinative.

> The fact that there are fewer participants in the adjudicative process than in the legislative process makes it easier for judges than for legislators to cut through the problem to a resolution. But it is precisely this ability to simplify the issues and to exclude interested participants that may put the judges in danger of fostering reductionist solutions.[9]

7. Ibid., p. 22.
8. Ibid., pp. 22–23.
9. Ibid., p. 23.

Advocates have an interest in simplifying the issues and holding out reductionist solutions as a means of inducing a judge to act. Interested parties are less likely to learn about litigation than about legislation, and hence are unable to reveal the complexity of issues.

Litigation is piecemeal / The judicial process prevents the courts from considering situationally related but legally unrelated issues. The court must focus on the problem presented:

> The lawsuit is the supreme example of incremental decision making. As such, it shares the advantages and the defects of the species. The outcome of litigation may give the illusion of a decisive victory, but the victory is often on a very limited point. The judge's power to decide extends, in principle, only to those issues that are before him. Related issues, not raised by the instant dispute, must generally await later litigation. So it is at least in traditional conception.[10]

Adjudication highlights certain factors and ignores others; because the subject of the litigation is treated out of context, the participants may make unwarranted assumptions about how the part relates to the whole.

Legal formalism / In interpreting laws as a means of solving educational problems, the courts focus on explicit rather than implicit phenomena, on formal rather than informal structure, on rationale rather than reality.

> Courts make, interpret, and expound *law*. Given their position in the institutional system, it is neither surprising nor illegitimate that the courts have a built-in emphasis on formal, manifest relationships, on those specified, for instance, in [legal documents]. Inevitably, much of the material required for expounding law is itself legal material, such as statutes and regulations. Moreover, the divergent patterns of informal relations that spring up around formal structures are not adequately reflected in those legal materials. Though the informal ethos and networks of relationships that exist in, say, juvenile court vary widely from one such court to another, the specified, formal functions of juvenile courts vary very little. Consequently, the bias of the judicial process for formal, mani-

10. Ibid., p. 35.

fest relationships leads the courts systematically to neglect or underemphasize the diversity that exists just below the surface of formal relationships. The more congruent informal patterns of behavior are with formal structures, the more accurate will be the courts' view of the facts. Unfortunately, however, such congruence can never be taken for granted.[11]

Schools, teachers, and education are the subjects of constitutions, statutory and case law, and regulations. Many of the mandates contained in these legal materials have been followed; many have simply existed on paper. These materials provide a rich resource of formal prescriptions which can be forced into operation by litigation. To the extent that the mandates are enforced, they encourage a formal approach to the problems of education.

The adjudicative process leads courts to assume the existence of uniformity /

The courts recurrently assume—and are given no information that would lead them not to assume—that they are working with more or less uniform situations for which a single rule will suffice. The problem is to frame the right rule. Repeatedly, however, the situations turn out to be diverse rather than uniform, and the single rule often operates perversely and disparately for just such reasons.[12]

This occurs because:

on the one hand, the piecemeal character of adjudication tends to distort social facts in the direction of isolating related phenomena; on the other hand, the emphasis on the individual litigants' case and the reliance on formal rather than behavioral materials both distort social facts in the direction of a usually fictitious uniformity.[13]

The casting of an educational problem in legal terms may result in a legalistic solution / The remedy may be inappropriate, given a broader definition of the problem:

The usual question before the judge is simply: Does one party have a *right*? Does another party have a *duty*? This should be

11. Ibid., p. 261.
12. Ibid.
13. Ibid., p. 262.

contrasted with the question before a "planner," whether legislative or bureaucratic: What are the *alternatives*? These are quite different ways of casting problems for decision.[14]

That is to say, a legal definition of a problem may lead to a formal solution. The difficulty of problem definition determining solution is exacerbated by litigation strategy because:

> plaintiffs' lawyers are likely to bring not the most representative case but the most extreme case of discrimination, of fraud, of violation of statute, of abuse of discretion, and so on.[15]

The resulting ruling may not be appropriate for the general case. Indeed,

> general law made from exceptional cases is not likely to be accorded much legitimacy by the knowledgeable bureaucrats and specialists who sense that the court was misled by unrepresentative cases.[16]

And, on the face of it, a decision perceived as not legitimate would be less likely to be obeyed.

CONCEPTIONS OF EDUCATION, TEACHER, AND SCHOOL REVISITED

In Chapter 3, we saw how the instrumental conception of education, the rationalistic conception of teaching, and the bureaucratic conception of the school satisfy the imperatives of educational policymaking. Legal formalism strengthens all of these conceptions partly because the attributes of adjudication lead the legal process to embrace these conceptions, partly because judges and lawyers share with other policymakers the same set of ideas about education, and partly because judges and lawyers have a view of bureaucratic life and human behavior that supports these conceptions of education.

The law, like the social sciences, comprehends reality through its own perceptual lenses. The law does not see everything; it sees only what the judge or lawyer is "trained" to see. And the law contains its own implicit theory for organizing the facts it perceives; in short, it has its own theories

14. Ibid., p. 34.   15. Ibid., p. 41.   16. Ibid., p. 267.

of human behavior and of organization. When called upon to interpret the purposes of education as depicted in law, the courts can be relied upon for a formal interpretation of the duties of the school or of the rights of students.

What theory of human behavior underlies court decisions in the realm of social and educational policy? Courts function as though they believe that their decisions will be obeyed. Persons affected by a judicial decree are assumed to be able to change their behavior to conform to the decree. Horowitz has created a construct which he terms "legal man."[17] He argues, in effect, that judges and lawyers believe in legal man in much the same fashion as economists believe in "economic man." Judges and lawyers behave as though they believe that they can predict with confidence how people will respond to changes in the law:

> [They] derive behavioral expectations from what might be called the logical structure of incentives. That is, courts may consciously formulate rules of law calculated to appeal to the interests of "legal man" in rather the same way as the marketplace is thought to appeal to the interests of "economic man." The problem with this, of course, is that it is deductive rather than empirical. There is no assurance that the judge has correctly formulated the structure of incentives: his logic and the logic of the actors affected by rules of law may begin from different premises.[18]

Here we begin to see how the courts can and will reinforce the rationalistic conception of the teacher, and, for that matter, of the educational administrator. The rationalistic educator is prepared to reconstitute his behavior in response to a judicial decree:

> Lawyers (and presumably judges) have inordinate faith in the power of the written word to shape behavior and a concomitant tendency to minimize the likelihood of behavior that deviates from the requirements of properly drafted regulations. There has indeed been a propensity, as I have said, to assume that properly framed court orders would be more or less self-executing.[19]

17. Ibid., p. 49.   18. Ibid.   19. Ibid., pp. 52–53.

The courts would comprehend the teacher in much the same way as CBTE comprehends the teacher. Both the courts and CBTE advocates appear to believe in a crude form of behaviorism which postulates that a behavior will occur if it is specified that it should occur. The educator's behavior (and presumably the process of education) can be changed by carefully constructing rules and regulations. But how is this to occur? What is the judges' theory of organization?

> Courts are not likely to possess expertise in the incentive structure of complex organizations. The adjudicative process is not likely to throw up sufficient material to enlighten them, and both lawyers and judges are likely to fill in the interstices with some highly stereotyped notions of "bureaucracy" drawn from their operational code.[20]

And what stronger stereotyped notion of how organizations function is there than that provided by the classical model of bureaucracy described in Chapter 3? If one wishes to change the aim or mode of official action, it is only necessary to frame a new rule. It is assumed that the incentive structure of the bureaucracy will change to accommodate the new rule.

ACCOUNTABLITY AND THE LAW

The word "accountability" as applied to education has generally referred to state level policies designed to affect local schools. The concept frequently denotes a legislative act—an accountability law—leading to the creation of an accountability plan to be followed by the school districts in the state.

But the idea of accountability in education has entered the judicial arena as well. In fact, it is an idea that is far from alien in this arena, for implicit in the general idea of accountability is the more specific notion of "legal accountability." Accountability legislation, of course, creates a legally enforceable relationship between the state government and the local school system. But, independent of this fact, accountability is beginning to be pursued through the courts.[21]

20. Ibid., p. 58.
21. Stephen D. Sugarman, "Accountability Through the Courts," *School Review* 82:2 (February 1974), 233–59.

The vocabulary of accountability through the law is different from the vocabulary of accountability elsewhere. The concepts employed by the courts are those which have gained meaning in other areas of litigation. They include "fraud," "damages," "negligence," "liability," "injury," "malpractice," and "treatment." Since accountability has recently become a fertile area of litigation in medicine, we can expect an increasing number of the concepts developed in that area to be applied to education as well.

The medical model has long fascinated educators. A certain apparent precision is associated with the medical process. There is a desired state known as health, although its definition is circular, since health is defined as the absence of injury and disease. The physician diagnoses an injury or a disease, i.e., the discrepancy between the actual state and the desired one. He prescribes a treatment which is calculated to reduce the discrepancy and bring about the desired state. Educators, particularly those who deal with children with severe learning problems, have been inclined to use medical vocabulary.

The medical analogy assumes added salience because lawsuits designed to induce accountability in education may have to depend upon precedents established in medical malpractice litigation. Stephen D. Sugarman has enumerated what constitutes professional negligence in medicine:

> Under the rules governing professional negligence, if a patient suffers an injury because a doctor should but fails to diagnose a disease, or if he misdiagnoses the disease, prescribes the wrong treatment, fails to warn the patient of the risks of treatment, carries out the treatment improperly, or any number of other things, the doctor is likely to be liable for the injury suffered.[22]

Proof of incompetence in education is difficult because there is little agreement on what constitutes competent performance on the part of a teacher. A charge of malpractice requires that the profession have a set of minimum standards of performance such that an expert witness can describe them

22. Ibid., p. 242.

to a lay jury, which then can compare a specific behavior with the norm. The professional is liable to a charge of malpractice when he fails to perform in accordance with the norm. He is not accountable for results, although in medicine there may be a more highly developed sense of an expected relationship between procedures and results.

Competency-based teaching may be seen as a means to define the norms of teaching. It would make it easier to note how a specific behavior deviates from the norm. The malpractice approach to accountability in education is facilitated and strengthened by the rationalistic model of teaching. In turn, the rationalistic model of teaching is potentially strengthened by malpractice suits. The more closely the teacher adheres to the standards of performance, to the dictates of CBTE and CBE, and to the norms of the profession, the less liable to a lawsuit will he be.

One of the limitations on the liability for negligence in education is that the *duty* of the school has not been specified in a manner conducive to legal enforcement.[23] What is the source of authoritative pronouncements on the duty of the school?[24] Possibilities include the state constitution, state statutes, state regulations, compilations of goals, etc. These documents contain an abundance of hortatory language probably too vague to be the basis for a complaint that a school is failing to fulfill its duty. Yet, as we have noted, the Supreme Court of New Jersey has asserted that it is the duty of the schools of the state to provide "thorough and efficient" education.[25] That phrase is now being given precise meaning by state law and regulations. But what of other general language? The process of interpolating meaning into such general language is a formal approach to defining the duties of schools. Once a formal statement is interpreted and put into operation, it reveals the duty of the state in legally cognizable terms.

The reduction of general hortatory language to educational objectives reinforces the rationalistic approach to education. On the one hand, the rationalistic tools are necessary to make the general language operative. Apparent precision is

23. Ibid., pp. 248–50.
24. Wise, *Rich Schools, Poor Schools*, pp. 112–18.
25. *Robinson* v. *Cahill*.

introduced by the mandate that the schools teach functional literacy or basic skills. Systems that are like PPBS and CBE facilitate and evaluate the efficacy of programs designed to promote functional literacy and basic skills. On the other hand, the very introduction of functional literacy or basic skills programs removes the major obstacle to negligence or malpractice lawsuits. The schools, by these systems, will have specified their own duties in a manner which reveals when the school system fails to perform these duties. The more explicit the school becomes about its purposes, the more liable it is to malpractice suits.

Sometimes legal concepts alter the educational ideas to which they are applied and, when borrowed from other substantive areas, may considerably alter how an educational problem is viewed. In the future we may see lawsuits designed to attack the schools' failure to impart functional literacy or basic skills. On another level, we may see challenges to the adequacy of the standards implied by functional literacy, basic skills, career skills, or moral skills. These concepts imply close articulation between the worlds of education and adult life. What if programs begun to improve this articulation fail to do so? If it is assumed that the student is being prepared to function more effectively in society, and if the programs fail to fulfill this promise, then we will no doubt see suits challenging the adequacy of the implied standards.

In conclusion, let us consider the word "treatment." A negligent physician may be sued for malpractice when he prescribes the wrong treatment or carries out the treatment improperly. A direct analogy can be constructed for a teacher. Yet, what is a "treatment" in education? It may be a specific curriculum or mode of instruction. The treatment may not work, in which case the teacher may have been negligent. Note, however, that we have quickly slipped into the view that education is something which the teacher, as society's agent, does *to* a student. Note also that this requires that there be something analogous to the desired state of health. Suddenly, we require a definition of an "educated person" or an "effectively functioning adult." From here it is but a short step to the utilitarian view that education is a treatment which society imposes on its members to prepare them to function in society.

REDUCING DISCRETION

While it is true that law and bureaucracy, as they have affected the practice of education, have evolved together, the rationalization of education by the law could not have begun without at least a rudimentary bureaucratic organization of schools. The law is rationalized as it is called upon to give meaning to legal concepts in the schools. The mutual dependence of law and bureaucracy was recognized by Weber, who observed:

> The rationalization of Roman law into a closed system of concepts to be scientifically handled was brought to perfection only during the period when the polity itself underwent bureaucratization.[26]

The further rationalization of the law, bureaucracy, and schools continues as a development in one arena affects developments in the others. Weber asserts:

> In principle a system of rationally debatable "reasons" stands behind every act of bureaucratic administration, that is, either subsumption under norms or a weighing of ends and means.[27]

Efforts to make education conform to legal norms are primarily, but not exclusively, concerned with the conditions under which education is delivered. The legal norms with which we are concerned here are "due process" and "equality."

However, the process of "subsumption under norms" frequently cannot be disentangled from the process of "weighing ends and means." Judges and lawyers behave as though they believe that there is no incompatibility between removing barriers to due process and equality and the attainment of organizational ends. The one is thought to facilitate the other, or at least not to hinder it. Courts review practices to determine whether they conform to the law. With a little difficulty, the courts can ask whether practices conform to the norms implicit or explicit in the law. With somewhat greater difficulty, they can ask whether the practices are consistent

26. Weber, *Essays in Sociology*, p. 219.
27. Ibid., p. 220.

with the law's purposes. With the greatest of difficulty, they can ask whether the ends of the law are attainable, given the means. To repair a faulty means-and-ends linkage requires knowledge that may not be available.

In the last chapter, we cited a definition of bureaucracy which contained four elements: a functional division of labor, the definition of staff roles as offices, the hierarchic ordering of offices, and operation according to rules of procedure. While judicially created educational policy operates on all characteristics of the school bureaucracy, it has its most important effects upon the rules of procedure.

Almost all judicial decisions which alter current practice limit the discretionary performance of school officials by proscribing or prescribing ends or means. Of course, lawsuits are brought by those who are aggrieved at the results of the schools' own decision-making process, precisely to limit official discretion. There are but two ways to accomplish this: by the establishment of a process which will be set in motion under prespecified conditions; and by the creation of a rule or rules which prescribe actions to be taken under specified conditions. In either case, an administrator or a body with administrative authority no longer has the administrative discretion which existed *ex ante*. Let us consider two cases: one concerned with due process and one with equality.

Due Process via Procedures

In *Goss* v. *Lopez*, the U.S. Supreme Court required that a student not be suspended from school without a hearing.[28] A student who is to be suspended from school from one to ten days for disciplinary reasons must be given a hearing before or promptly following the suspension. A principal who does not hold a hearing cannot suspend a student. To a modest degree, the *Goss* decision requires the school's decision-making process to mirror the judicial decision-making process. What is interesting about *Goss* is its likely impact on future decisions. For this reason, it is worth considering the majority and dissenting reasoning in some detail.

The majority opinion describes the view of the federal

28. *Goss* v. *Lopez*, 419 U.S. 565 (1975).

constitution, the states, local boards, and education that will prevail in this case:

> Although Ohio may not be constitutionally obligated to establish and maintain a public school system, it has nevertheless done so and has required its children to attend. Those young people do not "shed their constitutional rights" at the schoolhouse door. "The Fourteenth Amendment, as now applied to the States, protects the citizen against the State itself and all of its creatures . . . Boards of Education not excepted." The authority possessed by the State to prescribe and enforce standards of conduct in its schools although concededly very broad, must be exercised consistently with constitutional safeguards. Among other things, the State is constrained to recognize a student's legitimate entitlement to a public education as a property interest which is protected by the Due Process Clause and which may not be taken away for misconduct without adherence to the minimum procedures required by that clause.
>
> The Due Process Clause also forbids arbitrary deprivation of liberty.[29]

When a state establishes schools and requires children to attend, some constitutional protection is afforded—under the due process clause of the Fourteenth Amendment.[30] That clause requires the principal to give "notice" and hold a "due process hearing" before suspending a student.

In *Goss*, the Court stopped short

> of construing the Due Process Clause to require, country wide, that hearings in connection with short suspensions must afford the student the opportunity to secure counsel, to confront and cross-examine witnesses supporting the charge or to call his own witnesses to verify his version of the incident.[31]

In other words, for short suspensions the Court did not require the more elaborate procedures associated with complex hearings and trials.

Goss, taken by itself, is a limited intervention into the affairs of a school. In schools which already have procedures for suspensions it is no intervention at all. Moreover, *Goss* is

29. *Goss* v. *Lopez*, p. 574.
30. Those familiar with *San Antonio* v. *Rodriguez* may wonder why a similar analysis of education was not the starting point for the Court's analysis in that case. If education is a "property interest," why does not the Fourteenth Amendment also apply with respect to inequities in finance?
31. *Goss* v. *Lopez*, p. 583.

at most only a procedural, not a substantive, intervention, concerned only with disciplinary and not academic problems. And procedures and disciplinary matters are subjects about which the courts know a good deal.

However, the apparent limitedness of *Goss* may be deceptive, since its reasoning may easily be extended. The majority took pains to point out the limited problem with which *Goss* was dealing:

> We should also make it clear that we have addressed ourselves solely to the short suspension, not exceeding 10 days. Longer suspensions or expulsions for the remainder of the school term, or permanently, may require more formal procedures. Nor do we put aside the possibility that in unusual situations, although involving only a short suspension, something more than the rudimentary procedures will be required.[32]

Obviously, more severe punishments could require more elaborate procedures. Cases following *Goss* will doubtless explore whether and under what circumstances the accouterments of due process will be required: (1) the right to present reasons why the proposed action should not be taken; (2) the right to an unbiased tribunal; (3) the right to call witnesses; (4) the right to a record of the proceedings and a statement of reasons for the decision; (5) the right to have the decision based only upon the evidence presented; (6) the right to counsel; (7) the rights to confrontation and cross-examination; and (8) the right to appeal.[33] The latter would surely imply that once the appeal process within the school system is exhausted, the next step would be to the courts.

The apparent limitedness and the actual unlimitedness of *Goss* were the subject of the dissenting opinion:

> The Court today invalidates an Ohio statute that permits student suspensions from school without a hearing "for not more than ten days." The decision unnecessarily opens avenues for judicial intervention in the operation of our public schools that may affect adversely the quality of education. The Court holds for the first time that the federal courts, rather than educational officials and state legislatures, have the authority to determine the rules applicable to routine classroom discipline

32. *Goss* v. *Lopez*, p. 584.
33. R. Lawrence Dessem, "Student Due Process Rights in Academic Dismissals from the Public Schools," *Journal of Law and Education* 5:3 (July 1976), 295–304.

of children and teenagers in the process of elementary and secondary education by identifying a new constitutional right: the right of a student not to be suspended for as much as a single day without notice and a due process hearing either before or promptly following the suspension.[34]

The Court has conferred substantial protection against the loss of even a single school day. The dissenters did not disagree with the starting point of the majority opinion:

> Although we held in *San Antonio Independent School District* v. *Rodriguez* . . . that education is not a right protected by the Constitution, Ohio has elected by statute to provide free education for all youths age six to 21, with children under 18 years of age being compelled to attend school. State law, therefore, extends the right of free public school education to Ohio students in accordance with the education laws of that State. The right or entitlement to education so created is protected in a proper case by the Due Process Clause.[35]

Education is not a federally protected right except when the state provides education, and only in those circumstances in which the Supreme Court chooses to make it a federally protected right.

But the dissenters did perceive the expansionary capacity of *Goss*:

> No one can foresee the ultimate frontiers of the new "thicket" the Court now enters. Today's ruling appears to sweep within the protected interest in education a multitude of discretionary decisions in the educational process. Teachers and other school authorities are required to make many decisions that may have serious consequences for the pupil. They must decide, for example, how to grade the student's work, whether a student passes or fails a course, whether he is to be promoted, whether he is required to take certain subjects, whether he may be excluded from interscholastic athletics or other extracurricular activities, whether he may be removed from one school and sent to another, whether he may be bused long distances when available schools are nearby, and whether he should be placed in a "general," "vocational," or "college-preparatory" track.[36]

34. *Goss* v. *Lopez*, pp. 584–85.
35. *Goss* v. *Lopez*, p. 586.   36. *Goss* v. *Lopez*, p. 597.

Other discretionary decisions by school officials which impair a student's educational entitlement may cause even greater injury than the injury remedied by *Goss*. The dissenters concluded by noting that they could find no "rational and analytically sound distinction between the discretionary decision by school authorities to suspend a pupil for a brief period, and the types of discretionary school decisions described above."[37]

Goss was concerned with procedural due process in the context of a disciplinary problem. A later decision, *Missouri* v. *Horowitz*, did draw a distinction between disciplinary and academic problems, suggesting less stringent procedural requirements for the latter than for the former.[38] In this case the Court held that sufficient due process had been afforded. Although the decision was unanimous, three justices believed that the distinction between dismissal for disciplinary and for academic reasons was not relevant to the question of what procedures were required by the due process clause.

Equality via Regulation

The *Goss* principle may result in the reduction of administrative discretion by means of the requirement for due process hearings in a wide variety of circumstances. Possible extensions of the *Goss* principle are only now being devised. How these proposed extensions will fare and how they will be implemented remain to be seen. Each extension will replace administrative discretion—good and bad, fair and unfair—with due process hearings, the complexity of which will also need to be worked out. While we must wait to find out what the full effects will be, we already have some evidence of what the replacement of administrative discretion with regulations can mean.

A major purpose of the administrative structure of a school system is the allocation of resources to schools, including the assignment of children to schools and to classrooms. In fulfilling these responsibilities, a board of education must take into account a variety of legal, contractual, physical, and pedagogical considerations. The public schools

37. *Goss* v. *Lopez*, p. 599.   38. 98 S. Ct. 948 (1978).

of the District of Columbia have been the object of a number of court suits, federal regulations, and union agreements undertaken to rectify what was seen as an abuse or deleterious consequence of the exercise of administrative discretion of the school board in allocating resources to schools. The effects of these actions, particularly the court decisions, have been the subject of searching examination by Joan C. Baratz and Donald L. Horowitz.[39] Our examination here will begin with a 1971 decision (*Hobson* v. *Hansen*, II) which ordered that:

> Per pupil expenditures for all teachers' salaries and benefits from the regular D.C. budget in any elementary school shall not deviate more than plus and minus five percent from the mean of all elementary schools.[40]

The problem which the order was to solve was the maldistribution of resources in the schools; the legal principle invoked was equal protection; the solution was to be the equalization of expenditures on teachers' salaries.

The school system found that the easiest way to comply with the decree was the periodic transfer of special-subject or resource teachers, which was thought to be less disruptive than moving classroom teachers. Per pupil expenditures vary as a function of the number of pupils and the salaries of classroom and resource teachers. As pupil enrollment shifted, teachers shifted as well. Whether a school had older, higher-paid teachers or younger, lower-paid teachers determined class size and teacher-pupil ratio as well as the number of resource teachers. As Horowitz puts it:

> For equalization purposes, the school system has for the most part surrendered control over the movement of pupils and classroom teachers. Whatever "the equal protection of the laws" means abstractly in the District of Columbia schools it currently means transferring enough resource teachers annually, or more often if necessary, to equalize dollar values.[41]

39. Joan C. Baratz, *A Quest for Equal Educational Opportunity in a Major Urban School District: The Case of Washington, D.C.* (Washington, D.C.: The Education Policy Research Institute, 1975).

40. *Hobson* v. *Hansen* II.

41. Horowitz, *The Courts and Social Policy*, p. 150.

When administration by rules is substituted for administration by persons, the effects frequently cannot be predicted. The court decision was predicated on the assumption that poor children would benefit from the redistribution of teachers. An analysis by Horowitz revealed, however, that while many schools in the wealthier area of D.C. experienced a reduction in teacher services, some did not.[42] He cites two examples of schools which were affected differently from what was predicted:

> One relatively large school, located in a high-income, predominantly white section of the city, has had a steadily increasing enrollment over the last several years. There was a net enrollment increase of 13.6 percent between January 1973 and November 1974, and it was anticipated that for 1975–76 there would be another increase of several percentage points. Although the school lost one classroom teacher with the first implementation of the equalization plan in 1971, subsequent equalization rounds have been benign. In 1973, the school gained enough additional funds to hire its second full-time music teacher, and it now has a complete resource program, including a school orchestra and French instruction for third grade pupils and above. Since pupils at the school score high on achievement tests, the school can well afford to devote its additional funds to these enrichment programs.
>
> Another school is located in a primarily black, low-income area of the District. Enrollment at this school has been falling steadily. Since 1967, it has lost about half of its student body, which then numbered more than 1,000 pupils. From fall 1972 to fall 1974, the school experienced a 24 percent decline in enrollment. The annual decreases have been met by reducing classroom staff solely through attrition and reducing special-subject staff by involuntary transfers. At one time, the school had a complete resource program, conducted by full-time special-subject teachers. Now it lacks such a program in some areas, and covers others on only a part-time basis.
>
> In addition to its decline in enrollment, this school is saddled with a highly paid faculty. A decade ago, it was a "demonstration school," and special efforts were made to develop a strong staff. Teachers were encouraged to seek graduate training, which was then reflected in their salaries. (Some fifty

42. Ibid., p. 156.

percent of the teachers held masters degrees, and the average teacher salary was in the $12,000–$15,000 range.) With equalization, the highly paid staff quickly became a liability. Transfers of classroom teachers provide no answer because of seniority rules, and so the school pays for its high salary structure and its declining enrollment with the disintegration of its resource program.[43]

The equalization of per pupil expenditures on teachers' salaries was not the only externally imposed rule to which the D.C. Board of Education had to conform as it assigned teachers. The school system, since it wished to receive funds from Title I of ESEA, had to conform to "comparability guidelines" designed to ensure that Title I funds are used to supplement, not supplant, regular funds. Title I and its comparability guidelines were created to alleviate inequities in the allocation of resources in and between school systems. However, these guidelines were different in several important ways from the court decree. Baratz has compared the two:

Both formulas call for schools to fall within a ±5% range of the mean expenditures of regular budget funds. For the Court, however, the mean is figured by including all elementary schools, and comparing each school to that mean, whereas, in Title I comparability, the mean is computed on non-Title I schools, and each Title I school is then compared to that non-Title I school mean. The Title I formula computes the mean on the basis of salaries from all instructional staff (teachers, administrators, counselors, librarians, teacher aides, etc.) in the schools, whereas the 1971 *Hobson* compliance formula computes the mean expenditures only on the basis of classroom and special subject teachers. By the 1973–74 school year, both Title I and 1971 *Hobson* decree formulas had excluded special education staff. However, another major difference between the two formulas was that of longevity pay. Title I does not figure the longevity part of teachers' salaries into the mean expenditure for compliance, but does require that the longevity part of the salary payments be reported. Judge Wright, on the other hand, makes teacher experience and its concomitant longevity payments a central factor in compliance reporting and includes longevity and fringe benefits in the calculation

43. Ibid., pp. 156–57.

of mean expenditures. In addition, Title I guidelines call for comparability in per pupil expenditures for instructional materials, should the per pupil expenditure or staff ratios not be comparable.[44]

Baratz determined that it was *mathematically* possible for the school board to satisfy both the guidelines and the decree.[45] Whether it is educationally desirable is another question.

At least one additional set of rules extrinsic to the educational process limited the school system's discretion in assigning teachers—a contract with the Washington Teachers Union. The provisions of the contract discouraged the transfer of teachers with seniority. In fact, one of the factors which led to the Board's decision to comply with the equalization decree by transferring resource teachers was the provision in the contract which based seniority on exclusive assignment to a single school.[46] Only after satisfying the equalization decree, the Title I comparability guidelines, and the union contract could the school system begin to pay attention to educational considerations. By 1977, the difficulty of operating the school system by regulation was evident. Beginning with the 1977–78 school year, the school system was released from the specific requirements of the equalization decree; the Board of Education agreed to the principle of equal resource allocation.

THE RELIANCE ON SOCIAL SCIENCE

Generally, the purpose of adjudication with regard to educational policy is to guarantee a right or to require the performance of a duty. The court is called upon either to examine whether an action conforms to a legal norm or to determine whether means are permissible given ends, or ends achievable given means. Does an action deny equal protection or due process rights? Is a school system providing a minimally adequate education? Does suspending a student without

44. Joan C. Baratz, *A Quest for Equal Educational Opportunity*, pp. 181–83.

45. Ibid., pp. 198–99.

46. Horowitz, *The Courts and Social Policy*, p. 148. Resource teachers are generally assigned to several schools.

a hearing violate the norm of due process? Is classification on the basis of race or sex permissible, given the purposes of education? Will every child receive an equal, adequate, or appropriate educational opportunity, given prevailing practices of assigning students to schools and allocating resources to schools?

Although the courts arrive at their decisions by studying legal principle and precedent and by examining the facts, in the process they have frequently turned to social science. They appear to be favorably disposed toward a scientific basis for their decisions. The legal process appears to require that judges and lawyers behave as though they believe in predictability in human affairs. Judges and lawyers need to believe that determinate relationships exist within the individual, the social structure, and society's institutions. The belief may well be a fiction, but the process of adjudication appears to require this fiction.

INDETERMINACY AND HYPERRATIONALIZATION

Judges and lawyers have discovered, however, that the social science knowledge base does not always yield clear guidance for educational policy. While the search for a scientific basis for a court's decision is understandable, it frequently ends in the discovery that evidence is nonexistent, only moderately pertinent, inapplicable, or equivocal. Legal scholars even have a word to describe this state of affairs; it is "indeterminacy."[47] If "determinacy" in social affairs existed, then the task of judicial policymakers (not to mention other policymakers) would be easier, goes the argument.

It may be useful to contrast the concept of indeterminacy with the concepts of "loose coupling," "rationalization," and "hyperrationalization." A case may require a court to examine whether means are permissible given ends, or whether ends are achievable given means. If the situation is indeterminate, then the court will not *know* what effects changes in the one will have on the other. If means and ends are loosely coupled or

47. John E. Coons, "Law and the Sovereigns of Childhood," *Phi Delta Kappan* 58:1 (September 1976), 20. John E. McDermott, ed., *Indeterminacy in Education* (Berkeley, Calif.: McCutchan, 1976).

loosely related, then changes in the one may have no effect upon changes in the other. Thus, means and ends may be either tightly or loosely coupled, and the fact may be determined or undetermined—that is, known or unknown. If means and ends are purposefully organized and tightly coupled, the concept of rationalization applies. If a court acts to tighten the relationship between means and ends independently of the knowledge of whether that relationship can be tightened, or when the means and ends may be *incapable* of being tightly coupled, the concept of hyperrationalization applies. We will examine a form of hyperrationalization in Chapter 5 in the context of *Robinson* v. *Cahill.*

Redefinition of Issues

When courts seek to reduce indeterminacy by the use of social science evidence, as Henry M. Levin has observed, the use of such evidence frequently redefines the dispute.[48] For example, throughout school finance litigation, the courts could have accepted inequality of educational expenditures as evidence of a denial of the equal protection of the laws or of the guarantees of state constitutions. Differences in educational expenditures could have been taken as *prima facie* evidence of the unequal treatment of children, but the courts did not actually settle the school finance disputes on this basis.[49] Rather, they insisted upon considering or were pushed to consider the effects of these differences in expenditures. In some cases, plaintiffs, seeking to strengthen their arguments, introduced evidence of effects; in other cases, defendants, seeking to weaken the argument, introduced evidence of the lack of effects. In other words, it was explicitly or implicitly admitted that expenditures reflected differences in treatment; the courts then looked to proof of injury that resulted from low school expenditures. By seeking proof of injury, the legal

48. Henry M. Levin, "Education, Life Chances, and the Courts: The Role of Social Science Evidence," *Law and Contemporary Problems* 39:2, Part 2 (Spring 1976), 217–40.

49. *Hobson II*, of course, was resolved on this basis; the generalization refers to state cases. See Arthur E. Wise, "Minimum Educational Adequacy: Beyond School Finance Reform," *Journal of Education Finance* 1 (Spring 1976), 468–83.

process inevitably would and will be pushed to require not merely the elimination of objective differences in treatment, but also the remediation of the injury. By exposing the root causes of injury, the legal process must seek a remedy that goes beyond treatment to result.[50]

When social science evidence is introduced to help win a suit, it is used to reveal that an "injury" exists. If the court accepts that an injury exists, it thereby commits itself to ordering that the injury be remedied. The injury, however, is an artifact of the adjudicative process. In this fashion, because the need for desegregation has been argued on the basis of the harm caused minority children, we are led to expect improvements in test scores as the result of a desegregation decision. What was a moral and legal issue of segregation is transformed into an educational improvement issue. The injury constructed out of social science testimony to help win the case becomes the object of reform.

How the court chooses to interpret the evidence presented ought to bear some relationship to its decision. In the school finance cases, the courts found themselves squarely in the controversy generated by the Coleman Report and the criticisms of it.[51] Is there a demonstrable relationship between the cost of education and its quality? Can differences in school expenditures be shown to affect the outcomes of schooling, notably scores on reading and mathematics achievement tests? Since there is no general agreement among social scientists concerning this controversy, there could be no general agreement in the courts. Some courts were willing to assume that cost and quality are related and that low school expenditures cause educational injury; other courts were not willing to accept this assumption. When a court did accept this assumption, it also concluded that school finance practices violated the law.

The U.S. Supreme Court's decision in *San Antonio* v. *Rodriguez* appeared to turn in part on the Court's view of the

50. Glazer, "Towards an Imperial Judiciary?" p. 117.

51. James S. Coleman et al., *Equality of Educational Opportunity* (Washington, D.C.: Government Printing Office, 1966); Frederick Mosteller and Daniel P. Moynihan, *On Equality of Educational Opportunity* (New York: Random House, 1972).

relationship between educational costs and educational quality:

> On even the most basic questions in this area the scholars and educational experts are divided. Indeed, one of the major sources of controversy concerns the extent to which there is a demonstrable correlation between educational expenditures and the quality of education. . . . In such circumstances, the judiciary is well advised to refrain from imposing on the states inflexible constitutional restraints.[52]

The decision was to uphold the Texas system of school finance because it was not proved that the system failed to provide an adequate level of education for all children in the state. Subsequently state courts in Idaho, Oregon, and Washington upheld the constitutionality of their states' school finance system.[53] In each of these three cases, the courts did not accept the assumption of a relationship between cost and quality, thereby rejecting the argument that inequalities in school funds cause injury to some children.

On the other hand, state courts in New Jersey, California, and Connecticut have accepted the assumption of a relationship between cost and quality:

> We deal with the problem in those terms because dollar input is plainly relevant and because we have been shown no other viable criterion for measuring compliance with the constitutional mandate. The constitutional mandate could not be satisfied unless we were to suppose the unlikely proposition that the lowest level of dollar performance happens to coincide with the constitutional mandate and that all efforts beyond the lowest level are attributable to local decision to do more than the state was obliged to do.[54]
>
> . . . Uniformity and equality of treatment mean that, if there is a correlation or meaningful relationship between the amount of money expended by a school district . . . and the equality of education provided pupils by such expenditures, the state may

52. *San Antonio* v. *Rodriguez*, 411 U.S. 1 (1973).

53. Robert E. Lindquist and Arthur E. Wise, "Developments in Education Litigation: Equal Protection," *Journal of Law and Education* 5:1 (January 1976), 34.

54. *Robinson* v. *Cahill*, 303 A. 2d 273, 277.

not . . . permit . . . significant disparities in expenditures, between school districts.[55]

. . . The evidence in this case is highly persuasive that . . . there is a high correlation between education input and education opportunity (the range and quality of educational services offered to pupils). In other words, disparities in expenditures per pupil tend to result in disparities in education opportunity.[56]

These courts found that the effect of their states' school finance plans was to cause injury to some children. In so finding, the courts declared unconstitutional their states' school finance plans.

LIMITATIONS OF SOCIAL SCIENCE

We are left to wonder what the nature of the relationship is between the use of social science evidence and decisions reached. Does the court form an opinion about the cost-quality assumption and then arrive at its decision? Is that opinion part of the rationale for decisions? Or does the court formulate its decision about the school finance plan and then rationalize the decision by whatever means are available, including social science evidence?

At times it appears that the adjudicative process would be satisfied if there were congruence between legally enforceable principles and scientifically validated principles. A court would prefer to make decisions with sound knowledge of the facts of a case as well as the consequences of its decision. This sentiment surely lies behind the jurist's complaint that social science knowledge is not determinative of educational policy questions.[57] In fact, Harold L. Korn has argued that scientific knowledge should not enter a legal decision as a matter of evidence.[58] Rather, he expresses the hope that scientific knowledge could be incorporated into the rule of law. In this

55. *Serrano* v. *Priest*, No. 938, 254, Superior Ct. Cal. (April 10, 1974) (slip opinion), p. 51.

56. *Horton* v. *Meskill*, 31 Conn. Supp. 377, 332 A. 2d 113 (1974), pp. 117–18.

57. John E. McDermott (ed.), *Indeterminacy in Education: Social Science, Educational Policy and the Search for Standards* (Berkeley, Calif.: McCutchan, 1976).

58. Harold L. Korn, "Law, Fact, and Science in the Courts," *Columbia Law Review* 66 (1966), 1080–1116.

fashion, as scientific knowledge accumulated, it would be applied on a consistent basis to all cases.

> Law—whether statutory or judge-made—and the sciences both involve bodies of generalized, systematized, and transmissible knowledge. Indeed, law may be viewed in one sense as a cumulation of the knowledge about man, his behavior, and his environment that it is the task of all the other sciences to gather. This view would suggest that scientific learning entering the legal order should have a natural affinity for the generalized, systematized, and transmissible aspect of that order—the body of the statutory and judge-made "law"—rather than for the process of case by case "fact determination."[59]

The hope which Korn expresses remains thus far only a hope insofar as social science is concerned. Consistency in the application of social science knowledge has not occurred, nor does it appear to be warranted.

Social scientists themselves are calling for a new sense of modesty about their craft. Lee J. Cronbach, assessing the state of scientific psychology, has written:

> Social scientists generally, and psychologists in particular, have modeled their work on physical science, aspiring to amass empirical generalizations, to restructure them in more general laws, and to weld scattered laws into coherent theory. That lofty aspiration is far from realization.[60]

It would appear that the way in which the adjudicative process would prefer to use social science is at variance with its current potential.

The intrinsic difficulties of social science are compounded when efforts are made to use social scientific knowledge in the courtroom. For most of the history of the social sciences, it has been assumed that the search was for objective truth; but more recently, it has been realized that the outcomes of social science research are frequently determined by the values which an investigator brings to his research. The principal means by which social science knowledge is introduced into trials is through the actions of a disputing party.

59. Ibid., p. 1101.
60. Lee J. Cronbach, "Beyond the Two Disciplines of Scientific Psychology," *An American Psychologist* (February 1975), 101–20.

While the court strives to be objective, the parties to a dispute have little interest in objectivity.[61] A party will therefore introduce only evidence which serves his cause. The distortions which arise are endemic to the adversary process and to the current nature of social science. The term "forensic social science" has been used to describe studies which are conducted in support of a position in a policy dispute.[62]

EXPANDING LEGAL CONCEPTS

We have seen how certain legal concepts have been applied to some aspects of education. Once the concept of equal protection was applied to eliminate differences in treatment based upon race, the next logical questions were posed. Where else could equal protection not be denied on the basis of race? Could the presumed *effects* of past differences in treatment on the basis of race in schools be eliminated? In schools, on what other bases could equal protection be denied? Should differences in treatment based on local wealth or willingness to support schools be eliminated? The legal concepts of fraud, negligence, and malpractice have been given meaning in the context of the traditional independent professions—law and medicine. Might these concepts be applied to the "profession" of education? The idea of due process has been applied to suspensions from schools for disciplinary reasons. For what other reasons for dismissal might due process protection be required? For what other important decisions rendered by a school in behalf of a student might due process protection be required?

Each intervention of the judiciary into the operation of schools has contributed to a narrowing of our goals for education as the idea of accountability is given legal force. And each intervention has created centralization as the parameters of policy restrict the range of options at the local level.

61. Eleanor P. Wolf, "Social Science and the Courts: The Detroit Schools Case," *The Public Interest* 42 (Winter 1976), 102–20.

62. Alice M. Rivlin, "Forensic Social Science," *Harvard Educational Review* 43 (February 1973), 61–75.

The growing legalization of education is not, however, simply the result of court decisions. Glazer has described how the executive and legislative contribute to it:

> Just as the executive is required by the Court to institute procedures and rulings and rights it would prefer not to (as in the case of the EPA), the establishment of new ground for legal action is also the result of legislative and executive action, and the courts must enforce these new laws. Thus the reach of due process is extended not only by the courts—though I believe they have played the largest roles—but by legislatures. The Colorado legislature has recently required due process in all cases of dismissal or non-renewal of appointment in many of the state's colleges—an act which has been described as instituting "instant tenure." Due process is even more significantly extended by executive action implementing legislation, as in the recent HEW guidelines implementing non-discrimination by sex in federally-supported education activities.
>
> However, even if due process expands as a result not only of the actions of courts but also of legislatures and executives, it does so on the basis of the teaching of the Court, a teaching almost universally applauded by those who are considered qualified to judge. If the Court expands due process in every sphere, and teaches that this is the teaching of the Constitution, then it is no surprise if legislatures and executives follow that teaching in good measure on their own.[63]

In addition to the legalization of education which results from the direct actions taken by the three branches of government, further legalization occurs as schools and colleges not only respond to legal decisions but try, as well, to anticipate them. We can only guess about the nature of procedural, regulatory, and bureaucratic changes which institutions are imposing upon themselves in anticipation of externally imposed requirements.

Equal protection, due process, and malpractice are powerful concepts. Schools and colleges are still far from functioning fully consistently with these concepts. Nor are these the only legal principles likely to affect educational policymaking.

63. Glazer, "Towards an Imperial Judiciary?" pp. 113–14.

Before looking into the future, it is useful to underscore the point that in the logic of legal reasoning, legal positions once taken tend to be carried to their logical conclusion:

> The basic pattern of legal reasoning is reasoning by examples. It is reasoning from case to case. It is a three-step process described by the doctrine of precedent in which a proposition descriptive of the first case is made into a rule of law and then applied to a next similar situation. The steps are these: similarity is seen between cases; next the rule of law inherent in the first case is announced; then the rule of law is made applicable to the second case.[64]

So long as similarity between cases is perceived, the process advances.

THE RESPONSIBILITY OF THE STATE

It is an established principle that the schools are a state responsibility.[65] As we know, nearly all state constitutions vest responsibility for education in the state legislature. In all states except Hawaii, the state legislatures have delegated the responsibility for the operation of schools to local school districts. State delegation of operating responsibility to local units does not absolve the state from responsibility for the schools and especially does not absolve the state from the obligation to see that the Constitution is observed.[66] The principle that the state retains responsibility for schools is an enormously powerful one. Its use to settle legal disputes has been tempered by the tradition of local control, but, unfettered, the principle would appear to have the capacity for significant expansion.

The legal concept that the schools are a state responsibility has been invoked to resolve a variety of disputes. It has been used in decisions to establish the preeminent power of the state, to give school districts the limited status of quasi-corporations, to permit the state to create, alter, and dissolve school districts, and to establish the states' discretionary

64. Edward H. Levi, *An Introduction to Legal Reasoning* (Chicago: University of Chicago Press, 1948), pp. 1–2.
65. Wise, *Rich Schools, Poor Schools*, pp. 94–98.
66. Ibid., pp. 165–67.

authority over the raising and distribution of school funds.[67] More recently, the states have been reminded of their responsibility for schools in disputes concerning the federal Constitution. A number of desegregation decisions during the late 1950s and early 1960s made it clear that the state could be implicated in segregation practiced at the local level.[68] The school finance lawsuits were designed to compel the states to accept their full measure of responsibility for financing education.[69]

A 1977 U.S. Supreme Court decision concerned with segregation in Detroit concerned the implementation of certain remedial education programs and required the state to pay half the costs of these programs.[70] The district court had ordered the Detroit Board of Education to institute programs for remedial reading, in-service teacher training, unbiased testing, and counseling and career guidance. The Supreme Court affirmed the imposition of these programs "to restore the victims of discriminatory conduct to the position they would have enjoyed in terms of education had these four components been provided in a nondiscriminatory manner in a school system free from pervasive *de jure* racial segregation."[71] The Supreme Court also upheld the lower court's decision to require the state to pay for half the cost of the program. The state was thus held responsible for the existence of unconstitutional discrimination in Detroit and for the actions necessary to correct it. In this circumstance and perhaps others, the plenary power of the state in education, together with its obligation to conform to the Constitution, becomes a strong basis for state action in education. Moreover, under *Wood* v. *Strickland*, school board members can be held liable for damages if they *know* or *reasonably should know* that their actions violate the constitutional rights of students.[72] The latent potential of the concept of state responsibility cannot be overemphasized.

67. Ibid., Chapter 5.   68. Ibid., pp. 28–43.
69. Ibid., entire book.
70. *Milliken* v. *Bradley*, 45 L.W. 4873 (1977).
71. Ibid., p. 4877.
72. *Wood* v. *Strickland*, 420 U.S. 308 (1975).

The process of accretion of actual state responsibility has hardly begun. Of course, the state has long promulgated statutes and regulations which govern the *conditions* of education. What is new is that the state can be expected in the future to deal with actual school *operations*. The greater willingness to remit the adverse consequences of a school's policies to the courts, together with a corresponding willingness on the part of the courts to receive such litigation, means that the theoretical limit would be reached only when the state assumes full responsibility for school policies and *practices*.

The hammer that will drive the process of state accretion of responsibility is likely to be the concept of individual rights under federal or state constitutions. Thus, the right not to be segregated and the right not to be discriminated against in the allocation of funds will figure prominently in the process. The concept of duty—the responsibility which the state undertakes when it requires students to attend school—is also likely to emerge. The state's power is plenary; whenever an aggrieved party fails to secure a satisfactory judgment against the local school board, he can attempt to impugn the state school board. Any failure by the local school board can be described as a failure of the state. And once the state is held legally responsible for the failure, it is obviously responsible for ensuring a solution.

DUE PROCESS

The application of the concept of due process to schools and colleges is also a powerful one. Earlier in this chapter, we discussed the application of due process to dismissals from school for disciplinary reasons. This concept has so far been applied in cases involving the dismissal or non-renewal of faculty appointments, but will almost certainly be applied also to cases involving dismissal for academic reasons. "If due process is now something that must be taken into account . . . by schools and colleges . . . the logic of that position must be worked out."[73]

As lawsuits raise questions about the adequacy of procedures and the fairness of rules, schools and colleges must be-

73. Glazer, "Towards an Imperial Judiciary?" p. 113.

come more procedural and formal in their treatment of faculty and students. A university has been required by a court to readmit a medical student who had been expelled for marginal performance.[74] While it was clear that the student's performance was extremely poor, the university had never formally defined performance of "marginal quality." In other words, the court acted because the university had failed to rationalize its procedures sufficiently. One result is that a medical student of marginal quality may be permitted to become a practicing physician—a consequence which no one, except the student, wants. A second result is that this university and all others similarly situated—meaning all others with medical schools in the jurisdiction of this court—will set about to rationalize their procedures for expulsion. While this process of rationalization will prevent the recurrence of this particular error and perhaps other similar errors, the university's manual of procedures will grow. The university's academic procedures will, at the same time, assume a more judicial cast. The behavior of professors will become more circumspect as they come to conform to the procedures and rules. And possibly one more attorney will be added to the university's staff.

In order to evaluate these developments, we must ask: Are medical students, considered collectively, better off as a result of this decision? Are the individual rights of medical students better protected? Is the quality of medical schools, physician educators, and medical education likely to improve or to decline as a result of this decision? Is society now better protected? What is the relationship between this decision and medical school accreditation and physician certification?

Public and Private Institutions

A third major concept that could undergo similar change is the distinction between public and private institutions. (It is important to point out that the university referred to above is a private one.) Assaults on this distinction will continue to be made. An unsuccessful applicant to Harvard Law School, for example, argued (unsuccessfully) that, for purposes of the Fourteenth Amendment's due process clause, Harvard was a

74. *Washington Post*, September 11, 1978.

state institution, and that he had consequently been denied due process.[75] His reasoning was based on the fact that under the Massachusetts constitution the state legislature retains the power to alter the governance of this private university. Whether or not his was a frivolous argument, a federal court, as noted earlier, has intervened in a private institution in a similar case. As private institutions accept public money, as they acquiesce to being "coordinated" by 1202 Commissions,[76] and as they are increasingly regulated by state and federal law, the distinction between public and private may become increasingly susceptible to attack.

PROCEDURAL VERSUS SUBSTANTIVE

Courts have traditionally preferred to deal with procedural questions and have been reluctant to become involved with the substance of education. Judges believe that they have special insight into the uses of procedure that is denied them when it comes to matters of substance.[77] Nevertheless, court decisions which purport to deal only with procedural reform inevitably do affect the substance of education as well. As the number of such decisions increases, the impact will become more evident. Moreover, as the cases come closer to the heart of academic decision-making, the nature of academic decision-making and the educational experience will change. If the quality of education can be altered by procedures which affect the relatively small numbers of students affected by disciplinary and academic dismissal, what can we expect the ramifications on education to be as the procedures for decisions which affect all students are affected by actions of the court?

FUTURE IMPACT OF THE COURTS

Several other trends, noted earlier, can be expected to increase the judicial role in educational policymaking: (1) courts frequently must act when other branches of government are unable, unwilling, or do not know how to act; (2) as social

75. *The Chronicle of Higher Education*, October 18, 1976.
76. See Carnegie Foundation for the Advancement of Teaching, *The States and Higher Education* (San Francisco: Jossey-Bass, 1978), pp. 85–91.
77. Horowitz, *The Courts and Social Policy*, p. 49.

science findings identify injury, the courts can be called upon to root out that injury;[78] (3) courts are increasingly willing to formulate and impose solutions in order to ensure that the identified harm is remedied. These trends, when coupled with the expanding legal concepts we have discussed, suggest an increasingly stronger impact of the judiciary upon education.

We must be concerned not only with the impact of each expanding legal concept separately but with their cumulative impact as well. Each concept has its logical conclusion: state responsibility is fully satisfied when the state operates all schools; due process in schools is fully satisfied when the school emulates the court. The distinction between public and private is eradicated as private institutions must conform to the same principles as public institutions. The judicial distinction between procedural and substantive intervention erodes as the number of procedural interventions increases. Of course, the legal process can cease before the logical conclusion is reached if limiting principles are found.[79] Since expanding legal concepts tend to reinforce each other, the burden at the moment appears to be on those who wish to halt the process.

Although the future is difficult to predict, the state could in fact become what it is in legal document: the establisher and maintainer of schools and the guarantor of equal protection and due process rights. It remains to be seen to what extent the state will come to guarantee rights in private education and how much substance will be given to equal protection and due process. But, as we have noted, legal formalism pushes to the final locus of legal responsibility.

In the next chapter, we shall see how quickly and easily the state can assert its legal responsibility over local schools. We shall also see how "mere procedural reforms" can change the underlying conception of education and how social science, educational research, and evaluation help to formulate "the problem" and shape "the solution." We shall see, as we

78. Glazer, "Towards an Imperial Judiciary?" p. 116.
79. As noted earlier, in *Missouri* v. *Horowitz* the Supreme Court attempted to draw a distinction between dismissals for disciplinary and academic reasons.

examine the evolution of school finance litigation in New Jersey, the effects of the legalization of educational decision-making as the courts, the legislature, and the state department of education struggled with a succession of court decisions. We shall be looking at the hyperrationalization of the New Jersey schools.

CHAPTER 5

ROBINSON v. *CAHILL:*
THE HYPERRATIONALIZATION
OF THE NEW JERSEY SCHOOLS

Reading and speech deficiencies cannot be eliminated by judicial fiat; they will require time, patience, and the skills of specially trained teachers.

UNITED STATES SUPREME COURT
Milliken v. *Bradley*

HISTORY OF THE CASE

Robinson v. *Cahill* is the classic case study of the hyper-rationalization of education. This case, decided first in 1972, began as a challenge to the constitutionality of the system of financing elementary and secondary public schools in New Jersey, on the basis of the federal constitution's equal protection clause as well as the equal protection and education clauses of the state constitution.[1]

THE BOTTER OPINION

Superior Court Judge Theodore Botter began his opinion by noting:

The State Board of Education has overall control and supervision of public school education in the state . . . and is authorized to adopt rules and regulations for carrying out the state

---

1. 118 N.J. Super. 223, 287 A. 2d 187 (1972).

155

school laws. . . . The Commissioner is the chief executive officer of the State Department of Education. He is the agent of the State Board for all purposes.[2]

This description of responsibilities and roles of state officials—typical of most states—was to assume great importance.

The judge continued:

In most cases, rich districts spend more money per pupil than poor districts; rich districts spend more money on teachers' salaries per pupil; rich districts have more teachers and more professional staff per pupil; and rich districts manage this with tax rates that are lower than poor districts, despite "equalizing" [state] aid.[3]

The pattern of finance was familiar; it existed in nearly every state.

Judge Botter did not avoid the controversy concerning the relationship between the cost of education and the quality of education. He heard testimony from James W. Guthrie and Henry M. Levin, two of the authors of *Schools and Inequality*, a book which contained analyses challenging the *Coleman Report*'s conclusion that variations in resource inputs are unrelated to variations in educational outcomes.[4] Judge Botter's conclusion was clear:

So far as this court is concerned, the only evidence offered in the case does show correlation between educational expenditures and pupil achievement over and above the influence of family and other environmental factors.[5]

Although social scientists were in dispute about the results of research, the court was free to draw its conclusion.

Judge Botter then turned his attention to the New Jersey Constitution's Education Clause, first adopted in 1875:

The Legislature shall provide for the maintenance and support of a thorough and efficient system of free public schools for the

---

2. 287 A. 2d 187, p. 192.   3. Ibid., p. 194.
4. James W. Guthrie et al., *Schools and Inequality* (Cambridge, Mass.: MIT Press, 1971). Arthur E. Wise, "Review of *Schools and Inequality*," *Library Quarterly* 43 (January 1973), 68–69.
5. 287 A. 2d 187, 203.

instruction of all the children in the State between the ages of five and eighteen.

The judge's historical examination convinced him that the purpose of the law, as conceived in 1875, was "to make it a State legislative obligation to provide a thorough education for all pupils wherever located."[6]

> The word "thorough" in the Education Clause connotes in common meaning the concept of completeness and attention to detail. It means more than simply adequate or minimal.[7]

The judge noted that a lower standard of education, requiring only "rudimentary instruction," had been rejected.[8] Historical and contemporary interpretations of this "thorough and efficient" clause were to be the focal point of educational policymaking in New Jersey for years to come.

Judge Botter then turned his attention to another clause of the state constitution:

> All persons are by nature free and independent, and have certain natural and unalienable rights, among which are those of enjoying and defending life and liberty, of acquiring, possessing, and protecting property, and of pursuing and obtaining safety and happiness.

The New Jersey Supreme Court had held that "this clause contains an implied guarantee of equality comparable to the Equal Protection Clause" of the federal Constitution.[9]

Judge Botter cited the theses of Wise, Coons, and earlier school finance decisions (noted in Chapter 1) as support for his own holding:

> The Education Clause and the equality provisions of the New Jersey Constitution require a more certain and uniform basis than our statutory scheme now provides for the thorough education of each child.
>
> For the foregoing reasons I hold that the statutes of New Jersey do not provide the equality of educational opportunity which is demanded by our State Constitution. In my opinion the statutory scheme also violates the Equal Protection Clause of the Fourteenth Amendment.[10]

6. Ibid., p. 211. 7. Ibid. 8. Ibid. 9. Ibid., p. 212.
10. Ibid., p. 216.

For Judge Botter, the education clause, the phrase "thorough and efficient," the equality provisions of the New Jersey constitution, and the federal equal protection clause all meant that New Jersey was denying some of its children equality of educational opportunity. He did not, however, explicitly define equality of educational opportunity except to suggest that it had to do with the equalization of educational expenditures.[11]

THE STATE SUPREME COURT REVIEW

Between the Botter decision of 1972 and its review by the Supreme Court of New Jersey, the United States Supreme Court rendered a decision in a similar case, *San Antonio* v. *Rodriguez*, on March 21, 1973, which upheld the constitutionality of the Texas system of school finance, a system not unlike the one in operation in New Jersey.[12] The United States Supreme Court rested its decision upon the conclusion that the system did not violate the federal Constitution's equal protection clause.

Thirteen days later, on April 3, 1973, the Supreme Court of New Jersey rendered its decision.[13] It upheld the Botter decision, resting its decision upon the education clause and not upon either federal or state equal protection grounds. The court began by accepting the lower court's proposition of a relationship between dollars spent and the outcomes of education:

> There was testimony with respect to the correlation between dollar input per pupil and the end product of the educational process. Obviously equality of dollar input will not assure equality in educational results. There are individual and group disadvantages which play a part. Local conditions, too, are telling, for example, insofar as they attract or repel teachers who are free to choose one community rather than another. But it is nonetheless clear that there is a significant connection between the sums expended and the quality of the educational oppor-

11. Ibid., pp. 211 and 213.
12. 411 U.S. 1 (1973).
13. 62 N.J. 473, 303 A. 2d 273 (1973).

tunity. And of course the Legislature has acted upon that premise in providing State aid on formulas designed to ameliorate in part the dollar disparities generated by a system of local taxation. Hence we accept the proposition that the quality of educational opportunity does depend in substantial measure upon the number of dollars invested, notwithstanding that the impact upon students may be unequal because of other factors, natural or environmental.[14]

After reviewing the U.S. Supreme Court's decision in *San Antonio*, the New Jersey Supreme Court concluded that, in spite of some differences in school finance practices between Texas and New Jersey, the U.S. Supreme Court would have reached a similar decision in the New Jersey situation. The New Jersey court also concluded that the entire system of local government would be jeopardized by an application of the equal protection clause to school finance. It feared that if it used the equal protection clause to strike down school finance laws, other suits might challenge inequities in the provision of other local services. For this and other reasons, it rejected the use of its own equal protection clause. The court also concluded that its constitution's property tax clause was not a solid basis for its decision.

The court then examined the history of public education in New Jersey. When the public schools became free (1871), the proceeds of a statewide property tax were apportioned on the basis of the number of pupils and not on the basis of local property values. However, in 1881, a shift was made to a property value base because some counties were deliberately undervaluing their property in order to avoid their fair share of the state property tax burden. Thus the court noted:

> The state seemingly drifted into a formula of apportionment in which ratables rather than pupils became so prominent, not because ratables were deemed the fair basis for distribution of the tax proceeds, but as an antidote for an abuse with respect to valuation of the tax base. Had there been employed a direct remedy, i.e., statewide equalization of the assessments, thereby to insure an even distribution of the tax burden, it is likely

14. 303 A. 2d 273, 277.

that the per-pupil basis for distribution of the statewide tax proceeds would have retained its inherent equitable appeal.[15]

The court then turned its attention to the education clause—the clause containing the phrase "thorough and efficient." It immediately noted that "there appears to be no helpful history spelling out the intended impact."[16] Undaunted, however, the court continued:

> We can be sure the amendment was intended to embody the principle of the 1871 statute that public education for children shall be *free*. It is also plain that the ultimate responsibility for a thorough and efficient education was imposed upon the State. This has never been doubted.[17]

After examining other history, pertaining to matters of taxation, the court concluded:

> In the light of the foregoing, it cannot be said the 1875 amendments were intended to insure statewide equality among taxpayers. But we do not doubt that an equal educational opportunity for children was precisely in mind. The mandate that there be maintained and supported a "thorough and efficient system of free public schools for the instruction of all the children in the State between the ages of five and eighteen years" can have no other import. Whether the State acts directly or imposes the role upon local government, the end product must be what the Constitution commands. A system of instruction in any district of the State which is not thorough and efficient falls short of the constitutional command. Whatever the reason for the violation, the obligation is the State's to rectify it. If local government fails, the State government must compel it to act, and if the local government cannot carry the burden, the State must itself meet its continuing obligation.[18]

With these words, the court read "equal educational opportunity" into the thorough and efficient clause. This reading directed attention to students rather than to taxpayers. And "equal educational opportunity" was given a specific outcome definition:

15. Ibid., p. 291. "Ratables" are taxable properties.
16. Ibid.
17. Ibid.
18. Ibid., p. 294.

Today, a system of public education which did not offer high school education would hardly be thorough and efficient. The Constitution's guarantee must be understood to embrace that educational opportunity which is needed in the contemporary setting to equip a child for his role as a citizen and as a competitor in the labor market.[19]

Following the U.S. Supreme Court in *San Antonio*, which had allowed that schools *might* have a constitutional duty to prepare children to exercise the rights of citizenship, the New Jersey court offered a guarantee.[20] To the need to equip a child for his role as a citizen was added the need to equip him as a competitor in the labor market. And what had been "equal educational opportunity" was now "that educational opportunity."

While the court had begun to describe "thorough and efficient" in terms of educational outcomes, it did continue the lower court's concern with resources. It is interesting to note that from this point on, only when the court discusses resources does it use the phrase "*equal* educational opportunity":

> The trial court found the constitutional demand had not been met and did so on the basis of discrepancies in dollar input per pupil. We agree. We deal with the problem in those terms because dollar input is plainly relevant and because we have been shown no other viable criterion for measuring compliance with the constitutional mandate. The constitutional mandate could not be said to be satisfied unless we were to suppose the unlikely proposition that the lowest level of dollar performance happens to coincide with the constitutional mandate and that all efforts beyond the lowest level are attributable to local decisions to do more than the State was obliged to do.
>
> Surely the existing statutory system is not visibly geared to the mandate that there be a "a thorough and efficient system of free public schools for the instruction of all the children in this state between the ages of five and eighteen years." Indeed the State has never spelled out the content of the educational opportunity the Constitution requires. Without some such prescription, it is even more difficult to understand how the

19. Ibid., p. 295.
20. See Chapter 1, under School Finance Equalization.

tax burden can be left to local initiative with any hope that statewide equality of educational opportunity will emerge. The 1871 statute embraced a statewide tax because it was found that local taxation could not be expected to yield equal educational opportunity. Since then the State has returned the tax burden to local school districts to the point where at the time of the trial the State was meeting but 28% of the current operating expenses. There is no more evidence today than there was a hundred years ago that this approach will succeed.[21]

Yet, even as the New Jersey Supreme Court expressed its concern about resources, it underscored its belief in the need to spell out the content of the educational opportunity which the constitution requires—that is, the prescription.

The court proceeded to quote approvingly a state report which had asserted that "education is a State and not a local responsibility":

This means that the State has a responsibility not only to provide financial assistance to the local district but also to delineate the broad terms of operation of the local district, both financially and educationally.[22]

The dual concern over education and finance persisted:

We repeat that if the State chooses to assign its obligation under the 1875 amendment to local government, the State must do so by a plan which will fulfill the State's continuing obligation. To that end the State must define in some discernible way the education obligation and must *compel* the local school districts to raise the money necessary to provide that opportunity. The State has never spelled out the content of the constitutionally mandated educational opportunity. Nor has the State *required* the school districts to raise moneys needed to achieve that unstated standard. Nor is the State aid program designed to compensate for local failures to reach that level. It must be evident that our present scheme is a patchy product reflecting provincial contests rather than a plan sensitive only to the constitutional mandate.[23]

For the new finance system to be acceptable, it had to rest upon a clear definition of the state's educational obligation.

21. 303 A. 2d 273, 295–96.
22. Ibid., p. 297.
23. Ibid.

FURTHER OPINIONS

On June 19, 1973, the New Jersey Supreme Court gave the state legislature until December 31, 1974, to enact legislation compatible with the state constitution and to be effective July 1, 1975.[24] By January 23, 1975, no such legislation had been enacted and the court let stand existing legislation for the school year 1975–76.[25] On May 23, 1975, the court ordered the redistribution of $290,000,000 in state aid for the school year 1976–77 if the legislature did not by October 1, 1975, develop its own plan.[26] Although a new school finance plan had not been adopted, the state department of education had devised "guidelines" for the attainment by school districts of the goals of a thorough and efficient system of schools. The May 23 opinion, and dissents to it, considered these guidelines.

In the opinion of the court, Chief Justice Hughes refused to pass judgment on the guidelines:

> Nor can we adjudicate on a piecemeal or hypothetical basis. The validity of the tentative guidelines recently published by the Department of Education cannot now be passed upon, inchoate and hortatory in nature as they are. They would have to be considered in context with such legislative provision as may be enacted for their fiscal implementation, unless the judgment of this Court is likewise to be only hortatory and futile in that sense.[27]

The court did offer its approval of the efforts of the department of education

> to establish the components of a thorough and efficient system of education by formulation of standards, goals and guidelines by which the school districts and the Department may in collaboration improve the quality of the educational opportunity offered all school children. We assume that these efforts will move forward through the administrative process to a finality, and that the State, through the Commissioner of Education, will see to the prompt implementation of the standards, so determined, in the field. We would further expect that any problem attendant upon undue burdens on particular districts, in conforming to such standards, will have legislative attention.

24. 63 N.J. 196, 306 A. 2d 65 (1973) (*Robinson* II).
25. 67 N.J. 35, 339 A. 2d 193 (1975) (*Robinson* II).
26. 67 N.J. 333, 351 A. 2d 713 (1975) (*Robinson* IV).
27. 351 A. 2d 713, 719.

But by these comments we intend no present implication that any method of financing for the purposes stated, which would leave the present system of defraying the expense of education substantially unaltered, could fulfill the "thorough and efficient" constitutional norm.[28]

While the court was signaling its approval of the idea of establishing guidelines for a thorough and efficient system of education, it was also signaling that guidelines alone, without the redistribution of funds, were unlikely to meet the constitutional standard.

THE CASE FOR STANDARDS

Justice Pashman, in a separate opinion, argued that the court should have acted more decisively and more broadly. He was ready to "carry the Court into hitherto unexplored territories in the realms of constitutional law and equitable remedies."[29] His analysis presaged the shift from a concern for equality of educational opportunity to a concern for something else:

In *Robinson* I [the April 3, 1973 decision] the Court did not hold that disparate educational expenditures were *ipso facto* unconstitutional as a matter of constitutional equal protection. . . . Rather the Court found that [the education clause] imposed upon the State the duty to insure that a certain minimum level of educational opportunity is provided every student.[30]

For Justice Pashman, the import was clear:

The education clause requires that the State, having chosen to delegate administration of public schools to local school districts, must prescribe statewide standards for the operation of those schools so as to insure that all children are guaranteed an

28. Ibid.
29. Ibid., p. 725.
30. Ibid., p. 726. At this point, Justice Pashman observed in footnote 1:
This is, of course, only one possible definition of equality of educational opportunity. See *generally* McDermott and Klein, "The Cost-Quality Debate in School Finance Litigation: Do Dollars Make a Difference," *Law and Comtemp. Prob.* 38 (1974), 415, 416–23; Wise, "Legal Challenges to Public School Finance," *School Rev.* 82 (1973), 1, 15–19.
Both of these articles describe different understandings of "equality of educational opportunity."

opportunity for an education of a certain minimum quality. It must also establish a mechanism for compelling local compliance with such standards, and where, for financial reasons, a local school district cannot comply, it must provide a means for supplementing local resources.[31]

The state must establish statewide standards, the ultimate objective being

> to compel the State to assume these duties, which, to the grave injury of many children in this State, have gone long neglected. Until the State has at least adopted proper statewide standards, it is impossible for this Court to even determine to what degree the present disparities are resulting in inadequate education in some districts, although the findings of the trial court put it beyond question that lack of sufficient expenditures for education is seriously harming students in at least some school districts.[32]

Justice Pashman cited the research on the relationship between educational expenditures and educational outcomes, as he asserted that insufficient expenditures cause harm. If there had been a judicial determination that low expenditures cause harm, as there was, then two remedies could be imagined. One was to raise low expenditures in the certain knowledge (judicially determined) that the harm would be corrected; the other was to correct the harm directly, whatever the cost.

Justice Pashman read the education clause as imposing

> responsibility for formulation of statewide standards of educational quality upon the Legislature and, by implication, upon administrative agencies to which the Legislature properly delegates its authority.
>
> . . . .
>
> The Board and Commissioner are thus statutorily empowered to formulate statewide standards of educational quality. . . .[33]

"Statewide standards of educational quality" remained to be defined:

> I would remand the case in part to the State Board of Education to formulate statewide standards for educational quality

31. 351 A. 2d 713, 726.
32. Ibid., pp. 726–27.
33. Ibid., pp. 727–28.

and to evaluate each school district to determine whether it is in compliance with those standards and, if not in compliance, whether the district has the financial ability to comply without further State assistance.

. . . .

The product of such a remand would be both a set of standards and an evaluation of how much additional money would be needed to establish a "thorough and efficient" system of public schools in all school districts. . . . I would expect the Board to fully comply with the mandate of the Court upon such a remand in time for implementation of the Board's decisions in the 1976–77 school year.[34]

Within a year the Board was to define "statewide standards of educational quality" and assess the cost of bringing all school districts to those standards.

The majority opinion, while approving the idea of state guidelines, had avoided confronting the sharp differences of opinion in the state concerning the nature of the standards to be required. But for Justice Pashman:

The type of standards required by the education clause may be inferred from the language of that clause and the cases interpreting it. "Thoroughness" and "efficiency" are ultimately measures of the effectiveness of the public school system in performing its function—educating the children who attend it. . . .

[I]n *Robinson I,* we said:

The Constitution's guarantee must be understood to embrace that educational opportunity which is needed in the contemporary setting to equip a child for his role as a citizen and as a competitor in the labor market.

The statewide standards must, therefore, be cast in terms of the quality of education which the local school districts are actually providing to the students who attend them.[35]

By a combination of "inference" and examination of precedents (of which one of two was an earlier opinion in *Robinson*), it was determined that the statewide standards were to deal with the effectiveness of the school system in preparing chil-

34. Ibid., pp. 728–29.   35. Ibid., pp. 728–29.

dren for their roles as citizens and competitors in the labor market.

The controversy over standards concerned the merits of "input," "output," and "process" standards. Justice Pashman first tried to obliterate the distinction among the three by invoking the rationalistic model of education:

> The distinctions among these types of standards may in application be more illusory than real. Ultimately a well-conceived educational system requires that educational goals be formulated, that decisions be made as to what inputs of human and material resources are required, that the resources be properly allocated among students according to their needs in light of the goals, and finally that the success of the system in achieving its educational goals be evaluated and, based upon that evaluation, the choice of educational goals, the decision as to resource needs, and the process of allocating resources to students be revised.[36]

But Justice Pashman was quickly forced to acknowledge the differences between "output" and "process" standards:

> The Board and Commission have declared that their intention is to issue regulations which establish "process" standards. They define the "process" approach as "an educational system focusing on the delivery of resources to students in the most effective way, 'effective' being defined in terms of whatever works best for each individual learner." If this is indeed the thrust of the regulations to be issued, then they would not comply with the constitutional requirements.[37]

Justice Pashman had clearly allied himself with those who advocated output standards:

> The Commissioner has urged upon the Court the practical and theoretical obstacles to adopting and enforcing standards focused directly upon the question of whether public schools are in fact educating the students who attend them. Nevertheless, that question is precisely the one that is of most importance to children, their parents, and, ultimately, to society as a whole.[38]

36. Ibid., p. 729, note 6.   37. Ibid., p. 729, note 8.
38. Ibid., p. 729.

While Justice Pashman's opinion was a dissenting opinion, it marked the future more clearly than did the majority opinion.

THE PUBLIC SCHOOL EDUCATION ACT

On September 29, 1975, the state government enacted the Public School Education Act of 1975; this act was intended to be the Legislature's response to *Robinson*. On January 30, 1976, the New Jersey Supreme Court announced a new decision which involved a review of the act.[39] The court was deciding "whether the statute, *on its face*, did or did not meet constitutional requirements."[40] The court allowed that the review was theoretical, since the regulations implementing the statute had not yet been put into operation. Moreover, the funding and funds required by the statute had yet to be appropriated. The court, however, thought that the desirability of a speedy decision on the "facial" constitutionality of the act outweighed these considerations.

The court began the substance of its opinion by elevating the importance of educational considerations:

> It is, initially, of vital importance to note that this is the first time in the course of this litigation that we have had an opportunity to consider a plan intended to meet all aspects of a thorough and efficient education. *Robinson* I, as the opening sentence of the opinion makes clear, involved only "the constitutionality of statutes providing for the financing of elementary and secondary schools." It is of course true that the opinion says much that bears significantly upon aspects of the problem of public education other than the fiscal one. And although we have not hitherto been asked to examine the adequacy of the educational system in this State in other than financial terms, we have been constantly mindful that money is only one of a number of elements that must be studied in giving definition and content to the constitutional promise of a thorough and efficient education. Thus in *Robinson* IV we said,
>
> > [A] multitude of other [non-fiscal] factors play a vital role in the educational result—to name a few, individual and group disadvantages, use of compensatory techniques for the disadvantaged and handicapped, variation in availability of

39. 69 N.J. 449, 355 A. 2d 129 (1976) (*Robinson* V).
40. 355 A. 2d 129, 131 (emphasis added).

qualified teachers in different areas, effectiveness in teaching methods and evaluation thereof, professionalism at every level of the system, meaningful curricula, exercise of authority and discipline, and adequacy of overall goals fixed at the policy level.

We are now called upon to examine a legislative proposal that at once seeks to define the constitutional promise, identify the components of which it consists, establish a procedural mechanism for its implementation and afford the financial means necessary for its fulfillment.[41]

The court here explicitly allowed that its first *Robinson* decision concerned *only* the *financing* of education. Now, however, the financing of education was but one of a number of elements to be considered in determining "thorough and efficient education." A slight shift in wording was also to be noted. The expression "thorough and efficient education" had been substituted for the constitution's "thorough and efficient system" of schools.

The opinion then proceeded to cite—largely in approving tones—the Public School Education Act of 1975. The act began:

The goal of a thorough and efficient system of free public schools shall be to provide to all children in New Jersey, regardless of socioeconomic status or geographic location, the educational opportunity which will prepare them to function politically, economically and socially in a democratic society.[42]

The goal of the system is not the provision of equal educational opportunity to all children; it is the provision of "the educational opportunity which will prepare them to function . . . in . . . society."

The act listed the *major elements* to be required:

A thorough and efficient system of free public schools shall include the following major elements, which shall serve as guidelines for the achievement of the legislative goal and the implementation of this act:
   a. Establishment of educational goals at both the State and local levels;

41. Ibid., 132.
42. N.J.S.A. 18A:7A—4.

b. Encouragement of public involvement in the establishment of educational goals;

c. Instruction intended to produce the attainment of reasonable levels of proficiency in the basic communications and computational skills;

d. A breadth of program offerings designed to develop the individual talents and abilities of pupils;

e. Program and supportive services for all pupils especially those who are educationally disadvantaged or who have special educational needs;

f. Adequately equipped, sanitary and secure physical facilities and adequate materials and supplies;

g. Qualified instructional and other personnel;

h. Efficient administrative procedures;

i. An adequate State program of research and development; and

j. Evaluation and monitoring programs at both the State and local levels.[43]

The list of "major elements" introduced the idea of "the attainment of reasonable levels of proficiency in the basic communications and computational skills." The list of major elements did manage to include "an adequate State program of research and development" but somehow failed to be explicit about how schools were to be financed.

The act provided for "a rather elaborate monitoring arrangement."[44]

For the purpose of evaluating the thoroughness and efficiency of all the public schools of the State, the commissioner, with the approval of the State board and after review by the Joint Committee on the Public Schools, shall develop and administer a uniform, Statewide system for evaluating the performance of *each* school. Such a system shall be based in part on annual testing for achievement in basic skill areas, and in part on such other means as the commissioner deems proper in order to (a) determine pupil status and needs, (b) ensure pupil progress, and (c) assess the degree to which the educational objectives have been achieved.[45]

43. N.J.S.A. 18A:7A–5.
44. 355 A. 2d 129, 133–34.
45. N.J.S.A. 18A:7A–10 (emphasis added).

Although the list of major elements explicitly called for "a breadth of program offerings designed to develop the individual talents and abilities of pupils," the evaluation system was explicit only in requiring testing in the basic skills.

The commissioner and state board were given responsibility

> first, to maintain a constant awareness of what elements at any particular time find place in a thorough and efficient system of education, as this concept evolves through the inevitably changing forms that it will take in the years to come; second, to insure that there be ever present, sufficiently competent and dedicated personnel, adequately equipped to guarantee functional implementation so that over the years and throughout the State each pupil shall be offered an equal opportunity to receive an education of such excellence as will meet the constitutional standard.[46]

The words used to describe the responsibilities of the state officials strongly suggest operational rather than oversight responsibility. Moreover, the commissioner, upon finding an inadequacy, is authorized "to order necessary budget changes within the school district," or "in-service training programs for teachers and other school personnel or both."[47] If these steps are insufficient, the state board is authorized to "issue an administrative order specifying a remedial plan to the local board of education."[48] Concerning the authority granted to the commissioner under the act, the court said: "Nor does he wait for the matter to be presented to him. Directly or indirectly, *he is the initiator.*"[49]

The court concluded that the Public School Education Act of 1975 was constitutional, assuming that it was fully funded.[50] But the test of full funding was not the degree of equalization of school funds. Rather:

> The fiscal provisions of the Act are to be judged as adequate or inadequate depending upon whether they do or do not afford

46. 355 A. 2d 129, 134.
47. N.J.S.A. 18A:7A−15.
48. Ibid.
49. 355 A. 2d 129, 135 (emphasis added).
50. Ibid., p. 139.

sufficient financial support for the system of public education
that will emerge from the implementation of the plan set forth
in the statute.[51]

The court finished its opinion by promising or threatening to
intervene if the legislature did not by April 6, 1976 (slightly
over two months later) provide for full funding of the act. Of
course, until the plan was fully implemented, no one could
know what the cost would be.

One concludes from reading the majority opinion that
the legislature had not made *specific* proposals for changes in
state school finance practices. In fact, the legislature had incorporated several changes in the 1975 act; but the majority
chose to ignore these changes. Judge Conford, temporarily assigned to the New Jersey Supreme Court, issued a separate
opinion which called attention to the failure of the 1975 act
to correct financial deficiencies and to the failure of the majority to notice this fact.

> The court is departing from the course of fiscal justice to the
> school children of this State on which it embarked in so en-
> lightened a fashion in the 1973 *Robinson* decision and rein-
> forced so resolutely in the recent 1975 *Robinson* case.
>
> Introductorily, it is to be noted that in the 1975 *Robinson*
> opinion a majority of this court had no hesitancy in interpret-
> ing the 1973 decision of the court as identifying as "the princi-
> pal cause of the constitutional deficiency" of the previous sys-
> tem of financing public education in this State "the substantial
> reliance . . . upon local taxation, entailing as it does 'discordant
> correlations between the educational needs of the school dis-
> tricts and their respective tax bases. . . .' " In essential charac-
> ter, the 1975 act now under review retains the vitiating depen-
> dency upon local taxation for the bulk of the cost of financing
> local education, with its continuing substantial discordance
> among the school districts in relation to the ratio of the tax
> resources of the districts to the number of pupils enrolled in
> the schools. While the equalization support provisions of the
> 1975 act, designed to ameliorate the discordances mentioned,
> are an improvement over those of the previous law, . . . never-
> theless, as will be shown, a substantial proportion of the State's
> school districts, of the pupils enrolled therein and of the equal-

51. Ibid., p. 136.

ized assessed valuations represented thereby, remain unaffected by the support equalizing provisions of the 1975 act. In consequence, it must follow that the resulting absence of "equality of educational opportunity," which Chief Justice Weintraub found fatal to the constitutionality of Bateman in the 1973 *Robinson* decision, still condemns the validity of the 1975 act, at least in part.[52]

The specific financial features of the 1975 act, even if fully funded, would fall far short of providing "equality of educational opportunity," by which phrase Judge Conford meant to refer to expenditure equalization.

Judge Conford noted that the majority opinion

> ignores the adjudication in our prior decisions in this case that (a) inequality of educational opportunity is *per se* a denial of the guarantee of the Education Clause; and (b) discordancies in tax resources among the districts on a per pupil basis is presumptively a denial of equality of educational opportunity in the districts disadvantaged by such discordancies. It has been shown above that these pernicious conditions continue under the 1975 act.
>
> One can agree with the majority that the matter of achieving educational adequacy in our public schools has not heretofore been addressed by the Legislature in the comprehensive manner reflected by the 1975 act. It is salutary that this has now been done. But the matter of achievement of substantive excellence in the educational process was not the heart of the grievance which led to the filing of this action in the first instance.[53]

While the majority had become enamored with improving the educational process, the issue continued to be the financing of schools,

> . . . not the constitutionality of different methods of imparting education or of contending theories as to the merits of comparative educational goals or processes, unrelated to the matter of financing.
>
> The issue before the court ever since this litigation began always has been, and remains, the constitutionality of *the system of fiscal treatment* by the State of the districts in respect of

52. Ibid., pp. 143–44.
53. Ibid., p. 151.

education and the presumptive effect thereof upon the educational opportunities of pupils. The mere enactment of the 1975 act did not draw a curtain of irrelevance over the pre-existing system of financing education or obliterate the relationship of that system to that enacted in 1975. Nor did it, or any idealistic educational aspirations expressed therein, nullify the prior holdings of this court that there is a denial of equality of educational opportunity where one district can draw on substantially greater tax resources per pupil to support education than another district.

And so the fundamental issue before us has not, as one might gather from the majority opinion, been transmuted into the more remote future question of whether particular districts will on particular future occasions be shown to be inadequately financed for the administration of their educational function.[54]

But, for the majority, the reform of education had become a more important objective than the equalization of expenditures.

In a dissent, Justice Pashman argued that the act did not outline specific requirements. He set forth criteria for evaluating the regulations promulgated to implement the act. The first criterion was that the regulations be specific:

> They must prescribe the statewide standards of a constitutionally minimum quality education to which local school districts must adhere.
>
> . . . .
>
> [They must] set forth goals and standards that are specific enough to provide a meaningful way to evaluate local efforts and measure local performance.[55]

The second criterion was that the regulations provide for "standards of performance" and "levels of proficiency."

> It follows that, to be constitutionally and statutorily sufficient, statewide standards must define with some degree of specificity, the minimally required programs, facilities and attendant staff which each local district must provide in order to meet the mandate of a thorough and efficient educational system. Certainly, without requisite planning, facilities and staff, provision of an "equal educational opportunity" is impossible.

54. Ibid., p. 152.   55. Ibid., pp. 172–73.

Although these standards need not be rigid and inflexible (and may be subject to change in accordance with policy determinations by appropriate State agencies), they must specify, in some workable fashion, levels of constitutional adequacy for each of the above elements.

I draw special attention to one particular type of standard—standards of pupil performance. Without this type of standard it will be difficult to determine the success of individual school districts in preparing their pupils for active citizenship and productive lives. I find that, to conform to both constitutional and statutory requirements, the regulations promulgated . . . must contain standards of pupil performance.

These standards necessarily contemplate that the pupils of a district will attain a reasonable degree of proficiency in such basic skills as reading, writing and simple mathematics.[56]

Justice Pashman would have the state providing input, process, and output standards with the focus clearly on the basic skills.

The third criterion was that the regulations provide for "remedial plans" and "corrective action." In addition to regulating input, process, and output, which collectively might be taken to yield the cost of education, Justice Pashman considered the matter of finance separately. For him, the act and the regulations implementing it must "guarantee adequate and relatively equalized *expenditures per pupil* as well as equalized per-pupil tax resources."[57]

THE 1976 DECISION

On May 13, 1976, the New Jersey Supreme Court issued its sixth *Robinson* decision.[58] The legislature had failed by then to provide funds for the operation of the 1975 act. The court enjoined operation of any public schools in New Jersey, effective July 1, 1976, until the act was funded. The schools were closed for the first week in July. They reopened when the state adopted a statewide income tax which funded the specific financial features of the 1975 act. Whether these provisions afford sufficient financial support for the system of

56. Ibid., pp. 173–74.   57. Ibid., p. 179.
58. 70 N.J. 155, 358 A. 2d 457, 1976.

public education that will emerge remains to be seen.[59] In the interim, New Jersey has been struggling to operate its school system consistently with the constitutional mandate, whatever meaning that mandate may turn out to have.

TOWARD HYPERRATIONALIZATION

THE SHIFT IN THE MEANING OF "THOROUGH AND EFFICIENT"

The sequence of events in *Robinson* v. *Cahill* illustrates one theme of Chapter 1. The case began with a concern for equality of educational opportunity. While this concept was never given precise definition, it was implicit that the allocation of resources was equated with the allocation of opportunity. By 1976, when the decision began to be implemented, the ideal of equality of educational opportunity had been replaced by the concept of an adequate level of achievement. What caused the shift?

A conventional legal interpretation would postulate that this turn of events resulted from a revelation about the true meaning of "thorough and efficient." According to this interpretation, further historical inquiry and examination of judicial precedents led to the realization that "thorough and efficient" meant something different from what it had first seemed to mean. Differences in interpretation, then, were the result of differences in judicial craftsmanship.

Judge Botter's examination of the history of the "thorough and efficient" clause convinced him that its purpose was to make education a state responsibility. For him the contemporary meaning of "thorough"—completeness and attention to detail—was also important. He buttressed his conclusion by noting that the framers of the constitution had rejected the standard of "rudimentary instruction." Finally, for him, the meaning of "thorough and efficient" was similar to the meaning of equal protection.

When the New Jersey Supreme Court first undertook to interpret the clause, it first observed that there was *no helpful history*. This observation is curious, first, because it contra-

59. 351 A. 2d 129, 136.

dicts Judge Botter's conclusion and, second, because the court proceeded to an unambiguous inference. The inference was that equal educational opportunity was precisely in the minds of the framers of the state constitution. The court then inferred a contemporary meaning of these expressions as that opportunity needed to equip a child for his role as a citizen and competitor in the labor market. The court apparently saw no need for the modifier "equal." Perhaps it was implied. At any rate, equipping the child for adult roles became the operational meaning of "thorough and efficient." The search for a precise definition was on.

The court refused to endorse the state department's first efforts to establish guidelines, because they were "inchoate and hortatory." Justice Pashman was ready to insist that a certain *minimum* level of educational opportunity was to be provided. After struggling with the nature of standards necessary to ensure that end, he concluded that the standards had to deal with the effectiveness of the schools in equipping the child for adult roles. Although the connection between an education of a certain minimum quality and that output standard was not explicitly drawn, it was implicit. Soon the majority was ready to accept this position.

First, most members of the court needed to unencumber themselves of a concern for financial matters. By January 30, 1976, it appeared that all along they had really been primarily concerned with educational rather than financial matters. Indeed, thorough and efficient education—expressed in educational terms—was the goal. When the state legislature proposed some educational reforms, the court was prepared to accept these as fulfilling the constitutional obligation. The constitutional demand for a thorough and efficient system of schools could be satisfied by statewide standards, emphasis on the basic skills, and state supervision.

It should be clear that if the "thorough and efficient" clause had a precise historical meaning, it is not revealed in the opinions. For a while, "thorough and efficient" was taken to imply *equality* of something; later it was taken to imply a *minimum amount* of something. For a while, it was equated with opportunity; later it was equated with outcomes. For a while, it was connected to finance; later it was disconnected from financial considerations. At best, the "thorough and efficient" clause is a *tabula rasa* for the aspirations pressed upon or assumed by the court.

THE SHIFT IN THE APPLICABLE LEGAL NORM

A second conventional legal interpretation would seek to explain the shift in terms of the necessity of relying upon the "thorough and efficient" clause rather than upon the federal equal protection clause or the state equality provision. This interpretation would postulate that the different sources of legal authority would be found to have different meanings in the context of the dispute. The process of adjudication is likened to a search for the meaning of the general legal concept in a specific context. How should the operation of the New Jersey schools be made to conform to the legal norm?

For Judge Botter, the several sources of legal authority all led to the conclusion that New Jersey was not providing equality of educational opportunity. For him, whichever constitutional principle governed, the result would be the same. It should be emphasized that finding equality of educational opportunity in any of these sources is a matter of interpretation or interpolation, since the words are not contained in any of the statements of legal principle.

The New Jersey Supreme Court believed that it faced a problem as it was about to announce its first *Robinson* decision. It is evident that the New Jersey court had decided to affirm Judge Botter's decision before the U.S. Supreme Court decided adversely in *San Antonio*.[60] The New Jersey court was foreclosed from relying on the federal equal protection clause because the U.S. Supreme Court had ruled that Texas school finance practices did not violate it. The Supreme Court was reluctant to decide the case on the basis of the state equal protection clause. The elimination of these alternatives left the state Supreme Court with only the "thorough and efficient" clause. Still, the court began by reading it as implying equal educational opportunity. Consequently, the perceived need to rely on the "thorough and efficient" clause alone did not account for the shift from equal educational opportunity to the minimal outcome standard.

60. 303 A. 2d 273, 279–82.

The Shift in the Perception of the Problem to Be Solved

A third interpretation of the shift would postulate that a change occurred in the perception of the problem which the lawsuit was designed to solve. There appear to be at least three different problems which the litigation was intended to solve: (1) inequality of educational expenditures; (2) inequality among taxpayers in the support of schools; and (3) inequality in educational achievement. While all three problems were perceived as important, the emphasis varied over time. Toward the end, emphasis was placed upon the solution to the problem of unequal educational achievement.

Ambiguity was present from the beginning. Judge Botter had cited the work of Wise and Coons as authorities for his conclusion that the New Jersey school finance system denied equal protection rights. Wise, however, was concerned with the equalization of educational expenditures. He would have left the matter of raising revenues to finance expenditure equalization entirely in the hands of the legislature. Coons, on the other hand, had constructed an argument that would have equalized the rate of taxation for any particular level of educational expenditures. He would have let the expenditure level vary from school district to school district.[61]

Judge Botter concluded that the school finance system discriminated against both students and taxpayers—a conclusion which masked differences both in problem definition and problem solution. School expenditure equalization and taxpayer equalization are solutions to different problems. While these solutions are not mutually exclusive, they are not inevitably complementary.

Ambiguity about the problem to be solved was further compounded by faulty legal reasoning. It will be remembered that the New Jersey Supreme Court insisted upon resting its decision upon the "thorough and efficient" clause *alone*. It ruled that the clause implied equal educational opportunity for children and not statewide equality among taxpayers. Despite this ruling, the court persisted in making pronouncements about how school taxes should be raised. The legal

61. Arthur E. Wise, "Review of *Private Wealth and Public Education*" (by John E. Coons et. al.), *Saturday Review*, April 17, 1971, pp. 76 ff.

authority for these pronouncements is never specified.[62]

Even as the court continued to show concern for expenditure equalization and tax equalization, it began to suggest that the real problem was inequality of educational achievement. The court created the concept of the *constitutional guarantee*—the prescribed educational opportunity needed to equip a child for his role as a citizen and competitor in the labor market. Since ultimate educational improvement came to be the preferred solution, the problem would have to be redefined.

THE SHIFT FROM LIBERALISM TO CONSERVATISM

A fourth interpretation of the shift is that the climate had changed from the "liberalism" of the 1960s to the "conservatism" of the 1970s. The legal basis for school finance reform had its genesis in the liberal tradition of the 1960s, particularly in the expansion of individual rights created by the U.S. Supreme Court in the 1950s and 1960s. The precedents which formed the basis for arguing the unconstitutionality of school finance statutes began with *Brown* v. *Board of Education* and continued through cases concerned with wealth and geographical discrimination. However, by the time the school finance cases were being decided, the climate had become conservative. The U.S. Supreme Court had undergone a change in composition and orientation. The liberal social and educational programs of the 1960s had failed to have speedy effects. The nation's economy had contracted. It is possible that the shift in *Robinson* reflected or was part of the change in climate.

THE SHIFT IN THE VIEWS ABOUT EDUCATION

A fifth interpretation involves a change in the view of the nature of education. Is education a gift which society bestows upon the child, or is it a requirement which it imposes upon him? Education is seen as a gift when the focus is upon equality of educational opportunity. But when the focus is upon preparing the child for life, education is seen as a requirement. Education as a gift tends to be compatible with a variety

62. Arthur E. Wise, "Legal Challenges to Public School Finance," *School Review* 82 (November 1973), 1–25.

of educational objectives, including development of the individual and preparation for self-development. Education as a requirement tends to be compatible with instrumental education. Education is the treatment which society imposes upon the individual to prepare him to become a member of society. Throughout the history of American schooling, education has been seen both as a gift and a requirement, although the latter tends to emerge as the dominant view.

THE INFLUENCE OF SOCIAL SCIENCE

A sixth interpretation concerns how the use of social science evidence may have led to the redefinition of the problem. As Levin has said:

> Presentation of evidence on the relationship between educational expenditures and cognitive achievement implicitly narrows the context within which the effects of unequal expenditure patterns will be considered.[63]

Beyond defining the legal dispute, the use of social science legitimated achievement test scores in the basic skills as the proper measure of the outcomes of schooling. Low achievement scores became the legally defined harm which the lawsuit was to remedy. Social science evidence introduced to prove that low school expenditures cause harm resulted in the redefinition of the problem which *Robinson* was brought to solve. The initial concern with the maldistribution of resources gave way to a mandate to raise educational achievement. The U.S. Supreme Court had proposed that some "identifiable quantum of education" might be constitutionally required to prepare a student to exercise other constitutional rights. (See Chapter 1.) In *Robinson* that proposition was made a constitutional mandate.

FROM OPPORTUNITY AND EQUALITY TO ACHIEVEMENT AND ADEQUACY

Most of the themes described or analyzed in this book are to be found in the events associated with *Robinson* v.

63. Henry M. Levin, "Education, Life Chances, and the Courts: The Role of Social Science Evidence," *Law and Contemporary Problems* 39:2 (Spring 1975), 217–40, 237.

Cahill. This case shifted concern from equality of educational opportunity to adequacy of educational achievement. Many of the specific policies and technologies described in Chapter 1 were present. A strong tone of accountability permeates the litigation and associated legislation. The 1975 law, approved by the state Supreme Court, contains a classic statement of the rationalistic model. Goals will be established, made operative, and their attainment evaluated systematically. Emphasis will be on the acquisition of basic skills, for only these *must* be evaluated according to the law.

Curiously, neither the law nor the court opinions explain how the acquisition of reading and arithmetic skills prepares children to function politically, economically, and socially in a democratic society—the ultimate goal of a thorough and efficient system of schools. We have noted that one of the barriers to malpractice lawsuits is that in the past the duty of the school has not been precisely specified. Moreover, it is possible that as the state assumes a duty, the student gains a right. New Jersey has opened itself to two different malpractice lawsuits. A student may sue if he fails to acquire the basic skills, and he may sue if the basic skills do not prepare him to function effectively in society.

HYPERRATIONALIZATION ACHIEVED

Turning to some of the major themes of Chapter 2, it is clear that events in New Jersey contribute to the trends toward centralization, hyperrationalization, and goal reduction. With respect to centralization, *Robinson* seeks to actualize the formal authority already reposing in the state legislature, the state board of education, and the office of the commissioner of education. The force of logic is inexorable.

1. The legislature shall provide for the maintenance and support of a thorough and efficient system of schools.

2. The State Board of Education has overall control and supervision of public school education.

3. The commissioner is the agent of the State Board for all purposes.

4. If local government fails, the state government must compel it to act.

5. State goals must be established.

6. The commissioner shall develop and administer a uniform, statewide system for evaluating the performance of *each school.*

7. The commissioner shall maintain *constant awareness* and guarantee *functional implementation.*

8. Finally, the commissioner does not have to wait for an inadequacy to be brought to his attention. He is to be the *initiator.*

A stream of logic which begins with the notice that the legislature has formal authority over education leads to the conclusion that the commissioner has direct authority over individual schools. Centrally determined educational policy has led, at least in principle, to the central governance of schools in New Jersey.

Robinson represents the clear belief that the imposition of the rationalistic model will improve learning, particularly in the basic skills. In turn, it assumes that the rationalistic model and the basic skills emphasis will prepare students for their roles as citizens and competitors in the labor market. What is the meaning of these ends? Can they be made operational? If they have not been attained in the past, what reason is there for believing that they will be attained in the future? Are the reasons adequate? What new science or technology of education is assumed? The knowledge base in education gives no reason for believing that children or teachers who were not performing well prior to *Robinson* will perform well after it. The rationalization of education imposed by *Robinson* can only be described as hyperrationalization. Goal reduction and goal reductionism are also evident, as only testing for achievement in basic skill areas is mandated by the 1975 law.

INSTRUMENTAL EDUCATION

In Chapter 3, we noted the preference of the policymaking process for an instrumental view of education, that is, school is seen as the institution established by society to transform the person from child to productive, literate, and law-abiding citizen. *Robinson* enunciated that the schools must prepare children for their roles as citizens and workers. By sanctioning the 1975 law, the court also endorsed the goal of basic literacy. By implication, events associated with *Robinson* endorsed the concepts both of rationalistic teaching and bureaucratic schools. State-enunciated goals and statewide evaluation procedures inevitably strengthen these conceptions of teachers and schools.

LEGAL REASONING

The central theme of Chapter 4 is that the application of legal reasoning seems to reinforce the rationalistic conception of the educational process. The ostensible purpose of *Robinson* was to bring the operation of the schools of New Jersey into conformity with a provision of the state constitution. The result was the imposition of the rationalistic model.

The process of adjudication itself shapes the problem and the solution. Initially the problem of inequality in school finance had to be defined as a legal problem. It was framed as a denial of equal protection or of thorough and efficient education. The decision had to be rationalized against a legal principle that precedent permitted. The perceived need to rely on the "thorough and efficient" clause may have redefined the problem or restricted the choice of solution. Perhaps because the court was somewhat removed from the interplay of interest groups, it was more susceptible to proffered simplistic solutions. While *Robinson* was an extraordinarily comprehensive action by the time it was consummated, it nonetheless relied upon a simplified view of how school finance and educational processes and outcomes are related. Because the court was divining educational purpose from abstract constitutional language, it was driven to a utilitarian or instrumental view of education. The court either presupposed uniformity in the effects of schooling or was willing to impose uniformity of operation. The attributes of adjudication help to explain some of the changing focus of *Robinson*.

THE SHIFT IN PRIORITIES

As the policymaking system confronted the operating educational system, interest turned from increasing equality to increasing productivity.[64] Those who brought and sup-

---

64. The political context of *Robinson* is analyzed in Richard Lehne, *The Politics of School Finance Reform* (New York: Longman, 1978).

ported the lawsuit seemed to have as their ultimate objective the improvement of education for children. As they placed a lower priority upon resource equalization, they came to view it as a necessary but not a sufficient condition to achieve this end. This shift in priorities may well have made the interests of the reformers coincide with the interests of two other groups. On the one hand were those who opposed change in the manner of financing education. On the other hand were those who believed that rising expenditures for education should be countered by a demand for accountability in education.

For some, educational reform became the consuming issue. For others, the issue continued to be that school finance reform was not occurring. Still others were sustained by the belief that accountability would improve productivity in education. While reformers believed that education would be improved, conservatives were relieved by the distraction which educational reform provided. Perhaps no one would notice that financial reform had not in fact occurred.[65] In *Robinson* we see the complete course of hyperrationalization as we examined its development in Chapters 1 through 4.

65. In 1977–78, the gap between the district spending at the 95th percentile and the district spending at the 5th percentile actually increased. See Margaret E. Goertz, *Money and Education: Where Did the 400 Million Dollars Go?* (Princeton, N.J.: Education Policy Research Institute, 1978).

CHAPTER 6
ACHIEVING EQUITABLE
AND PRODUCTIVE EDUCATION

I promised you that I would put into the form of a bill my plan of establishing the elementary schools, without taking a cent from the literary fund. I have had leisure at this place to do this. I now send you the result. If 12 or 1500 schools are to be placed under one general administration, an attention so divided will amount to a dereliction of them to themselves. It is surely better than to place each school at once under the care of those most interested in its conduct. In this way the literary fund is left untouched to compleat at once the whole system of education by establishing a college in every district of about 80 miles square, for the 2nd grade of education, to wit, languages ancient and modern, and for the 3rd grade a single university, in which the sciences shall be taught in their highest degree.

I should apologise perhaps for the style of this bill. I dislike the verbose and intricate style of the modern English statutes, and in our revised code I endeavored to restore it to the simple one of the ancient statutes in such original bills as I drew in that work. I suppose the reformation has not been acceptable, as it has been little followed. You however can easily correct this bill to the taste of my brother lawyers, by making every other word a "said" or "aforesaid," and saying everything over 2 or 3 times, so as that nobody but we of the craft can untwist the diction, and find out what it means; and that too not so plainly but that we may conscientiously divide, one half on each side, mend it therefore in form and substance to the orthodox taste, and make it what it should be; or, if you think it radically wrong, say some-

thing else, and let us make a beginning in some way, no matter how wrong; experience will amend it as we go along, and make it effectual in the end.

THOMAS JEFFERSON *Letter to Joseph C. Cabell*

A NOTE ON HIGHER EDUCATION

All of the processes we have discussed largely in relation to elementary and secondary education are operating with potent effect on the system of higher education in the United States as well. The argument developed here is generally applicable to both public and private higher education. To fully develop the case for hyperrationalization in higher education, however, would require extensive treatment. This note will merely outline that treatment by examining the perceptions of spokespersons for higher education.

Before proceeding, it may be useful to review briefly some illustrations already drawn from higher education:

- Texas has imposed a planning, programming, budgeting system on all state agencies, including the state system of higher education.[1]
- Rhode Island has required a master plan to include higher education mandating the development of goals and objectives in terms of what men should know and be able to do.[2]
- Colleges have been castigated for focussing on the liberal arts rather than upon providing their students with salable skills.[3]
- Competency-based teacher education has been offered as a means to make colleges of teacher education accountable for results.[4]
- Lawsuits have caused institutions of higher education to rationalize their procedures.[5]

1. See Chapter 1, under Planning, Programming, Budgeting Systems.
2. See Chapter 1, under Planning Models.
3. See Chapter 3, under Some Historical Perspective.
4. See Chapter 3, under CBTE.
5. See Chapter 4, under Due Process.

CENTRALIZATION, HYPERRATIONALIZATION, AND GOAL REDUCTION REVISITED

Increasing centralization of educational decision-making has been the subject of substantial comment, particularly from some of the administrators of institutions of higher education. Stated sometimes stridently, the strength and volume of these comments signal a qualitative change in the nature of external influences, particularly the federal government. Dallin H. Oaks, President of Brigham Young University, has asserted:

> The last 20 years have seen increasing federal financing and increasing federal controls. Today there are no national commissions or national educational organizations speaking out for the freedom of higher education, and relatively few making the case for diversity. Along with federal financing, we have accepted federal controls, and higher education is well on its way to becoming a regulated industry. Heavily dependent on federal financing, higher education—like a business in financial peril—is in danger of a receivership in which its management would pass to an absentee creditor in Washington. The 20-year pattern of finance and control has created a regulatory mood in which institutions without direct federal financial support are nevertheless in danger of colonization by ambitious government regulators. The sovereign authority to make and execute educational policy is being taken away from the trustees, administration, and faculty of our universities and colleges. On more and more important questions, the policy-making authority is being claimed and exercised by remote government rule-makers.[6]

Derek C. Bok, President of Harvard University, has warned:

> Because of the value of autonomy and diversity there are obvious costs in attempting to influence universities through government rules. By limiting the discretion of university personnel, rules diminish initiative and experimentation. In addition, rules involve a transfer of authority from educational institutions to public officials. Since these officials have less experience in educational matters, they are more likely to

6. Dallin H. Oaks, "A Private University Looks at Government Regulation," Address to the National Association of College and University Attorneys, Dallas, Texas, June 18, 1976, pp. 1–2.

make mistakes, and the cost of these mistakes will be magnified enormously by the power of the federal government to affect almost the entire range of educational institutions. Because regulations must be reasonably uniform in nature, they also threaten to impinge upon the diversity of the system. It is almost impossible to draft a single set of rules, however plausible, that will fit the special circumstances of all the varied institutions that exist in this country.[7]

The presidents of four private universities in Washington, D.C., were moved to issue "A 1976 Declaration of Independence" from the federal government:

DECLARATION OF INDEPENDENCE

Because relationships between government and institutions of high learning have reached a critical state in this Bicentennial Year, we deem this the opportune moment to state briefly our basic beliefs and premises.

WE BELIEVE That a democratic society is best sustained when its institutions of higher learning are free to establish their own policies and programs in furtherance of high-quality education.

WE BELIEVE That bureaucracy has become so vast and complex in its operations that sound relationships between government and universities are hampered by overlapping and unduly restrictive procedures, and that a leveling and homogenizing process is being generated.

WE BELIEVE That the diverse educational needs of Americans are best met by colleges and universities which are themselves part of a pluralistic and diverse educational community.

WE BELIEVE That institutions of higher learning which are committed to serving the rising educational demands of contemporary society should be helped by government financial support.

WE BELIEVE That private institutions have a most solemn obligation to husband resources carefully through appropriate administrative and educational reform.

WE BELIEVE That our steadfast objective must be the maintenance of autonomy which preserves choices of both form and substance of subject matter which is researched and taught.

7. Derek C. Bok, "The President's Report, 1974–1975," *Harvard Today*, p. 10.

BE IT THEREFORE RESOLVED That we reaffirm our intention to maintain institutional independence from any external intervention which threatens the integrity of our institutions, including refusal of federal funds which carry such threats.[8]

University presidents clearly perceive central policy determination as limiting their autonomy.

While university spokespersons have reserved their strongest criticism for the federal government, they have also begun to comment on changes in state practices. The Carnegie Foundation for the Advancement of Teaching has noted the rapid increase of coordination and consolidation at the state level:

> In 1940, 33 states had no coordinating or planning or consolidating mechanisms covering the entire public sector; today, none are without them.
>
> In 1940, there were only two coordinating agencies (one of them, in New York, was regulatory) over public higher education; today there are 28—of which 19 are regulatory.
>
> In 1940, there were no commissions comparable to the present 1202 commissions; today they exist in 46 states.
>
> In 1940, 70 percent of public four-year campuses (other than teachers colleges) were governed by their own individual boards; today about 30 percent of all public four-year campuses are so governed.
>
> In 1940, only one state (New York) had some form of planning or coordination or regulation that covered private colleges and universities; today 49 have such arrangements—the one exception is Wisconsin.[9]

The Foundation regretted this centralization of authority at the state level:

> It reduces the influence of students and of faculty members and of campus administrators and of members of campus governing boards—all persons who know the most about institutions of higher education, and are the most directly involved in

8. "A 1976 Declaration of Independence," *The Chronicle of Higher Education*, April 19, 1976, p. 5.

9. Carnegie Foundation for the Advancement of Teaching, *The States and Higher Education* (San Francisco: Jossey-Bass, 1976), p. 85.

their operations. It also reduces their sense of responsibility. The governance of academic institutions should include an influential role for academics and for those in close relations with them.

This centralization seems to have had no measurable direct impacts on policies or on practices. No provable case can thus far be made that higher education is in any way better because of the centralization, except, where it has taken place, in the one area of careful advanced academic planning for higher education as a whole. It is, of course, not possible to know, however, what would have happened in the absence of the centralization that did occur.

The governance processes are worse. They are more costly, more cumbersome, more time-consuming, more frustrating, and place more power in the hands of those who are the furthest removed and who know the least.[10]

It is interesting to note the reinforcing effect of federal influence upon state influence. The "1202 Commissions," strongly encouraged by federal law, result, in turn, in coordination at the state level.[11]

Moreover, as coordination is extended to include private institutions, the distinction between private and public institutions begins to disappear. Already private institutions must have the approval of the state coordinating agency to establish

10. Ibid., pp. 11–12.
11. State Postsecondary Education Commissions

Sec. 1202. (a) Any State which desires to receive assistance under section 1203 or title X shall establish a State Commission or designate an existing State agency or State Commission (to be known as the State Commission) which is broadly and equitably representative of the general public and public and private nonprofit and proprietary institutions of postsecondary education in the State including community colleges (as defined in title X), junior colleges, postsecondary vocational schools, area vocational schools, technical institutes, four-year institutions of higher education and branches thereof. (20 U.S.C. 1142a) Enacted June 23, 1972. P.S. 92–318, sec. 196, 86 Stat. 324.

Comprehensive Statewide Planning

Sec. 1203. (a) The Commissioner is authorized to make grants to any State Commission established pursuant to section 1202(a) to enable it to expand the scope of the studies and planning required in title X through comprehensive inventories of, and studies with respect to, all public and private postsecondary educational resources in the State, including planning necessary for such resources to be better coordinated, improved, expanded, or altered so that all persons within the State who desire, and who can benefit from, postsecondary education may have an opportunity to do so. (20 U.S.C. 1142b) Enacted June 23, 1972, P.S. 92–318, sec. 196, 86 Stat. 325.

new programs and are subject to the review of existing programs for possible termination.[12]

And, of course, the contribution of the courts to centralization has been noted.[13] Court decisions already affect admissions policies, faculty hiring and firing, student discipline, and accrediting procedures. The role of the attorney in the administration of the university is well recognized.[14]

As we have noted with regard to the elementary and secondary schools, central policy determination is often associated with an increased rationalization of educational practice. When the policy objective is to promote fair treatment, new procedures such as adversarial due process hearings are introduced. When the policy objective is to promote equal treatment, new rules governing, for example, resource allocation are introduced. When the policy objective is to promote effectiveness, goals are prescribed by such techniques as competency-based education. When the policy objective is to promote efficiency, scientific management procedures such as PPBS are prescribed. Although the objectives are usually salutary, the policies frequently do not have their intended effects and sometimes have unintended effects. They often represent the misapplication of legal, scientific, and managerial rationality to education. And they often introduce a pernicious concern for quasi-legal procedures, arbitrary rules, measurable outcomes, and pseudoscientific processes. Hyperrationalization is at work in higher education.

The trend has not gone unnoticed; Earl F. Cheit has caustically observed:

> The new regime in higher education is one of review procedures, regulation, litigation, and demands for information. Together these now account for so much of the energies and attention of college and university officials that the whole House of Intellect could soon be buried in an avalanche of paper. The public events

12. Carnegie Foundation for the Advancement of Teaching, *Supplement to the States and Higher Education* (Berkeley, Calif.: Carnegie Council on Policy Studies in Higher Education, 1976), p. 44.

13. *The Second Newman Report: National Policy and Higher Education*, Report of a Special Task Force to the Secretary of Health, Education, and Welfare (Cambridge, Mass.: MIT Press, 1973), p. 57.

14. David Ray Papke, "Is There a Lawyer in the House," *Change*, April 1977, pp. 14–16.

of higher education now deal less with its goals than with its regulation. Meeting external demands for information and compliance with regulations has become a principal concern of institutional life. It is no longer surprising when the report of a college counsel is the longest item on the trustees' agenda.[15]

The Second Newman Report, assessing the merits of rationalization and competition, noted:

> On all sides today there are proposals to create voluntary or enforced coordination among institutions. The motivation is in part to enhance efficiency by division of labor, elimination of overlapping programs, use of common purchasing, assurance of programs and campuses of large enough size, and reduction of competition. All of this seems based on the assumption that there is one right way to produce a graduate, that education is like an assembly line with units of instruction that are interchangeable. If so, the only issues left for consideration are the quality of instruction and the cost per credit hour.[16]

The perception of hyperrationalization is very strong.

And, as we have also noted earlier, centralization and hyperrationalization are associated with goal reduction and goal reductionism. Educational policies for higher education have tended to reinforce narrowly utilitarian or instrumental aims. Research may have contributed to this result. William R. Herman has put forth a provocative argument:

> Fifteen years ago, it was evident to Theodore Schultz and Edward Denison that the growth in national products could not be fully explained by conventional measures of capital and labor. To account for the residual they devised independently a theory of human capital formation. In brief, they argued that knowledge and skills were as much capital as physical equipment; and that education, rather than merely consuming resources, was an investment that produced extraordinary dividends over the long run.
>
> The concept was startling and powerful and spawned a library of books and articles, not only on the investment potential of education and training but also on health and other human resources. But somewhere on the way to the national forum the

15. Earl F. Cheit, "What Price Accountability?" *Change*, November 1975, p. 30.
16. *The Second Newman Report*, pp. 84–85.

original concept of human capital as contributing extensively to national economic growth was forgotten. Almost as soon as the concept was born, human capital analysts turned their attention to identifying the personal benefits derived from an investment in education.

From that point on, while their contributions added much to economic theory, the findings also led to marked distortions in public policies relating to student and institutional aid. So long as the cost/benefit ratios were flattering, few people sympathetic to higher education either realized or admitted that the human capital perspective was converting higher education into nothing but an income-maximization strategy and nothing but vocational preparation. It was inherent in this view that, should the personal cost of education rise and the relative income benefits decline, disenchantment with the value of higher education would set in. And that is what is happening today.[17]

Policy interventions, perhaps buttressed by social science, have tended to reinforce vocational or career education. The four presidents of Washington, D.C., universities were moved to comment:

> The U.S. Office of Education has lent its considerable prestige and its considerable resources to career education. One possible unintended effect has been the erosion of arts and sciences as the core of liberal education. Increasingly, students are embarked on programs in which they hope to acquire more "saleable skills." Yet if the liberal arts tradition dies, the nation will be intellectually and culturally poorer.[18]

As Herman concluded, the question "is whether our institutions of higher education are merely means to increasing personal and national income, or whether, . . . they are ends in themselves, visible signs of our civilization."[19]

Goal reductionism enters higher education in the form of the "credit-hour," a proximate measure of the amount of instruction delivered to students. It measures only contact

17. William R. Herman, "The University as a National Asset," *Change*, June 1976, pp. 31–32.

18. "A 1976 Declaration of Independence."

19. Herman, "National Asset," pp. 36–37.

between faculty and students, ignoring all other faculty functions, including research. The use of the credit-hour in decision-making implies that the only purpose of the college is the instruction of students in classrooms. As centralization and hyperrationalization occur, the need for measures increases. Resource allocation decisions are based on the production of credit-hours on the assumption that credit-hours are an adequate proximate measure of the goals of higher education. If the comments that have been directed at centralization and hyperrationalization can be characterized as strident and caustic, then vitriolic would describe those that have been directed at the use of such measures as the credit-hour.[20]

RATIONALISTIC TEACHING

Higher education so far has escaped the efforts to tighten the relationship between means and ends that has characterized the elementary and secondary schools. While instrumental education has begun to be emphasized, as noted in the preceding section, so far no mandatory legislation requires colleges to become more effective. Colleges have become more bureaucratic, however:

> Higher education is also specially vulnerable to any force that increases bureaucratization. In the past fifteen years, most educational institutions have found their administrative staff growing much more rapidly than the size of their faculties. The volume of paper work has also risen enormously, and the amount of committee work has expanded at an extraordinary rate.
>
> There are many reasons beyond government intervention for the growth of campus bureaucracy. The added size of many colleges and universities has created new administrative complexities. The emergence of statewide sytems of higher education has removed many decisions to more distant centers of authority. Financial constraints have led to tighter, more detailed budgetary controls. Student activism and the concerns of new constituencies, such as women and minority groups, have uncovered new problems to be solved.

20. See, for example: W. Lewis Hyde, "The Great Faucault Pendulum Caper," *The Chronicle of Higher Education*, August 16, 1976, p. 16. Carter A. Daniel, " 'Stop!' I Screamed, 'Stop, Stop, Stop!' " *The Chronicle of Higher Education*, September 13, 1976, p. 32.

These developments have had noticeable effects upon the internal life of educational institutions. The growing sense of impersonal bureaucracy has impaired relations between faculty and administration already strained through the process of belt tightening and budgetary restraint. Students have likewise experienced less flexibility and informality in their dealings with the administration. Detailed rules and computerized forms have replaced much of the individual treatment which students formerly experienced in attempting to resolve their academic and personal problems. It is this sense of depersonalization that provoked the plaintive slogan of Berkeley students in the "sixties": "I am a human being: Do not fold, spindle or mutilate."[21]

Yet, policymakers may not be far from mandating educational achievement in higher education. Several recommendations by the Southern Regional Education Board point in this direction:

> Statewide planning in postsecondary education must be assigned a high priority. Improvement of the planning and decision-making process at both the institutional and the state levels is essential.
>
> Education and training for employment is a crucial need for high school graduates in the South. Specific training programs below the baccalaureate should remain a primary function of two-year colleges, vocational-technical schools, and proprietary schools, but the relationship between education and employment requires careful attention at all levels of postsecondary education.
>
> The academic community has within its own ranks the potential for self-generated reform. That reform should be based on a systematic assessment of educational outcomes and impact, and should lead to improved faculty performance and productivity.[22]

Vocation and career objectives are given emphasis. Statewide planning is to be employed. Finally, the attainment of educational outcomes will presumably improve because of systematic evaluation. Thus, externally created educational objectives

21. Bok, "The President's Report," pp. 12–13.
22. Southern Regional Education Board, *Priorities for Postsecondary Education in the South* (Atlanta, Ga.: SREB, 1976), pp. iv–v.

will be mediated by the bureaucratic structure of the college and will come to rest with the faculty for implementation.

Although competency-based education has never been mandated by law (except for schools of education), the federal government has supported its adoption on an "experimental" basis. The Fund for the Improvement of Postsecondary Education has had as one of its objectives the promotion of CBE. The assumptions governing CBE for higher education are similar to those for elementary and secondary education. First, it is assumed that competence can be defined in measurable terms:

> Competence is the state or quality of being capable of adequate performance. Individuals are described as competent if they can meet or surpass the prevailing standard of adequacy for a particular activity. While competence does not equate with excellence, it does imply a level of proficiency that has been judged to be sufficient for the purposes of the activity in question. Recently the concept of competence or competency has entered the language of educational reform to describe efforts to reformulate the structures of postsecondary education on the basis of clearly defined objectives.[23]

Second, it is assumed that the objectives for education must be derived from outside the institution, and particularly from the labor market:

> [There is] the problem of congruence between educational objectives and individual and social needs. Given the changes in the technological and social context that have taken place over the past two decades, the evidence that many graduates are ill-prepared for their vocations and professions, and the changing labor market, a careful re-examination of institutional objectives seems not only appropriate but necessary.[24]

Third, it is assumed that an explicit statement of objectives will improve the quality of teaching:

> The presence of more explicit objectives and more precise criteria for the award of credentials may persuade educators to take

23. Fund for the Improvement of Postsecondary Education, *Special Focus Program: Education and Certification for Competence* (Washington, D.C.: FIPSE, 1975), p. 7.
24. Ibid., p. 8.

greater responsibility for the attainments of their clients by examining the efficacy of the curriculum and the pedagogy that they offer. The diversity of learners in terms of their attitudes, aptitudes, and circumstances necessitates greater diversity among institutions and alternative modes of teaching and learning within institutions.[25]

Finally, the attainment of competence must be assessed systematically:

> The determination of criteria of competency is one of the most difficult problems to be addressed. Typically, they would correspond to levels of performance required for entry into roles outside the academic setting. In some cases, this may be determined by research; in others, such as the general skills associated with liberal education, this may prove difficult or excessively costly. In all cases, however, the criteria must be based on evidence sufficient to ensure that they will not be viewed as arbitrary or rhetorical and thus be rendered inoperational.[26]

The requirement for systematic assessment almost inevitably leads to emphasis upon minimal entry-level skills.

Unlike most CBE legislation, the Fund does recognize the need to reorganize the delivery and certification functions if CBE is to work. It fails, however, to provide a compelling rationale for the four assumptions upon which the program is based. The definition of competence is necessarily arbitrary or subjective;[27] educational objectives may be derived from elsewhere than the labor market; there is no evidence that precisely stated behavioral objectives will improve teaching or learning; and the need for systematic assessment of objectives inevitably narrows the objectives sought.

It is, of course, the case that participation in Fund-sponsored projects is voluntary and experimental. It is also the case that the development of objectives and the conduct of the program are the responsibility of the institution.[28] In

25. Ibid., p. 9.
26. Ibid., p. 15.
27. Gene V. Glass, "Standards and Criteria," unpublished paper.
28. However, the Fund suggests (p. 13):

The constituencies which have legitimate interests in the formulation of these competencies are many, and include learners, faculty members, administrators, trustees, governing board, public agencies, professional associations, accrediting and licensing boards, practicing professionals, employers, and representatives of the

these respects CBE, as fostered by the Fund, is different from CBE as required by state law. Nonetheless, the factors which lead the policymaking system to favor CBE in elementary and secondary education are also present in higher education.

Conclusion

While the forces of hyperrationalization are affecting higher education with the same potency as elementary and secondary education, in some respects the trends in higher education are more obvious because they represent a more pronounced shift from the tradition of institutional autonomy. The creation of coordinating councils and the development of multi-campus state university systems are visible signs of the change in the authority structure of higher education.[29] So far, the hyperrationalization of higher education has resulted primarily from efforts to increase equality and fairness and, to a lesser degree, from efforts to increase institutional efficiency. While higher education has generally been spared efforts to increase institutional effectiveness, such efforts are likely to begin as the policymaking system consolidates control over the operating system.[30]

INCREMENTAL BUREAUCRATIC CENTRALIZATION

If the dominant forces now operating on the educational system play out to their logical conclusion, incremental bureaucratic centralization will be the inevitable result. The pressures to solve educational problems through policy interventions appear unremitting, and the allure of solving problems of unfairness by the imposition of procedures is increasing. The attractiveness of solving problems of inequality by

---

public interest. Thus, while the Fund assumes that the definition and specification process will most frequently be initiated and led by post-secondary educational institutions, the development of these objectives may involve the cooperative effort of constituencies both internal and external to educational institutions.

29. *The Second Newman Report*, pp. 53–56.

30. Congress has, for example, considered requiring medical students to receive six weeks of training in underserved areas, on the assumption that they would alter their career plans. (See Bok, "The President's Report," p. 11.)

the imposition of rules is also growing, and the political need to solve problems of low productivity is making increasingly unrealistic demands on current scientific knowledge about education. The ad hoc repair of the operating educational system by the policymaking system appears destined to continue unabated.

Efforts to make schools and colleges more equitable or more productive will continue to result in the central determination of policy. In the process, the bureaucratic conception of the school will be strengthened. While educators may be inclined to resist the excessive rationalization of their activities, they likely cannot resist forever. Moreover, the unionization of teachers and collective bargaining are likely to contribute to increasing rationalization. Unions will seek new rules and procedural safeguards, and management will counter with new rules and procedures of its own.

Centrally determined policies require central bureaucratic structure to plan, monitor, and evaluate their implementation. Central structures such as state departments of education and coordinating commissions of higher education will grow in size and influence. Because these agencies act for the state, there is a great temptation to bring all institutions—public and private—within their purview. As noted in Chapter 4, legal principles, once established, are capable of considerable extension. Ultimate authority for education is at the state level. To the extent that the principle of state authority is invoked, state responsibility is increased.

It is not possible to predict whether federal or state authority will predominate in the future. In part, the answer to the question may turn on the amount of revenue provided by each level of government. The federal government's influence grew enormously between the mid-sixties and the mid-seventies with a share of school expenditures that never exceeded 8 percent. The National Education Association argues for increasing the federal share to one-third. In larger part, the answer to the question will turn on the locus for problem solution identified by the polity. For a long time the locus was the local institution. For a while the locus was the federal government. More recently, attention has tended to fix at the state level. There is the possibility, exemplified by the Education for All Handicapped Children Act, for federal law to strengthen the role of the state. Of course, as the role of the state is strengthened, so, too, is the federal role. More effective management by the federal government can be achieved by its relating to fifty or so sub-units rather than to thousands.

As suggested in Chapter 2, there are limits to incremental bureaucratic centralization. One occurs when authority over the operating educational system has been fully centralized. Another occurs when the goals of the operating educational system have been exhaustively prescribed. A third occurs when the means of the operating system have been fully prescribed—that is, when all important decisions are made either in due process hearings or according to rules, and the curriculum is designed and administered in accord with scientific principles. The continued application of these rationalities reinforces incremental bureaucratic centralization.

ALTERNATIVE SOLUTIONS

As we look for alternatives to an increasingly dismal prospect, it may be useful to summarize in a series of propositions:

1. The more educational policies are promulgated by higher levels of government, the more bureaucratic will become the *conception* of the school. The dominant conception is of a centrally determined system of education serving narrow, utilitarian ends employing rationalistic means.

2. To the extent that educators reject the bureaucratic conception of the school, educational policies will fail. The beliefs that education must be liberating and that schools cannot be standardized and routinized buttress this rejection.

3. To the extent that educators accept the bureaucratic conception of the school, the more bureaucratic will the schools become *in fact*. Quasi-judicial procedures, rigid rules, pseudoscientific processes, and measurable outcomes *can* be implemented.

4. Problems of inequity in the allocation of educational

opportunities, resources, and programs can be solved by policy intervention. They may be otherwise insoluble. The cost will be some bureaucratization; it is a cost which many will be prepared to accept.

5. Problems of low productivity in the educational system generally cannot be solved by policy intervention. It is, of course, possible to reduce costs—with an indeterminate effect upon quality. It is also possible for schools to adopt pseudoscientific processes and measurable outcomes. Given the state-of-the-art of educational science, it is doubtful, however, that productivity will increase.

6. While teachers as individuals resist the conception of their role implied by excessive rationalization, teachers' organizations may contribute to it.

7. To the extent that the public or interest groups address demands to policymakers rather than to the educational system, centralization and hyperrationalization will increase.

8. To the extent that the public or its representatives insist upon *measuring* the effects of educational policies, goal reduction and goal reductionism will occur.

These propositions raise profound questions about the proper role of each level and branch of government in the governance of education. What are the principles which do, could, or should limit the role of each level of government in educational policymaking? Why do interest groups shift their attention from one level of government to another? Are state and local boards of education vestigial? One approach to answering these questions would be to examine the legal responsibilities of each level and branch of government. This approach would probably not be productive, however, because, for example, while the federal government was given *no* responsibility for education by the federal Constitution, the state governments were given *all* responsibility for education by their state constitutions. Current reality varies substantially from legal form.

Or, one could examine the political leverage enjoyed by each level of government. It is obvious, for example, that change wrought at the federal level affects more children than change wrought at the local level, making higher levels of government more attractive targets for inducing change. In the same way, general government is more powerful than education government. The state legislature has more leverage than the state board of education or the state coordinating commission for higher education. The short answer to the question of what role can be played by higher levels of government and general government is "whatever role they choose," subject only to the restraints of tradition and politics.

Or, one could attempt to limit governmental roles by emphasizing the line between policymaking and operational responsibility. In fact, however, this line is far from clear. When a higher level of government intercedes in education, it does so to accomplish a purpose. If the purpose is not achieved, the tendency is to make the policy guidance more specific. Sufficiently specific policy guidance becomes an operational prescription. It is difficult to divide responsibility by a *procedural* distinction.

A fourth approach is the substantive one to be argued here—*that schools and colleges should be held responsible for the production of education, while other levels and branches of government should be held responsible for ensuring equity within schools and colleges.* In those instances where the schools are not accomplishing a national or state purpose, before the higher level of government acts it should first be determined whether education can, in fact, serve that purpose and whether policy can be devised that will cause the schools to deliver the education desired.

Let us now look at four possible alternatives to the incremental bureaucratic centralization of the educational system. As we do, the reader is forewarned that there are no easy solutions. Equity and productivity issues, now intertwined, will be hard to disentangle. Moreover, the forces associated with hyperrationalization in education reflect more general social trends. It is not clear that the educational system can be changed without changes in these broader trends.

Planned Bureaucratic Centralization

One alternative is planned bureaucratic centralization which begins with the assumption that bureaucratic centralization is inevitable for the reasons already noted, and also assumes that planning is superior to ad hoc bureaucratic centralization. It assumes that the design of a new system of goverance for education can overcome some of the dysfunctions accompanying incremental change.

At present, a fully developed structure for governance and decision-making exists at the institutional level. Policymakers repair that structure by prescribing changes in the inputs, processes, and outcomes of the institution. Often changes in one element are made without considering their consequences for the other elements. Often the changes introduce procedural complexity without achieving intended reforms, and mandate outcomes without confronting the difficult question of how those outcomes are to be produced. Always the changes come from those who have formal authority but who do not have operational responsibility.[31] Authority divorced from responsibility may increase the tendency to frame unrealistic expectations and to call upon the schools to solve social problems.

Planned bureaucratic centralization could overcome some of these difficulties. At the very least, those charged with operational responsibility might not have to confront contradictory, overlapping, and duplicating policy guidance. Authority, responsibility, and control over the incentive structure could be aligned. Those who wish to design centralized educational systems have two types of models to study—national educational systems elsewhere in the world, and large-city school systems in the United States. Many of these, of course, enroll larger numbers of students than do some states. Similarly, multi-campus state universities may reveal the kind of coordination which could emerge from continuing efforts to coordinate institutions of higher education within a state. It is possible to design and manage large educational systems.

RESPONSIBLE LOCAL CONTROL

A second alternative might be a reversion to local control in the belief that local officials would no longer discriminate against minority persons, women, the handicapped, and the otherwise educationally disadvantaged. This presupposes

31. Laurence Iannaccone, "Using Research in School Reform," *The Generator* 7:2 (Spring 1977), 5.

that local institutional officials have learned the lessons which court decisions and federal regulation have been designed to teach and that they would make decisions consistently with these precepts. Responsible local control also recognizes that improvements in productivity are not likely to result from centrally determined policy. Alternatively, demands by the public for accountability, basic skills, career education, etc., could be addressed to local officials rather than to state or federal officials.

Responsible local control is not likely to be a satisfactory resolution, however. First, there is no reason to believe that local officials would not revert to their former discriminatory behavior; second, other problems of equality, particularly those connected with inequalities in tax bases or inadequacies in institutional resources, would be difficult to solve.

THE RATIONALISTIC SOLUTION

The rationalistic solution begins with the premise that the failings of educational policy are due to their inadequate conceptualization and/or their premature application. The rationalistic solution recognizes the inevitability of the technocraticization of society and its institutions. Those who support the rationalistic solution must believe that, over time, research and development will devise policy tools which will not distort educational purposes. Thus, in the drive to make schools accountable for results, goals will determine which tests are devised rather than available tests determining the goals to be selected. Advocates of CBE, rather than merely adding it to an existing school structure, will first cause the underlying structure to be redesigned to accommodate CBE.[32] Efforts will be made to understand the causes of low academic achievement before solutions are imposed. Realistic assessments of the causes of social problems will be made before the schools are directed to solve them. Supposed productivity-improving devices will be tested before being implemented. Innovations will be adopted only when the incentive structure can be made to accommodate them.

32. William G. Spady, "Competency-Based Education: A Bandwagon in Search of a Definition," *Educational Researcher* 6:1 (January 1977), 9–14.

The rationalistic solution would attend also to problems of inequity and their solution. It will endeavor to assess the efficacy of rules and procedures in attaining the objectives of equality and fairness. It will examine the role of quotas in encouraging compliance. It will study the role of incentives, disincentives, proscriptions, and prescriptions in reaching desired ends. It will strive to understand and eliminate the dysfunctional consequences of rules and procedures. It will use information derived from study to construct sophisticated rules. It will use information to assess the costs and benefits of elaborated procedures.

The rationalistic solution is theoretically compatible with a mix of central and local control. Sensitive policy tools presumably could appropriately be used to allocate authority, responsibility, and tasks to the different levels of governance. The final apportionment would depend upon where the burden of proof lay. Should centralization of a function occur only when local decision-makers fail to act? Or would centralization occur whenever the technology allowed it?

THE RATIONAL SOLUTION

The rational solution is based upon two premises. The first is that problems of inequity are not likely to be resolved at the local or institutional level. Inequalities in the allocation of resources, opportunities, and programs are generally problems which arise out of the conflicting interests of majorities and minorities and of the powerful and the powerless. Because local institutions are apparently the captives of majoritarian politics, they intentionally and unintentionally discriminate. Moreover, the frame of reference for judging 'inequality" is generally larger than a single institution. A judgment of inequality is reached from a comparison of resources, opportunities, and programs across school districts, states, and institutions. Consequently, we must rely upon the policy-making system to solve problems of inequity in the operating educational system.

The second premise is that problems of low productivity cannot, at least in the foreseeable future, be solved by policy intervention. No science or technology of education can form a firm basis for policy intended to improve productivity.

There are as yet only crude devices which can be incorporated into policy. These devices purport to be productivity-improving, but most have yet to demonstrate their worth. Consequently, control over the operation of schools should revert to local officials; efforts to improve educational productivity can and should continue at the institutional level.

Efforts to eliminate inequity will then result in central determination of some policy. In turn, some bureaucratization, rationalization, proceduralization, and regulation will occur. However, these processes will be justified because they can ensure results. Rationalization which does not achieve its intended results should end.

Evaluating the Alternatives

Incremental bureaucratic centralization is the most probable estimate of the future. Planned bureaucratic centralization is improbable because it would require major determination and leadership to be achieved. Moreover, it would violate such sacred traditions as local control and institutional autonomy. Responsible local control is improbable because many interest groups would have to surrender recently attained and powerful levers for change.

The rationalistic solution is plausible, for it promises amelioration of our educational ills and the sharing of educational governance among all three levels of government. It is merely plausible, however, because both policymakers and educators may tire of a possible succession of productivity-improving innovations which do not work. The rational solution is plausible because it permits many interest groups to achieve their objectives and because it perpetuates a mix of control. It is merely plausible because it would require a reversal of the trend toward regulating schools and colleges in the belief that such regulation will cause them to improve. Because it requires higher levels of government to appropriate funds to resolve inequalities, it contradicts the principle that those who appropriate funds should control their expenditure. That principle itself is, of course, contradicted by those policymakers who support revenue-sharing. (Revenue-sharing is a system whereby one level of government appropriates funds to another level of government which becomes responsible for the expenditure of those funds.) If the sentiments which favor revenue-sharing gain strength, then the rational solution becomes more plausible.

I need hardly restate my conclusion that incremental bureaucratic centralization is not desirable. One's opinions of planned bureaucratic centralization will depend upon how one judges national school systems elsewhere in the world, on the one hand, and upon how one judges large-city school systems in the United States, on the other hand. Responsible local control risks a retreat from the egalitarian gains of the last two decades. One's opinion of the rationalistic solution depends upon one's beliefs about the likely progress of educational research. My preference is clearly for the rational solution which recognizes, on the one hand, the need to regulate in the interests of equity and, on the other hand, the limits of the knowledge base available for improving productivity.

OTHER ALTERNATIVES

Could educational vouchers be an antidote to growing rationalization?[33] Economists recognize competition as an alternative to rationalization as a means to allocate resources and to foster quality. Educational vouchers made available by government to parents have been proposed as a way to introduce a competitive market to education. The concept is that parents exercising choices among institutions would cause institutional quality to rise. Aside from the practical and political problems of actually introducing a voucher system, there are two reasons for believing that a voucher system might not be an effective antidote to excessive rationalization. First, vouchers *appear* to create a situation in which policymakers would have less control over the operating system. Second, in the event that vouchers were adopted, the policymaking system, under pressure from various interest groups, would be likely to engage in extensive rationalization to ensure the quality and equality of inputs, processes and outcomes.

33. See generally John E. Coons and Stephen D. Sugarman, *Education by Choice: The Case for Family Control* (Berkeley, Calif.: University of California Press, 1978).

Could procedures to decentralize and debureaucratize be antidotes to centralization and bureaucratization? The very terms suggest the antitheses of the concepts we have been examining; therein lies the explanation. Decentralization has been tried in some large systems. Its problem has been and continues to be that critical decisions—particularly those concerned with personnel—remain with the central authority. While it might be possible to decentralize operational control, it is not clear that formal authority can be decentralized.[34] Moreover, needs for coordination, economies of scale, collective bargaining, racial integration, and other factors militate against decentralization.

The dismantling of bureaucratic structures, the reduction of hierarchy, and the loosening of control are similarly elusive objectives. They are presumably compatible with the idea that the teacher is a professional who should be free, insofar as possible, to practice his profession and with other romantic notions of the teacher as a lone practitioner. It is an unlikely reform because it fails to take into account the polity's apparent need for control.

Could community control of education or citizen participation in educational decision-making be antidotes to centralization?[35] After all, centralization and rationalization are merely means to ensure that the schools are responsive to the polity. If the polity were directly in control, then the need for rationalization would be obviated. However, community control and citizen participation share the deficiency of decentralization which they presuppose. For these reforms to work, authority must be decentralized. And the polity to which the schools must be responsive is larger than the polity which is represented in the school's community. Community control and citizen participation tend to serve the dominant political interests in the community; minority interests within the community may not be well served. For these reasons, it is unlikely that community control and citizen participation can be more than minor forces for change.

34. Tyll van Geel, *Authority to Control the School Program* (Lexington, Mass.: Heath, 1976), p. 118.
35. See generally National Committee for Citizens in Education, *Public Testimony on Public Schools*, ed. Shelly Weinstein (Berkeley, Calif.: McCutchan, 1975).

CONCLUDING CONCERNS

The relationships among policy, ideology, research, and reality are complex and deserve serious examination. This book has concentrated upon the ideology implicit in educational policy. Some attention has been given to the ways in which research shapes that ideology. Only a little attention has been given to empirical examination of how policy actually affects the reality of school operation. Clearly, substantial research on the relationship between ideology and school practice is required.

I have been particularly critical of the misuse of social science and educational research. In fact, the concept of hyperrationalization is meant to direct attention to the need for serious research in education. Rationalization, as opposed to hyperrationalization, cannot occur unless the relationships between organizational means and organizational ends are known. And, in education, we are very far from having sound knowledge about these relationships.

The concept of hyperrationalization is doubtless applicable to other public sector activities. Centralization of other public and private sector activities is, of course, also occurring. This book should shed some light upon hyperrationalization and centralization elsewhere. In turn, studies of other sectors may shed more light upon education.

The role of the researcher and of research needs to be examined also. A discovery or new technique is frequently put to premature use, and researchers bear some responsibility for this. The temptation is for too much educational research to be conceived of as applied research or policy-relevant research. The result too often is that neither knowledge nor practice gains. The need to solve the fundamental problems of education is too great to continuously waste resources on the search for easy solutions. *We need to resolve the paradox of educational policy: the support for educational policies which presuppose a science of education is great, while political support for research leading to the improvement of education is meager.* Because of the economics of research, we must look to the federal government to support it. The costs are high in relation to the necessarily unpredictable outcomes.

The benefits—when they occur—are available to the nation.

The rationalistic vision of the educational system has strong implications for educational leadership. The system would require managers who are good bureaucrats rather than strong educational leaders. The system would value those able to manage a process without being disturbed by larger questions of the role of education in society. Those best able to manage rules and procedures would be preferred over those who worry about the direction of education. And what kinds of persons would be willing to serve as members of local school boards and as members of college boards of trustees?

Schools and colleges are being shaped by the belief that a law or a judicial decree can correct educational problems. Describing the growing tendency to solve problems by judicial means, Chief Justice Warren E. Burger said: "The 'enemy' may be our willingness to assume that the more refined and deliberate the procedure, the better the quality of justice which results." He termed it "possible" that lawyers and judges, "aided and abetted by the inherently litigious nature of Americans," have tended to "cast all disputes into a legal framework that only legally trained professionals can deal with in traditional legal ways."[36] If this is so, then the American educational system has a very large challenge before it.

The forces associated with hyperrationalization threaten a number of traditions in education. They threaten local control of public education and institutional autonomy in higher education. They threaten teacher professionalism in schools and collegial governance in colleges. They threaten the independence of private education at all levels. They threaten the role of educational governance structures separate from general government. They threaten liberal education and the belief that education is important as an end in itself. These traditions have evolved to serve important *societal* functions. While it is wise to abandon traditions whose functions we no longer value or can otherwise accommodate, it is unwise to destroy traditions whose functions we value or cannot otherwise accommodate.

Schools and colleges can become more equitable. Schools

36. Chief Justice Warren E. Burger as quoted in the *Washington Post*, May 28, 1977.

and colleges can become more efficient and effective. However, the two questions to be asked of every educational policy are: will it have the intended effect? and what other effects will it have?

The policies we have examined reveal a struggle for power over who will rule our nation's schools and colleges. If the forces associated with hyperrationalization are not checked, who will be the winners and losers in the struggle for power? The winners will be the elected and appointed officials associated with general government who are making educational policies in areas formerly reserved to educational governance structures. The losers will be members of state boards of education.[37] Their more important functions have been supplanted by the actions of general government. The winners will be the staffs of state departments of education (and corresponding federal staffs). With each new policy, they tend to gain new responsibilities. The losers will be members of local boards of education and institutional boards of trustees who were accustomed to thinking that it was their job to set educational policy. The losers will be administrators of private institutions who will see their discretion diminished. Probable winners will be school administrators. On the one hand, they will have new responsibilities and new mechanisms to control their institutions. On the other hand, they will be subject to new constraints. Major losers will be teachers who will see their professional autonomy replaced by a bureaucratic conception of their role. The most tragic loss will be to the students who are cast as objects being prepared to assume their place in society. Lastly, our society will be the worst loser, for it is the tendency of educational policies to cast the welfare of the individual as subordinate to the welfare of the state. Nothing less is at stake in this struggle for power than individual freedom in a democratic society.

37. At the moment, state coordinating commissions for postsecondary institutions appear to be in ascendancy vis-à-vis institutional level boards of trustees. However, this appearance is probably due to the recency of their creation. In the future, it will become clear that their influence is similar to that of state school boards.

INDEX

Achievement tests: role in desegregation, 5; to measure school outcomes, 8–9; in Title I funds allocation, 11–12, 36; decline in scores, 26–27; Florida requirements, 37; policy role, 72–73; results, as goal of teachers, 98–99; teachers' view of, 99–100; in basic skills, 110–111. *See also* Minimal competency

Accountability: movement, terms used by, 12–13; goals of, 14; Ohio system, 17; legislation, volume of, 18; in relation to minimal competency, 24–27, 42; role of, in malpractice concept, 29–30; in Maryland law, 38; in Mississippi law, 39; in Oklahoma law, 40–41; in Virginia law, 39–40; in relation to goal reduction, 59; ineffectiveness of, 80; defined in 1913, 84–85; in relation to output measures, 99; response to teachers' demands, 104–105; movement, as competency-based education movement, 110–111; at state level, 126. *See also* Bureaucratization; Hyperrationalization; Scientific management

Administrative discretion: reduced by judicial intervention, 48–49, 131–139; in resource allocation, 135–139

American Federation of Teachers, 105

Baratz, Joan C., 136, 138–139

Basic skills; in Florida, 43; in elementary schools, 59–61; as goals, 110–111

Behavioral science, contribution to rationalistic teaching model, 97–98

Bidwell, Charles, 95–96

Bobbitt, Franklin, 83–84

Bok, Derek C., 188–189, 195–196

Botter, Theodore (Judge), 155–158, 176–179

Bowles, Samuel, 115–117

Brigham Young University, 188

Brown v. *Board of Education*, 3–5, 180

Bureaucracy: defined and described, 62–64; Weberian model of, 62–64; values implicit in, 88; models of, 88–90; situation of, leading to litigation, 120; acceptance of rules, 126; dependence on law; 130; effect of legal decisions on, 131. *See also* Schools; Scientific management

Bureaucratic rationalization, 81

Bureaucratization: factors promoting, 48; response of teachers, 63; as rationalization, 63–65; rationalization and hyperrationalization in, 65–66; of teachers organizations, 105–106; of higher education, 106, 195–196; relation to legalism, 118–119. *See also* Centralization; Hyperrationalization;

213